The Believers Church:
A Voluntary Church

Studies in the
Believers
Church
Tradition

Studies in the
Believers Church Tradition

The Studies in the Believers Church Tradition series was established with the aim of publishing scholarly works in the field of the so-called "Believers Church" or "Free Church" tradition. Included in this tradition are a wide range of church communions having their roots either in the 16th century Anabaptists (sometimes considered part of the "Radical Reformation") or 17th century English Separatists. Emphases common to these various traditions include an appreciation of voluntarism and an understanding of the Church as a gathered community of believers baptized as adults upon the confession of faith.

The sponsor for this publication series is the Centre for Anabaptist and Baptist Studies (CABS), a venture of cooperation between Conrad Grebel College and McMaster Divinity College.

1. William H. Brackney, ed., *The Believers Church: A Voluntary Church. Papers of the Twelfth Believers Church Conference held at McMaster Divinity College, October 17-19, 1996.*

The Believers Church:
A Voluntary Church

Papers of the Twelfth Believers Church Conference
held at McMaster Divinity College,
October 17-19, 1996

Edited with an Introduction by

William H. Brackney

1998

Canadian Cataloguing in Publication Data

Believers Church Conference (12th: 1996: McMaster Divinity College)
   The believers church: a voluntary church: papers of the twelfth Believers
Church Conference

(Studies in the believers church tradition, ISSN 1480-7432)
Conference held at McMaster Divinity College, Hamilton, Ont., Oct. 17-19,
1996.
Includes bibliographical references and index.
ISBN 0-9683462-0-0

1. Free churches — Congresses. I. Brackney, William H. II. Title.

BR115.V64B44 1966   280'.4   C98-930913-4

THE BELIEVERS CHURCH:
A VOLUNTARY CHURCH

Copyright © 1998 by Pandora Press
51 Pandora Avenue N.
Kitchener, Ontario, N2H 3C1
All rights reserved

Co-published with Herald Press,
Scottdale, Pennsylvania/Waterloo, Ontario

International Standard Book Number: **0-9683462-0-0**
Printed in Canada on acid-free paper

Book and cover design by Clifford Snyder

05 04 03 02 01 00 99 98 10 9 8 7 6 5 4 3 2 1

Dedicated to

John Howard Yoder

(1927-1997)

In Memoriam

Contents

Introduction

William H. Brackney

The subject of voluntarism is much in the media and has long received attention in believers church literature. Franklin H. Littell, for instance, in his groundbreaking doctoral dissertation of 1951, observed of the Anabaptist tradition that "the church must be a voluntary association . . . gathered by a freely and comprehensively conceived evangel."[1] Likewise, Sidney E. Mead found that one of the great characteristics of Christianity in the United States was its voluntariness.[2] Voluntarism is a powerful force which caused anxiety in the ancient and magisterial churches and set the modern church free for mission.

What is meant by voluntarism? How does it intersect with Christian experience? It is a multifaceted concept which evolves in the course of Christian history. It stems from an emphasis upon the will — that which is uncoerced, spontaneous in nature, derived from one's own choice or consent. Theologically interpreted, voluntarism defines both divine and human attributes: God's own self-giving character and human capability, itself a gift of God. Theologians have realized that voluntarism raises human worth and posits a strong anthropology; this has often caused timidity and strong opposition from rigid determinists.[3]

Biblical scholars have not had much to say about voluntarism. It may be a too obvious facet of the Judao-Christian heritage. In the Old Testament narratives, for instance, there is ample evidence of voluntary behaviour, as in the life of Moses or King David. Similarly in the New Testament, the apostles wrestle with their desire to follow their inner directions in spiritual matters. Voluntary associations may be found from the Nazarites to the prayer bands described in the Acts of the Apostles. It

William H. Brackney is principal of McMaster Divinity College and professor of historical theology at McMaster University, Hamilton, Ontario.

[1] Franklin H. Littell, *The Anabaptist View of the Church: A Study in the Origins of Sectarian Protestantism*, rev. ed. (Boston: Starr King Press, 1958), 46, 118.

[2] Sidney E. Mead, *The Lively Experiment* (Boston: Seabury Press, 1957), 45.

[3] See for instance, my *Christian Voluntarism in Britain and North America: A Bibliography and Critical Assessment* (Westport: Greenwood Press, 1996), 1-14, for a scholarly elaboration of these themes.

may even be argued that the gospel is an invitation to offer oneself, just as Jesus voluntarily gave his life for others. The early Church was essentially a voluntary association of believers, constituted by their faith in Christ and their free choice to follow his teachings.

Church history was built strongly on the principle of voluntary association, derived in large part from the Roman context. There are numerous examples in the early and medieval church of voluntary association, such as burial societies and brotherhoods and women religious, and this dimension of voluntarism became extremely important for organizational and theological purposes. A religious voluntary association came to be a gathering of persons united for a common purpose, committed to each other in the accomplishment of their goal and characterized by democratic participation and management of their association. This could be seen in various types of church polities (the Albigensians and Waldensians, for example), as well as in independent organizations. Many of the medieval renewal movements and religious orders (like the Carthusians and Beghards) had their origins in the voluntary assent to a rule or ideal, later institutionalized by discipline and warrant of the Church. In the Reformation, particularly among the Anabaptist traditions, voluntary associations of believers covenanted themselves to be the church in small collections of those who shunned hierarchical organizations and the use of the sword in spiritual matters. This manifestation became a primary example of the voluntary thrust.

Voluntarism as an idea or principle has also had differing emphases in various political contexts. As already noted, voluntarism among the Anabaptists meant a "Free Church" or "Freiwilligkeitskirche," thus giving birth to the modern term. Anabaptist confessional statements and Baptist confessions are replete with expressions of voluntarism. The doctrine of the believers' church has fully articulated the nature of voluntarism: a church voluntarily gathered, of those who voluntarily covenant with God and each other, and who voluntarily support its objectives with their personal resources. But this voluntarist ecclesiology fast outdistanced the believers' churches and was in evidence even among the established churches. Nonconformity in Britain was affirmed in the Act of Toleration in 1689, and the Dissenting Deputies (composed of Baptists, Congregationalists, and Presbyterians) in the eighteenth century had large influence in the making of public policy. In nineteenth-century Britain, Thomas Chalmers (1780-1847) called for a voluntary church, by which he meant that churches should be supported by those who are members and not by the government. This church was, to use the contemporary term, "disestablishment." In the mid-seventeenth century, Puritans and later Anglicans developed voluntary associations for mission and educational purposes, and an entirely new rationale for Christian voluntarism emerged. By the mid-nineteenth century, the overwhelming dynamism of the Christian movement in all of its variations in Britain was found among the voluntarists.

In the United States voluntarism describes not just a Free Church, but a smorgasbord of religious opportunities; cults, sects, churches, and denominations all behave as though they must care for their own needs. Not only did the frontier experience provide ample room for every possible kind of religious expression to exist, but the long drive to establish religious liberty and disestablishment in the legal frame of the U.S. Constitution ensured that voluntarism would be a part of the American way of life. A number of watchdog agencies from many denominational and independent perspectives in the U.S. now observe very closely the course of church-state relations to ensure that religious voluntarism is protected. Voluntarism has become the cherished property of Protestants, Catholics, Jews, and the non-religious communities as well. Governments and social agencies now build expectations upon the "third sector" or those who operate without church or state support.

In the twentieth-century North American scene, voluntarism is the force which produces the parachurch organization and generates change and renewal in the institutional churches, and this has brought about much anxiety and negative feelings between religious organizations claiming overlapping constituencies. In Canadian usage, voluntarism describes a peculiar arrangement where educational institutions are selectively identified to receive recognition and support on a matching basis to their own popularity and resources. In recent years, however, this has led to a debate within the Evangelical community and the smaller denominations about favoritism towards select groups recognized in nineteenth-century canons.

The theological underpinnings of voluntarism provide a major contribution to evolving Christian thought. For centuries theologians and philosophers have debated the freedom of the will, a subject which has separated Augustine and Pelagius, Luther and Erasmus, Calvin and Arminius, to name just a few. If one stresses too much the action of human initiative, the sovereignty of God is diminished; on the other hand, an excessive determinism deprives human beings of their own freedom, seen as a gift of God in creation. This debate was more than a sideline, it was a major determinant of orthodoxy. Once resolved to the satisfaction of a majority of mainstream Christians, a new dynamism and power in the providence of God was set forth in the church and the world which greatly extended the gospel of Jesus Christ. A key aspect of this discussion was the impact of the Renaissance and later the Enlightenment, whereby human capability was given new value in social and political contexts. John Locke, for instance, did much to advance the currency and vocabulary of religious voluntarism in Western thought.

Voluntarism has had a pronounced impact upon Christian experience in the West, both before and since its recognition as a valid phenomenon. Yet we understand too little how voluntarism has an impact and how it transforms Christian life and structures. The believers churches have spent too little time understanding the voluntary claim in their own identity and how this gift to other Christians has had a runaway effect upon virtually every other category of Christian life. Hence the underlying rationale for the theme of the Twelfth Believers Church Conference in the Canadian context.

The theme of the Believers Church Conference held at McMaster Divinity College, in Hamilton, Ontario on October 17-19, 1996 focused upon the meaning and implications of voluntarism. Papers were invited, and voluntary (!) responses were evaluated according to their suitability for the general theme. Overall, the planning committee attempted to encompass various angles on the idea of voluntarism, exhibiting several scholarly methodologies. The Conference featured papers from a wide variety of perspectives (reproduced in this volume), plus responses. We realized that voluntarism, while an historic characteristic of believers churches, now belongs to the general social fabric. Hence we were pleased that Catholics, mainstream Protestants, and Pentecostals were involved.

A second feature of the Conference was interactive. A panel discussion elaborating upon the Toronto Blessing as a current manifestation of voluntarism, as well as a second panel discussion about the nature of parachurch organizations, especially in the Canadian context, and how they operate as voluntary associations, were well-received. Mainstream, evangelical, and Pentecostal representatives were part of the first panel; the Canadian Bible Society, InterVarsity Canada, and the Salvation Army were all represented in the second discussion. A third feature of the Conference was focused in addresses presented by Virginia Hodgekinson and Brian Stiller on the growth of Christian voluntarism in the religious organizational life of the United States and Canada, respectively. Hodgekinson works for the Independent Sector in Washington, D. C. (her paper was not available in written form). Stiller has long been associated with organized Evangelicalism across Canada.

The first section of this volume has an historical or sociological focus. David Priestley, a Baptist historical theologian, examines the basis of ecclesiology which emerged from the various segments of English Protestantism in the seventeenth century, with particular focus on the Independents or Congregationalists. He finds several key elements in the Congregationalist understanding which elucidate the voluntary spirit, including the basis of church membership, leadership, and inter-congregational cooperation. Michael Haykin, a Baptist church historian, further exhibits the character of voluntarism in the life of William Fraser, a nineteenth-century Scottish-Canadian preacher who pioneered church development in Upper Canada. Fraser was a product of the Haldanite Revival in Scotland and was zealous for evangelism, missions, and education. He was a quintessential Canadian voluntarist of his era.

Next, Brian Hogan, a Canadian Catholic historian, brings an entirely new perspective to voluntarism as he examines the evolution of voluntary Catholic organizations such as Catholic Action and the Institute of Social Action in the twentieth century. Undergirded by a changing theological attitude illustrated in Vatican II and a more voluntary socio-political environment, Hogan argues that Catholic voluntary associations have been transformative vehicles for both participants and their environments. Mennonite sociologist Leo Driedger then relates voluntarism to individualism, and finds that in times of social change Mennonite initiative and individualism shaped new social patterns and institutions. Using an impressive array of empirical and family data, Driedger analyzes types of individualism, and finds that Mennonites use initiative and assertiveness extensively for the service of others – the essence of the voluntary character.

Finally, two writers discuss the contemporary character of voluntarism on the Canadian scene. Brian Stiller, a Pentecostal minister and well-known Evangelical leader in Canada for over two decades, reflects on the power of voluntarism, especially in the Canadian Evangelical community, and argues that Evangelicals must retain a high commitment to voluntarism because of its being part of the Evangelical character. James Beverley, a theologian who has followed recent manifestations of the revival impulse in Canada, looks carefully at the phenomenon of the Toronto Blessing and concludes that it is everything a voluntary manifestation should be, but he is sceptical about the background influences and dismayed by the tone and level of criticism by some churchmen who are themselves part of the larger voluntarist community. The Toronto Blessing was selected as an obvious voluntarist phenomenon which has drawn interest worldwide.

Section two offers several critiques of the idea of voluntarism, especially as it relates to religious experience in the late twentieth century. Scott Holland, a Church of the Brethren pastor in Pennsylvania, wrestles with Anabaptist identity and declares that the tradition has given itself much to decision and discipleship but little to mystery and grace. By drawing upon the Pietist heritage in particular and mysticism as well, he reminds us in the believers church tradition of the importance of individuals, which is fundamental to the voluntarism we affirm. His is a call for more radical poetics and practical virtuosity.

James Reimer and Joyce Bellous next offer critiques from very different perspectives. James Reimer, a Mennonite historical theologian, surveys medieval voluntarism and then introduces the recent work of Anglican theologian Joan Lockwood O'Donovan to understand better classical believers church theologians Balthasar Hubmaier and Pilgram Marpeck. Reimer argues that voluntarists (and especially those in the believers church traditions) are caught between classic realism and nominalism, and ultimately must acknowledge that human agency is derived from, dependent upon, and accountable to divine agency.

Joyce Bellous, an educational specialist, likewise raises very important questions about the philosophical premises of Christian voluntarism and the impact of voluntarism on the process of Christian discipleship. She questions the nature of voluntarism as always "benevolent"; she also raises a process question about the nature of a believer's growth into what she calls the "fullness of Christ."

The final two papers look forward. James McClendon, a Baptist theologian who has redefined "baptistic" themes in previous work, defines voluntarism in his own experience and its evolution in modern Baptist experience with examples from the United States and Canada. With other Baptists, McClendon calls for new attention to Bible study, shared discipleship, a free common life in Christ, and liberty without coercion. These are elements which place the believers churches in good position to respond to demands on the church in the years ahead. From a different perspective, Reformed theologian George Vandervelde challenges the believers churches to follow their voluntary emphases and seriously engage the ecumenical dialogues in the broader church. A re-examination of church and voluntary faith, he believes, will strengthen the believers churches while also opening new avenues of theological understanding for other churches. The believers church ecclesiology is a great gift to the larger church.

It is the collective hope and prayer of the planners and participants of the Twelfth Believers Church Conference that this stimulating gathering will generate new discussions and studies of the character of voluntarism, and that those in the historic believers churches will be strengthened in their resolve and open to others in the Body of Christ who value this great tradition.

The editor wishes to express appreciation to James Reimer, co-editor of the series *Studies in the Believers Church Tradition*, to Arnold Snyder and the staff of Pandora Press for their helpful suggestions and patient and meticulous care during the production process, and to Mrs. Terri Galan at McMaster Divinity College for her good work in fulfilling many obligations between the conference and the publication. Gratitude is also expressed to the Board of Trustees of McMaster Divinity College for their support of the twelfth Believers Church Conference and this series.

William H. Brackney, Convenor and Editor
Principal, McMaster Divinity College

1

Believers' Assembly or Believers Church:
A Seventeenth-Century Rationale for Congregational Polity

David T. Priestley

> *I believe in the Holy Spirit,*
> *the holy catholic church,*
> *the communion of saints,*
> *the forgiveness of sins.*

We in the believers churches are identifiable primarily by our restrictive answer to the question, "Who constitute the church?" We make the quite voluntarist reply: true believers in Christ, people who personally accept the Gospel, intentional Christians, voluntary disciples, or (in the terminology of seventeenth-century Puritans), "visible saints." Preoccupied with whether people have "genuine faith," evangelicals effectively have reduced the question of Christianity to one of whether an individual believes, expressed frequently as: "Are you saved? Have you been converted?"[1] The believers church movement, however, is about the *church*, not simply about believing; i.e., it is about a voluntarist *church* no less than a voluntarist faith. This paper will examine the specific proposal that seventeenth-century Independents made for the shape of the believers church.

Sixteenth-century radicals rejected the medieval tradition of a comprehensive national or ethnic church. Nevertheless, continental Anabaptists and then English Puritans took for granted that the Christian life is a "churched" life; faith and church are voluntary, but not optional. Hence, they laboured to shape biblical structures for life together as the Body of Christ. The theological premise for their biblical study lay in the phrases like those of the Apostles' Creed that sketch the arena and work

David T. Priestley is professor of historical theology at Edmonton Baptist Seminary in Edmonton, Alberta.

[1] Stanley J. Grenz, *Revisioning Evangelical Theology* (Downers Grove, IL: InterVarsity Press, 1993), 164-69, joins in current expressions of uneasiness with this truncated Gospel.

of the Holy Spirit: "the holy catholic church, the communion of saints, the forgiveness of sins." One betrays one's vision when the question of the church is reduced to "Who are saints?"

The seventeenth-century Puritans, as did the sixteenth-century Reformers, accepted the traditional understanding that the church's ministry of forgiving sins is an exercise of the "keys of the kingdom of heaven" that Christ gave to Peter (Matt. 16.19). Protestants denied that the keys are the monopoly of a hierarchy stretching from Rome into the smallest European village. Luther, for example, insisted that those who by faith lay hold of the God who graciously justifies are freed not only *from* priestly oppression but *to be* priests to one another: "we are worthy to appear before God and to pray for others and to teach one another the things of God."[2] By "the priesthood of the believer," he intended to express the sacred privilege every Christian has, in the midst of any earthly vocation and situation of life, of declaring that God unconditionally accepts the unrighteous and of demonstrating that Christ frees us from the bondage of sin, death, and the devil.[3] Believer priests exercise the keys of the Kingdom when they proclaim in their speech and life that God justifies by grace alone through faith alone. The church, then, is the assembly of priests willingly gathered under the One they have chosen to order their worship, those whom they have "charged with the administration of the Word of God and the sacraments."[4] They assemble to announce again and experience anew the Gospel in order to return to vocational responsibilities in the liberty the Spirit creates.[5]

---

[2] Martin Luther, "The Freedom of a Christian" (1520) in *Luther's Works* 31 (Philadelphia: Muhlenberg Press, 1957), 355.

[3] Gustaf Wingren, *Luther on Vocation* (Philadelphia: Muhlenberg Press, 1957).

[4] Martin Luther, "To the Christian Nobility of the German Nation," *Luther's Works* 44 (Philadelphia: Fortress Press, 1966), 130.

[5] See Robert H. Fischer, "Luther on the Priesthood of All Believers," *Baptist Quarterly* 17:7 (July 1958), 293-311. Cf. John Owen, "Digression on the priesthood of all Christians" in "The Duty of Pastors and People Distinguished" (1644), *The Works of John Owen*, ed. William H. Goold 13 (repr. Carlisle, PA: Banner of Truth Trust, 1967), 19-29. Luther's proposal for "those who want to be Christians in earnest" ("The German Mass" [1526] in *Luther's Works* 53 [Philadelphia: Fortress Press, 1965], 63f.) is the point of departure for Donald F. Durnbaugh's paradigm in *The Believers' Church* (New York: Macmillan, 1968), 3-33.

In England, the question of the church took another turn in response to the Elizabethan Settlement of 1559. Some purists were vehemently dissatisfied with the limitations of these reforms. A small number initiated Separatist churches in Elizabeth's time. They anathematized the state church while they struggled to formulate a congregational rationale and practice, a church whose members were "of the willing sort," in Robert Browne's famous phrase.[6] Under James I, doctrinaire Presbyterians hoped for the restructuring of the Church of England on the Scottish pattern. Other Puritans argued for a "middle way" between Separatism and presbyterial government which would be a voluntary church, though authorized by Parliament as the form for the Church of England.

The English ecclesiological debate came to a head in the Assembly of Divines that Parliament appointed in 1643 to advise it on how Scripture and the teachings of the Reformation ought to be embodied in the Church of England. By that time, three parties were arguing that their respective polity was the sole dominical design; depending on whom one asked, episcopacy, independency, or presbytery was *jus divinum* for the Church.[7]

In their *Apologetical Narration*, the Westminster Independents observed that there is in Scripture "a complete sufficiency as to make the man of God perfect so also to make the churches of God perfect . . . if the directions and examples therein delivered were fully known and followed."[8] Ten years later, one of them insisted that in Scripture all of

> these appointments, institutions, and ordinances of Christ –
> baptism, the Lord's Supper, particular churches, the ministry,
> church censures, singing of psalms, and the like – are laid on

[6] Robert Browne, "A Treatise of Reformation without Tarrying for Any" in *The Writings of Robert Harrison and Robert Browne*, ed. Albert Peel and Leland H. Carlson, Elizabethan Nonconformist Texts 2 (London: George Allen and Unwin, 1953), 162.

[7] J. R. DeWitt, *Jus Divinum: The Westminster Assembly and the Divine Right of Church Government* (Kampen: J. H. Kok N. V., 1969); cf. Robert S. Paul, *Assembly of the Lord: Politics and Religion in the Westminster Assembly and the "Grand Debate"* (Edinburgh: T. & T. Clark, 1985).

[8] Thomas Goodwin et al., *An Apologetical Narration Humbly Submitted to the Honourable Houses of Parliament* (London, 1643), 9.

such universal and perpetual grounds as to continue until Christ's coming again.[9]

This essay looks at the seventeenth-century proposal that these appointments, which are "Christ's only law for the church," constitute the principles of congregationalism. "Independency" was its other name, derived from its insistence on the autonomy of each church from the jurisdiction of other churches. It saw itself as the beneficiary of the thought and experiences of the continental Reformed churches, of the New England churches, and of "the fatal miscarriages and shipwrecks of the Separation."[10] Prime advocates for "the congregational way" were William Ames (1576-1633), John Bunyan (1628-1688), John Cotton (1584-1652) with other New England divines, John Owen (1616-1683), and the Westminster and Savoy "Independents."[11]

Their constant appeal was to Christ, "the only Lawgiver to the Church." John Owen awkwardly stated the principle:

> The church is the house of Christ, his family, his kingdom. To act [i.e., exercise] any power in its rule which is not his, which derives not from him, which is not by his legal grant or to act

---

[9] William Bridge, *A Vindication of Ordinances* (London: 1653), 5.

[10] Goodwin et al., *Apologetical Narration*, 4-5.

[11] Alan P.F. Sell, *Saints: Visible, Orderly, Catholic—The Congregational Idea of the Church* (Allison Park, PA: Pickwick Publications, 1986). The specifically "Independent" literature (publications in the time of the Westminster Assembly) begins with Goodwin et al., *Apologetical Narration*. John Cotton was often quoted by friend and foe: see his *The Keys of the Kingdom of Heaven* (London: 1644); *The Way of the Churches of Christ in New England* (London: 1645); *The Way of the Congregational Churches Cleared* responded to criticisms (London: 1648). A three-part volume by New England authorities was *Church Government and Church Covenant Discussed* (London: 1643). It consisted of Hugh Peter, "An Answer of the elders of the several churches in New England to Two and Thirty Questions;" Richard Mather, "An Apology of the Said Elders in New England for Church Covenant" [1639]; and John Davenport, "An Answer to Nine Positions about Church Government." Thomas Hooker, *A Survey of the Sum of Church Discipline* (London: 1648) was prefaced by an Independent commendation when it appeared.

any power by ways, processes, rules, and laws not of his appointment is an invasion of his right and dominion.[12]

Disciples of the Lord have only a ministerial power in forming and practising church life; they are authorized to do only as He commanded. Hence, the Scriptures are to be investigated rigorously to discern polity in general and policy as specific issues arise. Their polity has seven characteristics.

The first characteristic is "visible sainthood." The confession that the church is "the communion of saints" was taken quite literally by non-separating Congregationalists; hence, they deserve investigation as a seventeenth-century English believers church.

In 1672, John Bunyan published an essay subtitled "With who, or who not, I can hold Church-fellowship, or the Communion of Saints." There he declared, "my principles are such as lead me to a denial to communicate in the things of the Kingdom of Christ with ungodly and open profane."[13] Thirty-five years earlier John Cotton had written: "Let no member come in but he that *knows Christ*."[14] The New England divine explained, in a book published during the Assembly debates, that the church is to consist of those who know "the principles of religion" (doctrine), have "experience in the ways of grace" (faith), and are known for "their godly conversation among men" (obedience). Contrariwise, those who are "ignorant and graceless or scandalous" patently are not saints and are ineligible for communion with saints.[15] Faith is wilful and obedience is determined. The Savoy "Platform of Church Polity," appended to the Independents' revision of the Westminster Confession, stated: "The members of these churches are saints by calling, visibly manifesting and

---

[12] Owen, "The True Nature of a Gospel Church and its Government," *Works* 16, 33.

[13] "A Confession of my Faith and A Reason of My Practice," *The Miscellaneous Works of John Bunyan* 4 (London: Oxford University Press, 1989), 135-36.

[14] John Cotton, "Sermon at Salem" in *John Cotton on the Churches of New England*, ed. Larzer Ziff (Cambridge, MA: Belknap Press, 1968), 59.

[15] Cotton, *Way of the Churches of Christ*, 54.

evidencing . . . their obedience to that call of Christ . . . ."[16] Called, they resolved to obey.

The Congregationalists uniformly asserted that the rock on which the church is built (Matt. 16:18) is those who confess as Peter did, i.e., who have a conviction wrought by God, not by human pedagogy, persuasion, reasoning, or coercion. Those who choose to believe like that, said William Ames, experience real changes, not merely a change of state (justification); there are

> genuine effects seen in degrees of beginning, progress and completion (2 Cor. 4.16: "the inner man is renewed day by day"). Sanctification is the real change in man from the sordidness of sin to the purity of God's image (Eph. 4.22-24).[17]

Owen, once a Presbyterian, likewise came to affirm visible godliness as the prerequisite to incorporation into the church; candidates for embodiment in a particular visible church are:

> such as, in the judgement of charity, entitle them to all the appellations of "saints, called, sanctified"– that is, visibly and by profession – which are given to the members of all the churches in the New Testament.[18]

The likely source of the term beloved of Independents for the church's latitude in "trying" membership candidates is John Calvin (1509-1564). Members of the church, the French evangelical explained, are those whom the church, by a "judgement of charity," believes do honestly confess the faith and evidence the life.[19] Among the English Puritans, these strictures were not to be exercised with legalistic rigour; they claimed a latitude "as

---

[16] "Of the Institution of Churches and the Order appointed in them by Jesus Christ," art. 8, in Williston Walker, ed., *The Creeds and Platforms of Congregationalism* (Boston: Pilgrim Press, 1960), 404.

[17] William Ames, *Marrow of Theology*, I.29.1-2, 4 (Boston: Pilgrim Press, 1968), 167-68.

[18] Owen, "True Nature," *Works* 17.

[19] John Calvin, *Institutes of the Christian Religion* IV.1.8, 9.

would take in any member of Christ, the meanest in whom there may be supposed to be the least of Christ."[20]

Obviously, people may be moral though unregenerate; others are hypocrites. Since human judgement as to who are saints cannot be infallible, the church inevitably is mixed. Nonetheless, it flies in the face of common sense, let alone the purpose and law of Christ, to welcome into the church of the faithful those who made no pretence of godliness, those who were "notoriously and flagitiously wicked," if not quite "pests of the earth."[21]

"Give none offence" (1 Cor. 10:32); "approve things that are excellent; . . . be sincere and without offence" (Phil. 1:10); "as He who has called you is holy, so you be holy in all manner of conversation" (1 Pet. 1:15) are texts the Congregationalists often adduced. Consecration to God entails separation from the world; moreover, saints become visible only as they show evidence of separation. The traditional rationalization for encouraging a mixed church, they argued, was based on specious use of the parable of the wheat and the tares (Matt. 13:24-30), the type of Noah's ark (Gen. 7:7-9), and analogous texts. Saints were visible. So, too, was the church Christ ordained.

The second characteristic of congregational polity was the "particular visible church." Hugh Peter expressed the Congregationalist sentiment and the New England practice plainly: "We do not know any visible church of the N. T. properly so called but only a particular congregation."[22] Cotton bluntly called the notion of an universal visible Church a "chimera." And the "invisible church" was a yet greater abstraction that served no practical purpose; it may even perniciously distract us from radical intentional discipleship. The church must be visible; Owen took it as given "that all church power and authority, for the administration of all the ordinances and institutions of the gospel, was intrusted with a particular congregation."[23]

---

[20] Goodwin et al., *Apologetical Narration*, 12.

[21] Owen, "True Nature," *Works* 16, 11.

[22] Peter, "Two and Thirty Questions," 9-10.

[23] Owen, "A Discourse concerning the administration of Church Censures," *Works* 16, 233. This is an emphatic principle, not simply a pragmatic observation about "the persistently communal nature of religion"–James P. Wind and James W. Lewis, *American Congregations* 1 (Chicago: University of Chicago Press, 1994), 2.

Each such visible church possessed the full competence and power Christ promised to the Church. The particular church alone had the power of the keys, the seals, the censures, the offices, the communion, and the authority by which spiritual life was sustained and enriched. Christ instituted the church to sustain the faith and cultivate the growth of believers (Eph. 4:12); it is the human instrument through whose teaching, admonition, sacraments, and common life the purposes of redemption are realized in the saints.

The visible church was, by Christ's institution, inevitable. Saints were necessarily drawn into deliberate church fellowship with other saints. Calling to Christ's people invariably was entailed in calling to Christ. Bunyan imaginatively applied details of Noah's story to express the essentiality of church life. The various animals who came to Christ (*sic*) in the ark, he observed, did so "by a special instinct from heaven of the fruits of a divine election." Analogously, saints also entered the ark of the church, not by nature or arbitrary human resolve, "but as being by a divine hand singled out and guided thither. . . ."[24] On the other hand, it was an act "of the obedience of faith to the authority of Christ," i.e., it is a voluntary act, the willing choice of the believer who recognized there is no other option where Christ is King.[25] Whether one emphasises divine constraint or human volition, "churchmanship was inescapable"; saints were always "orderly."[26]

Nevertheless, the saints do not arbitrarily organize churches; the Lord irresistibly brings them into existence. Hence, they are to be "gathered churches" of believers who cooperate in their calling rather than churches comprehending all residents in a parish. A commitment to Him to walk as He has ordained begets our commitment to each other to mutually encourage the common fulfilment of that obligation.

The third characteristic of congregational polity, therefore, was the "covenant." The church was intentional. Godly people, members in good standing of pure and true churches in several places, may assemble occasionally, even for spiritual edification, yet that does not constitute them a church.[27] What distinguished the circumstantial assembly of the

---

[24] Bunyan, "An Exposition on the Ten First Chapters of Genesis and Part of the Eleventh," *Miscellaneous Works* 12, 206-7.

[25] Owen, "True Nature," *Works* 16, 27.

[26] Sell, *Saints: Visible, Orderly, Catholic*, 3.

[27] Cotton, *Way of the Churches of Christ*, 10.

faithful from a particular visible church is the voluntary covenant the saints make among themselves and with the Lord. A particular church comes into being when, in Ames's words: "Believers bind themselves individually to perform all those duties toward God and toward one another which relate to the purpose of the church and its edification." Gathered, they will to be united. This bond is self-consciously a "communion of *saints*" for it is constituted with the intention of encouraging "holy communion with God among themselves."[28] Such believers, Owen asserted,

> enter into a church-state . . . by mutual confederation or solemn agreement for the performance of all the duties which the Lord Christ has prescribed to his disciples in such churches and in order to the exercise of the power wherewith they are intrusted according to the rule of the word.[29]

The covenant idea was pervasive in the "federal theology" of English Puritanism as well as among continental reformers.[30] It distinctively applied the classical Christian understanding that the Church is God's New Israel. As God contracted with Abraham and with Israel under Moses, He also contracts with those who commit themselves trustingly to obey the divine will more fully revealed through Christ. And as Israel renewed its covenant ordinarily in the cycle of annual festivals, the ordinary meetings of the Christian church are services of renewal and reinforcement of the new covenant.

When John Cotton preached (as quoted above): "Let no member come in but he that *knows Christ*," his text was Jer. 50:5: "They shall ask the way to Zion with their faces thitherward, saying, 'Come and let us join ourselves to the Lord in a perpetual covenant that shall not be forgotten.'" Under the same text, Richard Mather (1596-1669) fulsomely described a church covenant as the following:

---

[28] Ames, *Marrow*, I.32.14-18, p. 180-81.

[29] Owen, "True Nature," *Works* 16, 25.

[30] Charles S. McCoy and J. Wayne Baker, *Fountainhead of Federalism: Heinrich Bullinger and the Covenant Tradition* (Louisville: Westminster/John Knox, 1991); J. Wayne Baker, *Heinrich Bullinger and the Covenant: The Other Reformed Tradition* (Athens, OH: Ohio University Press, 1980).

a solemn and public promise before the Lord whereby a company of Christians, called by the power and mercy of God to fellowship with Christ and by His providence to live together and by His grace to cleave together in the unity of faith and brotherly love and desirous to partake together in all the holy ordinances of God, do in confidence of His gracious acceptance in Christ bind themselves to the Lord and one to another to walk together by the assistance of His Spirit in all such ways of holy worship in him and of edification one towards another as the Gospel of Christ requires of every Christian church and the members thereof.[31]

This expressed a self-conscious voluntarism.

The church provided for all in its covenant the seals of the covenant. Any child (or grandchild) of an admitted saint should be baptized in infancy, as Israelites analogously circumcised the newborn. But such baptized persons were not admitted to the "privileges" of the Gospel, to full communion in church order, until the church judged them fit to exercise the keys. From the obvious impropriety that "openly ungracious and profane" people should be admitted to the Lord's Table, the New England churches

infer the necessity of their personal profession of their faith when they come to years and taking hold of church covenant, whereby we mean only a renewing of covenant or a new professing of their interest in God's covenant and walking according to it when they shall be adults.[32]

So the second seal of the covenant, the sacrament of the Lord's Table, and the other privileges of the church were granted only to those whom the church judges to be "visible saints." The Lord's Table is a place of self-evaluation and church discipline. Participants are expected to exercise discernment of their own spiritual walk. Relations with others must be restored before one received the seal:

[31] Mather, "Apology for Church Covenant," 3.
[32] Peter, "Two and Thirty Questions," 20.

[T]herefore, if you bring your gift to the altar and there remember that your brother has ought against you, leave there your gift before the altar and go your way; first be reconciled to your brother and then come and offer your gift (Matt. 5:23, 24).

If one does not take the initiative to sustain fellowship, the Table must be refused to those who have violated their promise of obedience and submission. The voluntarism of membership was understood to entail closed communion; only those whom the church had authority to censure, i.e., those who are in covenant in that particular church, may participate at the Table.

The flagrantly wicked may not mock the Gospel by participating in the Table. The impenitent have no right to the Table which is fenced by the church's collective discernment. The restored jubilantly return to the place of nurture after the church judges them to have returned to proper conformity to the standards of the Gospel. The reader should note, the *church* judges.

The fourth characteristic of this polity was congregationalism. The power of the keys, in contrast to any episcopal or clerical pretension, was exercised by the whole congregation in itself or through its officers when the Gospel was declared and its common judgement was determined. The congregationalist polemicists and politicians spent much more time addressing the responsibility of the church to arrive at common judgements to discern the mind of Christ than discussing its function to publicize the Gospel. The keys were an unavoidable responsibility, although often identified by them as a "Gospel privilege."

Church censures manifested the responsibility and power of the keys. Congregationalist discussion of the subject of the power of the church usually opened by discussing discipline. "Tell it to the church," Christ instructed the disciples (Matt. 18:17).

The seventeenth-century congregationalists reasoned that discipline presupposed the church's prior authority to identify and incorporate its members. Without power to admit members, they inferred, it could have no authority to censure them. Consequently, the church must discriminate among those who presented themselves for admission. It did not do this presumptuously or arbitrarily; it acted only on the criteria recorded in God's word. Christ has made the law; the church administered it.

"Christian," finally, was a title the church bestowed on those it determines fit the name, not a label one claimed for oneself.

The candidate freely confessed personal faith and related experience of grace; the church reasonably and charitably judged the words and life of the petitioner. To present oneself for membership implied one agreed to embrace the covenant among the believers, founded on the covenant God apparently already has effected in one's heart. The pledge might be formally voiced in question and answer, or in personal confession or "relations," or tacitly understood from the interest of the candidate. The church also, by accepting the new member, made its pledge of watchcare and aid to attain "the full stature of Christ" (Eph. 4:13). The mutual voluntarism of this procedure is patent.

The fifth characteristic of congregational polity was a strong eldership. Christ not only ordained the church to consist of saints and to be for their communion and edification; He graciously identified officers by whom the saints are to be led and fed (Eph. 4:11; 1 Tim. 3:1-13; 5:9-10; Titus 1:5-9). Elders may preach and teach; these were the pastors and doctors of the church. Elders governed; they were the "ruling elders" who directed the church's deliberations and announced and enforced its judgements. Deacons served at the Lord's Table and at the tables of those who preach and teach as well as of those who suffer want. Widows tended the sick and needy. While pastors and doctors and widows deserved the material support of the church, ruling elders and deacons served at their own cost, unless they qualified as among the needy.

Officers were chosen from among those in the church whom the Spirit had gifted for the ministry pertaining to the office. Christ not only designated offices, they believed; by the Spirit, He went on to provide the saints to fill them. Without the charismatic overtones of much modern talk of spiritual gifts, these Puritans took seriously the promise that God would provide what and who each church needs. They were certain that the gifts of prophecy, miracles, tongues, and interpretation were limited to the primitive church as also the offices of apostle and evangelist were; but the rest were much discussed. Ministry, teaching, exhortation, generosity, rule, mercy (Rom. 12), wisdom, knowledge, faith, discernment (1 Cor. 12), and pastors and teachers (Eph. 4) were gifts that the church identifies in members whom it then calls to places of service. "Improving of gifts" was assumed; spiritual endowment did not ensure instant excellence.

Church rulers, as the church itself, had only a ministerial power, not a right to legislate. They governed only according to the instructions

Christ laid down; they may formulate no statutes of their own. This applied to specific questions of local issues no less than to the larger question of polity. Owen remembered the attractive phrase that says the ministers' role is not to dominate but to be "helpers of your joy" (2 Cor. 1:24).

While many may see congregationalism as democracy in the church, the seventeenth-century independents acknowledged considerable authority in the offices of pastor, teacher, and ruling elder. The power of the church enabled the congregation to identify and elect its leaders; the power of the church also required the discernment and consent of the congregation in matters of discipline and doctrine.

Yet the leaders clearly took the lead. The ruling elder presented the issues; the pastor expounded the applicable biblical teaching; the elders aired the options. Members could comment or question. Finally, the ruling elder put the question to the church. The consent of the church in election, admission, censure, or other resolution of common concern could be given by silence as well as by affirmation.

The sixth characteristic of congregational polity was discipline. By Christ's design and ordinance (Matt. 16:19; John 20:23), the church was the means by which the Kingdom is opened and shut. In worship and sacraments, in teaching and self-government, the church proclaimed the good news of wrath and redemption. It exercised the keys of the Kingdom. It was the arena in which sins were forgiven and retained, the society where liberty and condemnation were declared, the institution by which human destinies were revealed.

The initial submission of the Christian was to Christ as King. The function of the church was to further Christ's royal dominion. Believers, gathered by the Spirit, covenanted together to walk in the way Christ indicated. Their mutual care and aid entailed correction. The first text that warrants conceiving of the church as particular is one that deals with correction between disciples. Matt. 18:15-20 records Christ's instruction: "Tell it to the church;" the "it" one tells the church is the brother's trespass and his refusal to acknowledge and rectify it, despite the appeals of the offended party and the admonitions of others invited to help. The incestuous couple at Corinth were to be disciplined by the church: "By the name of our Lord Jesus Christ, when you are gathered together . . . with the power of our Lord Jesus Christ . . . deliver such a one to Satan" (1 Cor. 5:4-5). This punishment "by many" had limits, however; by collective action, when repentance is evident, the whole church is to "forgive and comfort lest perhaps such a one should be swallowed up with overmuch sorrow" (2 Cor. 2:6-7).

In judicial terms, "charges were laid" against saints by any party they offend or by anyone cognizant of public scandal they commit, provided the steps of brotherly appeal and of small group admonition have been followed without success. Elders received the accusation, investigated the case by interviewing all involved, deliberated over Scripture and reason, and presented the matter with their recommendation to the church. The church then followed the elders' proposal as being the mind of Christ and removed the recalcitrant one from membership. To put a fine point on it, a judgement was made that the erstwhile brother/sister failed to manifest the holiness expected of saints; and until behaviour changed, until reconciliation and restitution occurred, the onetime "saint" could no longer be reckoned one of Christ's.

There was a soteriological dimension in this definition and practice of the church; Bunyan expressed it in five neat lines:

> to show the church wherein she should
> in all her actions so herself behave
> as to convince the faulty she would save
> his soul; and that 'tis for this very thing
> she does him unto open judgement bring.[33]

The church, by its testing at the time of admission and its subsequent censure, demonstrated to everyone the seriousness of Christ's call and the power of the keys entrusted to her. Specifically to the ungodly, it shows the possibility of a real salvation; to the excommunicate, the likelihood of a real damnation.[34]

The seventh characteristic of Independency was its cooperativeness. The subtitle of Cotton's *Way of the Churches of Christ in New England* was "the way of churches walking in brotherly equality, or coordination, without subjection of one church to another." No authority was vested in any inter-congregational office or agency. Hence, the polity came to be called Independent, not always with complimentary intent. However, the

---

[33] Bunyan, "Discourse of the Building, Nature, Excellency, and Government of the House of God" (1688), lines 1151-54, *Miscellaneous Works* 6 (1980).

[34] John von Rohr, "*Extra ecclesiam nulla salus*: an Early Congregational Version," *Church History* 36 (1967), 107-21.

Independents made no pretence of absolute congregational autonomy. In the first place, each church sought to be subject to the will of Christ. Then, should a church be unable to discern the mind of Christ on an issue (through ignorance or sin), it was to call on the neighbouring churches to send their elders and experienced brethren to advise them.

The key case and text for this principle and practice was the Jerusalem council (Acts 15). In its voluntary exercise of inter-church consultation, congregationalism made visible the larger unity of the churches of Christ. Such councils or synods can have no jurisdictional authority because churches have no covenant of mutual care and submission among themselves; they can only advise. Hence, while a church must excommunicate the obdurate and impenitent for violating covenant with the particular visible church of which one is a member, the only censure among churches can be to withdraw fellowship from the congregation that refuses to correct itself when advised that it was breaking some essential of Christian faith or life expressed or entailed in the Law of Christ.

* * *

Presupposing both the traditional centrality of the church to define and nurture Christians and the traditional authority of Scripture, seventeenth-century congregationalists argued for a church polity that incorporated "visible saints" of "a willing sort" into particular gathered churches under the headship of Christ. These saints covenanted to obey all the commands of Christ and to encourage one another to grow into the fullness of Christ by example and admonition, by word and sacrament, by charity and discipline. They elected gifted members to offices of preaching, teaching, and government in the church as Christ directed in His word and by the Spirit. Admission and excommunication were extreme instances of the church's authority to bind and loose. While each church enjoyed the full competence of the keys independently of any outside authority, fraternal responsibilities required them to invite and heed the counsel of neighbouring churches.

They understood their polity for a believers church to be Christ-ordained. Reason subject to Scripture and the Spirit should arrive at this congregational shape for the church; and the will subject to Christ, the only King and Lawgiver in the Church, should exert every effort to realize this gracious provision for Christian growth. Polity is not *adiaphora*; it must be obeyed as *jus divinum*. It was not an option though it was thoroughly voluntarist.

The specifics of their proposal were not an end-station. The federalism of this seventeenth-century covenant theology led inexorably to broader exercise of the congregation's authority, relaxing the Puritan oligarchy of elders into a greater equality of responsibility and participation. The incongruity of appealing to the civil magistrate to validate a believers church for an entire nation (or particularly, of limiting the civil franchise to visible saints) or of sustaining the entrenched practice of baptizing the unconscious and unwilling was apparent to some in their ecclesiastical family even as the thought summarized in these pages was being hammered out.

The voluntarist convictions these believers churches of the seventeenth-century deduced from Scripture and elaborated out of the church's traditions is a heritage the church of the twenty-first century dare not ignore. Believers may assemble in any random pattern as they will. But if we of a later generation are to constitute ourselves as a particular visible church, we must remember that some English forebears believed that Christ has made lasting "appointments, institutions, and ordinances" for the Church. Our willing conformity to their guidance will be a conformity to Christ, not to an English ancestry, to a design no less dominical because it once was extracted and extrapolated by Puritan churchmen and their Congregational and Baptist successors.

2

Voluntarism in the Life and Ministry of William Fraser (1801-1883)

Michael A.G. Haykin

Fundamental to the Baptist tradition since its emergence from the Puritan/Separatist matrix in seventeenth-century England has been the quality of voluntarism.[1] The faith characteristic of Baptists has been "an eager, free and full surrender to the Lord, and in the Lord to one another."[2] When, for instance, Thomas Helwys (c. 1575-1615) returned to England from the Netherlands in 1612 to plant the first Baptist church on English soil and to face certain persecution as a consequence, he published a plea for religious liberty. In it he sought to persuade his monarch, James I, that although he rightfully had the "power to take our sonnes & our daughters to do all his services of war, and of peace," he had no right exercising this power over men and women when it came to religious matters.

> Doth not the King knowe that the God of Gods, and Lord of Lords, . . . hath reserved to himself a heavenly kingdom, and that with this kingdome, our lord the King hath nothinge to do . . . but as a subject himself, . . . For mens religion to God, is betwixt God and themselves; the King shall not answer for it, neither may the King be judg betwene God and man.[3]

Michael A. G. Haykin is professor of church history at Heritage Baptist College and Theological Seminary in Cambridge, Ontario.

[1] In the words of William H. Brackney: "A voluntary spirit lies at the very heart of the Baptist self-understanding," *The Baptists* (Westport, Connecticut/London: Praeger Publishers, 1994), 71.

[2] Geoffrey F. Nuttall, *Visible Saints: The Congregational Way 1640-1660* (Oxford: Basil Blackwell, 1957), 106-107. Nuttall uses these words of the seventeenth-century founders of Congregationalism, but they are equally applicable to their Baptist cousins.

[3] *A Short Declaration of the mistery of iniquity* (1612) in H. Leon McBeth, *A Sourcebook for Baptist Heritage* (Nashville, Tennessee: Broadman Press, 1990), 71-72. For Helwys, see Ernest A. Payne, *Thomas Helwys and the First Baptist Church in England* (London: The Baptist Union of Great Britain and Ireland, 1962); B.R. White, "Helwys, Thomas" in Richard L. Greaves and Robert Zaller, eds., *Biographical Dictionary of British Radicals in the Seventeenth Century* (Brighton, Sussex: The

Since the Christian faith is ultimately a voluntary matter, to use force and compulsion would be destructive of its very essence.

The same voluntaristic spirit is discernible in another early Baptist text, the *First London Confession of Faith*, drawn up in 1644 by an association of seven Calvinistic Baptist congregations in London. In the ecclesiological section of this confession these churches set forth their conviction that a local church "is a company of visible Saints, called and separated from the world, by the Word and the Spirit of God, to the visible profession of the faith of the Gospel, being baptized into that faith, and joyned to the Lord, and each other by mutuall agreement."[4] This statement combines both tradition and innovation. First of all, it recalls traditional Puritan definitions of the church. For instance, in 1572 John Field (d.1588), co-author of *An Admonition to the Parliament*, one of the most important tracts of Elizabethan Puritanism, could define the church as "a company or congregatione of the faythfull called and gathered out of the worlde by the preachinge of the Gospell."[5] The mention of "mutuall agreement" in the *Confession*, though, is indebted to the Congregationalist conviction that a church can exist only where men and women voluntarily profess their belief in the gospel and willingly agree to join themselves together for worship and to be subject to corporate discipline.[6]

Although Baptist congregations could be found in most parts of England and Wales by the beginning of the eighteenth century, there were virtually none in Scotland until the last few decades of that era. The national church, Presbyterian in its ecclesial structure, had become so fused with Scottishness that Baptist principles seemed completely alien to the Scottish mind. Extremely influential in this regard was the first theological standard of Scottish Presbyterianism, the *Scots Confession*. Drawn up in 1560 by John Knox (c. 1513-1572) and five other Reformed

---

Harvester Press, 1983), II, 76-77; Timothy George, "Between Pacifism and Coercion; The English Baptist Doctrine of Religious Toleration," *The Mennonite Quarterly Review* 58 (1984), 36-39, passim.

[4] *The First London Confession of Faith* XXXIII [William L. Lumpkin, *Baptist Confessions of Faith* 2nd. ed. (Valley Forge: Judson Press, 1969), 165].

[5] Cited in Edmund S. Morgan, *Visible Saints: The History of a Puritan Idea* (Ithaca/London: Cornell University Press, 1963), 14.

[6] For a discussion of this understanding of the church, see especially Nuttall, *Visible Saints*, 101-30.

ministers, this text was adamant in its opposition to believer's baptism: "we damne the error of the Anabaptists, who denies baptisme to apperteine to Children, before that they have faith and understanding."[7]

The first noteworthy appearance of Baptist communities on Scottish soil was in the brief period between the defeat of the Scots by Cromwell's New Model Army at the Battle of Dunbar on September 3, 1650, and the death of Cromwell eight years later. Many of Cromwell's army officers were Baptist in their convictions, and they wasted no time in establishing congregations in the towns where they were garrisoned. Cromwell himself had sought to convince the Scottish Presbyterians of the rightness of tolerating expressions of biblical Christianity other than their own. "Is all religion wrapped up in that or any one form?" he asked the Scots. "We think not so. We say, faith working by love is the true character of a Christian; and, God is our witness, in whomsoever we see any thing of Christ to be, there we reckon our duty to love, waiting for a more plentiful effusion of the spirit of God to make all those Christians, who, by the malice of the world, are diversified, and by their own carnal-mindedness, do diversify themselves by several names of reproach, to be of one heart and one mind, worshipping God with one consent."[8] Scottish Presbyterians, though, remained unconvinced and the restoration of Charles II to the throne in 1660 extinguished all of these Cromwellian expressions of voluntary religion.

Sixty years were to pass before a voluntary church was once again found in Scotland. It was in the 1720s that John Glas (1695-1773), minister of the Presbyterian work in Tealing, gradually came to the conviction that Christ's kingdom is one that is completely spiritual and as

---

[7] *Confessio Fidei Scoticana* XXIII in Philip Schaff, ed. and David S. Schaff, revised, *The Creeds of Christendom* (1931 ed.;repr. Grand Rapids: Baker Book House, 1983), III, 474. My attention was drawn to this text by its inclusion in D. B. Murray, "The Seventeenth and Eighteenth Centuries" in D. W. Bebbington, ed., *The Baptists in Scotland. A History* (Glasgow: The Baptist Union of Scotland, 1988), 9-25.

[8] *A Declaration of the Army of England upon their March into Scotland To all that are Saints, and Partakers of the Faith of God's Elect, in Scotland* in Wilbur Cortez Abbott, *The Writings and Speeches of Oliver Cromwell* (Cambridge: Harvard University Press, 1939), II, 285-86.

such independent of both state control and support.[9] A church of some seventy believers was formed in the parish of Tealing, and over the next couple of decades Glasite congregations could be found in Dundee, Perth, Edinburgh, and booming textile centres such as Paisley and Dunkeld. Although the Glasites were never numerous, Glas's views cast a wide net of influence. The "Scotch Baptists," also known as the "McLeanite Baptists" after their chief theologian and apologist, Archibald McLean (1733-1812), were essentially a product of Glas's ecclesiological vision.[10] James Haldane (1768-1851) and his older brother Robert (1764-1842), fulsomely described by one historian as "the Wesley and Whitefield of Scotland,"[11] were also deeply influenced by Glas, especially after 1803 when they began to move towards Baptist convictions.[12]

Within a few years of their conversion in the mid-1790s both of the Haldanes were undertaking extensive preaching tours of the Highlands and the Orkneys, where their preaching often drew large crowds. Robert had inherited considerable wealth and when the brothers founded the Society for the Propagation of the Gospel at Home (SPGH) in 1797, the first

---

[9] Murray, "Seventeenth and Eighteenth Centuries," 13-14. For Glas, see idem, "The Influence of John Glas," *Records of the Scottish Church History Society* 22 (1984), 45-56.

[10] On the Scotch Baptists, see Murray, "Seventeenth and Eighteenth Centuries," 19-24.

[11] Percival Waugh, "The Converging Streams–1800-50," in George Yuille, ed., *History of the Baptists in Scotland from Pre-Reformation Times* (Glasgow: Baptist Union Publications Committee, 1926), 55.

[12] Murray, "Influence of John Glas", 53-54. The standard life of the Haldanes is Alexander Haldane, *The Lives of Robert and James Haldane* (1852 ed,; repr. Edinburgh: The Banner of Truth Trust, 1990). For more recent studies, see D. B. Murray and D. E. Meek, "The Early Nineteenth Century" in Bebbington, ed., *Baptists in Scotland*, 30-32; Deryck W. Lovegrove, "Unity and Separation: Contrasting Elements in the Thought and Practice of Robert and James Alexander Haldane" in Keigh Robbins, ed., *Protestant Evangelicalism: Britain, Ireland, Germany and America c. 1750-c. 1950.* (Oxford: Basil Blackwell, 1990), 153-77; Kenneth J. Stewart, "Restoring the Reformation: British Evangelicalism and the 'Reveil' at Geneva 1816-1849" (Unpublished Ph. D. Thesis, University of Edinburgh, 1991), 59-66, 126-69; Deryck Lovegrove, "Haldane, James Alexander" in Donald M. Lewis, ed., *The Blackwell Dictionary of Evangelical Biography* 1730-1860 (Oxford/Cambridge, Massachusetts: Blackwell Publishers Ltd., 1995) 1, 501; Kenneth J. Stewart, "Haldane, Robert" in Lewis, ed., *Blackwell Dictionary of Evangelical Biography*, I, 501-02.

itinerant society concerned with the evangelization of the Highlands, he used his wealth to finance the promotion of this venture. Robert's generosity was displayed in the support of the Society's itinerant preachers, the publication of religious tracts and Bibles, the purchase and building of Congregationalist worship centres, and the creation of a seminary, which trained nearly three hundred students in the nine years of its existence from 1799 to 1808. It has been estimated that Robert spent some 70,000 pounds in home missionary ventures related to this Society between 1798 and 1810.[13] Central to its raison d'etre was the conviction that large areas of Scotland had no adequate instruction in evangelical Christianity. Also prominent was the non-denominational character of the organization. "It is not our design to form or to extend the influence of any sect," the founders declared. "Our sole intention is to make known the everlasting gospel of our Lord Jesus Christ." Those who ministered under its auspices were thus expected to "discourage all bitter party spirit, wherever they discover it."[14]

These aims reflect the catholicity typical of British evangelicalism in the 1790s. At the first general meeting of the London Missionary Society in 1795, for example, the Congregationalist minister David Bogue (1750-1825) preached to a euphoric crowd on the "Funeral of Bigotry." "Here are Episcopalians, Methodists, Presbyterians, and Independents," he declared, "all united in one society, all joining to form its laws, to regulate its institutions, and manage its various concerns. Behold us here assembled with one accord to attend the funeral of *bigotry*."[15] In the congregation that day was Samuel Pearce (1766-1799), the pastor of

[13] R. F. Calder, "Robert Haldane's Theological Seminary," *Transactions of the Congregational Historical Society* 13 (1937-1939), 59-63, 53; D. W. Lovegrove, "Haldane, Robert" in Nigel M. De S. Cameron, David F. Wright, David C. Lachman, and Donald E. Meek, eds., *Dictionary of Scottish Church History & Theology* (Downers Grove, Illinois: InterVarsity Press, 1993), 386.

[14] Cited in Deryck W. Lovegrove, "Unity and Separation: Contrasting Elements in the Thought and Practice of Robert and James Haldane" in Keith Robbins, ed., *Protestant Evangelicalism: Britain, Ireland, Germany and America c. 1750-c.1950.* (Oxford: Basil Blackwell, 1990), 155.

[15] Cited in Roger H. Martin, *Evangelicals United: Ecumenical Stirrings in Pre-Victorian Britain,* 1795-1830 (Metuchen, New Jersey/London: The Scarecrow Press, Inc., 1983), 43.

Cannon Street Baptist Church, Birmingham. Caught up by Bogue's stirring declaration, he wrote home ecstatically to his wife, Sarah; "You my love will join me in a hearty amen to so evangelical a wish."[16]

The SPGH was only one of a host of voluntary associations formed during this period. For instance, the Bedfordshire Union of Christians, created in 1797 like the SPGH, saw Baptist ministers like John Sutcliff (1752-1814) of Olney, Buckinghamshire, working side by side with Congregationalist pastors such as Samuel Greatheed (d. 1823) and Thomas Hillyard (d. 1828). In the stated goals of this English parallel to the SPGH, mention was made of bringing the light of the gospel into the "dark and depraved" areas of Bedfordshire and neighbouring counties of the East Midlands, as well as restoring "the universal Church of Christ to some measure of its primitive harmony and unity; and thereby to remedy the positive and obvious evils, which have been produced by discord among Christians.[17]

In 1808, however, the Haldanes aroused considerable controversy in the churches that they had planted and financed when they embraced believer's baptism by immersion. Not surprisingly, their advocacy of believer's baptism brought about the collapse of the SPGH, though it was a major stimulus to the Scottish Baptist movement. Of the forty-one Baptist churches existing in Scotland by 1810, twenty-three had their origins between 1808 and 1810, and most of these were linked to the controversy surrounding the Haldanes' move from Congregationalism to Baptist convictions.[18]

Now, a number of these Baptist causes were Gaelic-speaking congregations in the Highlands, or the Gaidhealtachd, where Gaelic was the mother tongue. The Presbyterian Church in the Lowlands, where

[16] Letter to Sarah Pearce, September 28, 1795 (Samuel Pearce Letters, Angus Library, Regent's Park College, Oxford University).

[17] S. Greatheed, *General Union Recommended to Real Christians* (London: 1798), xvii. For further discussion of the Bedfordshire Union of Christians, see Michael A.G. Haykin, *One heart and one soul: John Sutcliff of Olney, his friends and his times* (Darlington, Co. Durham: Evangelical Press, 1994), 305-08.

[18] Murray and Meek, "Early Nineteenth Century," 32; D. E. Meek, "The Highlands" in Bebbington, ed., *Baptists in Scotland*, 284-85. On this controversy, "The Independent and Baptist Churches of Highland Perthshire and Strathspey," *Transactions of the Gaelic Society of Inverness* 56 (1988-90), 281-87.

English and Scots—the latter, like English, a derivative from Old English
—were primarily spoken, had been convinced for much of the seventeenth
and eighteenth centuries that "true" religion and "civilized" behaviour
could only be inculcated through the medium of English and Anglo-
Scottish culture.[19] Although some provision was made for ministry in
Gaelic and there were a few attempts in the seventeenth century to publish
a full translation of the Scriptures in Gaelic, a Gaelic New Testament did
not appear until 1767 and a complete Bible not until 1801.[20] The
appearance of this translation, however, was linked to a growing
realization among Scottish Lowland evangelicals that Gaelic was critical
for the evangelization of the Highlands. Various missionary efforts in
cross-cultural contexts, in particular that of the Serampore Baptists in
India, had inspired Scottish Lowland evangelicals like the Haldanes to
reflect on the mission field immediately to their north.[21] Moreover,
missionaries such as the Serampore Trio—William Carey (1761-1834),
Joshua Marshman (1768-1837), and William Ward (1769-1823)—were
keenly aware that the proclamation of the gospel in the vernacular was
vital for the success of their enterprises. Not for a moment did they regard
the languages and dialects of the Indian sub-continent as too "barbaric"
for the transmission of the gospel.[22] Similarly, Scottish evangelicals who
became involved in the evangelization of the Highlands from the 1790s
onwards were increasingly conscious of the importance of Gaelic for
accomplishing this task.

---

[19] Victor Edward Durkacz, *The Decline of the Celtic Languages. A Study of Linguistic
and Cultural Conflict in Scotland, Wales and Ireland from the Reformation to the
Twentieth Century* (Edinburgh: John Donald Publishers Ltd., 1983), 9-14; Jane Dawson,
"Calvinism and the Gaithealtachd in Scotland," in Andrew Pettegree, Alastair Duke and
Gillian Lewis, *Calvinism in Europe, 1540-1620* (Cambridge: Cambridge University
Press, 1994), 252. See also the remarks of Donald E. Meek, "Language and Style in the
Scottish Gaelic Bible (1767-1807)," *Scottish Language*, 9 (Winter, 1990), 1.

[20] For this Bible, see especially Donald E. Meek, "Bible (Versions, Gaelic)" in De S.
Cameron, Wright, Lachman, and Meek, eds., *Dictionary of Scottish Church History &
Theology*, 75-76.

[21] On the broad impact of Carey and his colleagues, see William H. Brackney, *Christian
Voluntarism in Britain and North America: A Bibliography and Critical Assessment*
(Westport, Connecticut/London: Greenwood Press, 1995), 43-45.

[22] Durkacz, *Decline of the Celtic Languages*, 100.

Of the various Gaelic-speaking Baptist congregations in the Highlands, "the largest and most productive" was that at Grantown-on-Spey, Morayshire.[23] In fact, one of the factors said to have induced James Haldane to submit to believer's baptism was the example set by the pastor of this church, Lachlan Mackintosh (d. 1857), who had been converted under Haldane's preaching in 1803.[24] Mackintosh publicly announced his commitment to Baptist views in 1807 and was baptized the following year. With the backing of his congregation, the Grantown-on-Spey church was then re-organized as a Baptist work and in time became, in the words of Donald Meek, a "nursery of powerful Baptist preachers."[25] A central reason for the impact of the Grantown church was undoubtedly the arrangement made by Robert Haldane for itinerant missionaries to study under Mackintosh during the 1820's.[26] Also critical in the growth and influence of this church was the man who succeeded Mackintosh as pastor in 1826, Peter Grant (1783-1867), who had been converted through the preaching of his predecessor.[27]

Grant, whose pastorate lasted till his death in 1867, was the possessor of considerable evangelistic, teaching and hymn-writing gifts. Under his ministry the church became the centre of an extremely vigorous movement of evangelism and outreach in the Strathspey Valley and far beyond. Here, fledgling Baptist preachers were nurtured in a strongly voluntaristic Christianity, which, yoked to a deep commitment to believer's baptism, enabled them to challenge the established Presbyterianism of the Highlands.[28] In certain districts of the Highlands, notably the north-west,

---

[23] Donald E. Meek, "Mackintosh, Lachlan" in Lewis, ed., *Blackwell Dictionary of Evangelical Biography*, II, 725.

[24] For Mackintosh, see Meek, "Independent and Baptist Churches," 282; idem. "Mackintosh, Lachlan" in Lewis, ed., *Blackwell Dictionary of Evangelical Biography*, II, 725-726.

[25] "Independent and Baptist Churches, 287.

[26] Haldane, *The Lives of Robert and James Haldane*, 494-495.

[27] For Grant, see Donald E. Meek, "Grant, Peter" in Lewis, ed., *Blackwell Dictionary of Evangelical Biography*, I, 467. Donald Meek is currently preparing a paper on Grant for the first International Conference on Baptist Studies at Regent's Park College, Oxford, in the summer of 1997 under the provisional title of "'The Glory of the Lamb': The Gaelic Hymnody of Peter Grant."

[28] Meek, "Independent and Baptist Churches," 287.

"the Men" (na Daoine), a "spiritual elite who acted as the custodians and leaders of experimental religion" of Highland Presbyterianism, were powerful enough to prevent Baptist congregations taking root.[29] In other areas, though, particularly Perthshire and the Inner Hebrides, Baptist congregations were planted which flourished and which would in time provide men and women who would be in the forefront of the Baptist movement in Canada. One such Baptist, William Fraser, is the main subject of the rest of this paper.

Early years in Scotland, 1801-1831

Born in 1801 into a farming family, William Fraser was raised among the rugged and imposing scenery of Strathspey.[30] His parents belonged to the Church of Scotland but theirs was a nominal Christianity. So Fraser grew up regarding himself as a Christian, completely unaware of the fact that he needed to experience conversion. Around the age of sixteen, a number of Scripture passages awakened him to the true nature of his spiritual condition. Not long after, he heard Peter Grant preach and, in the words of the Irish-Canadian Baptist John Dempsey, he was "enabled to receive the Lord Jesus as his own Saviour."[31] Soon after his conversion Grant spoke to him about his need to declare his faith publicly in believer's baptism. Having been raised in the Church of Scotland, Fraser wrestled with this request for some time. Eventually, though, he came to the conviction that this was the only baptism known by the New Testament

---

[29] Meek, "Highlands," 287. On "the Men," see D. E. Meek, "Men, The" in De S. Cameron, Wright, Lachman, and Meek, eds., *Dictionary of Scottish Church History and Theology*, 558-59.

[30] For the following details of Fraser's life, I am indebted to John Dempsey, "The Late Rev. W. Fraser," *The Canadian Baptist*, 28, No. 38 (October 4, 1883), 8, *idem*, "William Fraser, The McMaster University Monthly, 8 (1898-1899), 241-48; Donald E. Meek, "Evangelicalism and Emigration: Aspects of the Role of Dissenting Evangelicalism in Highland Emigration to Canada," in Gordon W. MacLennan, ed., *Proceedings of the First North American Congress of Celtic Studies* (Ottawa: Chair of Celtic Studies, University of Ottawa, 1988), 27-31; idem, "Fraser, William" in De S. Cameron, Wright, Lachman, and Meek, eds., *Dictionary of Scottish Church History and Theology*, 336.

[31] "William Fraser," 243.

church, a conviction from which he never wavered. He was baptized by his pastor, Lachlan Mackintosh, and joined the Grantown-on-Spey church.

From 1823 to 1825 Fraser studied at the Haldane seminary in Grantown-on-Spey under Mackintosh's supervision.[32] Having completed his studies, he served as an itinerant preacher for a year in the Highlands and adjacent regions of the Lowlands. Trekking over the wildest of hillsides in all types of weather would have built up reserves of physical fortitude and stamina, which would serve him in good stead later during his pastorate in the Ottawa Valley. Fraser's ministry during this year would have consisted of two circuits. The "home circuit" would be covered during the winter months, while the longer circuit, undertaken during the summer, might well take over two months to cover.[33] Having to preach often in the open air would also have developed Fraser's skills as a communicator and Baptist apologist.[34]

On more than one occasion as he spoke Fraser probably would have had to deal with local authorities or "the Men." Christopher Anderson (1782-1852), pastor of the Baptist cause in Richmond Court, Edinburgh, and one of William Carey's most faithful British supporters, describes in his diary an encounter with local authorities that was not at all atypical. In 1805 he was present at the formation of Bellanoch Baptist Church, Argyllshire, whose first pastor was Donald McVicar (f. 18(-1820), who had studied under the Haldanes and emigrated to Canada i he 1810's.[35] The day following the actual constitution of the church an open-air baptismal service was being held when the factor of the Bellanoch landlord, Malcolm of Poltalloch, appeared on the scene and, in the words of Anderson, "said he had a general order to stop all such preaching on the estate, and would call out the Volunteers if we did not desist!"[36] And on at least one occasion Fraser,

[32] Dempsey wrongly states that this seminary was in Edinburgh ("William Fraser," 243). On the seminary in Grantown-on-Spey, see also Haldane, *The Lives of Robert and James Haldane*, 331.

[33] *Ibid.*, 288.

[34] Meek, "Independent and Baptist Churches," 276, 287.

[35] On McVicar, see Donald E. Meek, "McVicar, Donald," in Lewis, ed., *Blackwell Dictionary of Evangelical Biography*, II, 733.

[36] Hugh Anderson, *The Life and Letters of Christopher Anderson* (Edinburgh: William P. Kennedy, 1854), 26-27.

preaching on the isle of Lewis, "spent four hours of a Sabbath day discussing on the inability and sinfulness of infant baptism." This reference was made by one of the more liberal ministers on the island, John Cameron, who further referred to Fraser and other like-minded Baptists as a "swarm of dissenters who came to Lewis to pounce upon the poor people, like common carrion."[37]

In 1826 Fraser was asked to oversee the Baptist work in Uig on the Isle of Skye. This church had come into being around 1808.[38] Four years later a chapel, capable of accommodating 300 people, was built beside the River Conon, where outdoor baptisms were held. During Fraser's first year of ministry the membership of the church grew to around sixty, and it was said that a "considerable number," as many as three hundred, attended the worship services of the church. The large difference between members and adherents/"listeners" was typical of most Highland Baptist churches during this period. As Donald Meek has observed, "the level of adherency for a single church would have ranged from five to ten times the size of the membership."[39] A number of these Baptist churches, moreover, appear to have had difficulty retaining adherents/listeners over the long run. In part this was due to the fact that the voluntarism of their church life clashed with the nature of Highland society, which was strongly based on extended family networks. The latter was better suited to Presbyterianism.[40]

On July 27, 1828, Fraser was "set apart to the pastoral office by prayer, with fasting" in the presence of his congregation and a number of pastors. One of the pastors, Dugald Sinclair (1777-1870), an itinerant preacher who prepared the soil for the emergence of a number of Gaelic-speaking Calvinistic Baptist churches in the Inner Hebrides, gave the charge to Fraser from Acts 20:28 ("Take heed therefore unto yourselves, and to all the flock, over the which the Holy Ghost hath made you overseers, to feed the church of God, which he hath purchased with his

---

[37] Cited in Meek, "Independent and Baptist Churches," 289.

[38] *Ibid.* 333-39.

[39] *Ibid.*, 293.

[40] *Ibid.*, 293-94.

own blood" [KJV].[41] Over the next four years, however, a goodly number of the church members emigrated, and by 1831 church membership was down to twenty-three.

Between the last quarter of the eighteenth century and 1870 waves of emigration swept over the Gaelic-speaking Highlands, transplanting entire communities of Highlanders to the American continent. During this period an estimated 185,000 Scots left their homeland for Canada.[42] Reasons for emigrating were various. Many went to Canada in order to escape the winds of change sweeping over the Highlands and thus to preserve their pastoral way of life. Traditional methods of farming were being phased out, cottage industries were losing ground in the face of industrialization, and clan chiefs were turning the people off the land to make way for more lucrative sheep-farms or deer-forests.[43] In addition, the years following the British victory over the French in the Napoleonic Wars spelled general economic depression throughout Great Britain. The kelping industry, a main source of livelihood in many areas of the Inner and Outer Hebrides, virtually collapsed overnight, and many were driven overseas out of economic necessity. Fraser himself decided to emigrate in 1831,[44] but his reasons appear to have been primarily religious in motivation.

[41] *Report of the Baptist Home Missionary Society for Scotland, chiefly for the Highlands and Islands,* (1829), 33-36; Meek, "Evangelicalism and Emigration," 30. Sinclair emigrated to Ontario in 1831, where he assumed the pastoral leadership of what would eventually become Poplar Hill Christian Church, Ilderton. For Sinclair, see especially Donald E. Meek, "Dugald Sinclair: The Life and Work of a Highland Itinerant Missionary," *Scottish Studies* 30 (1991), 59-91.

[42] Stephen J. Hornsby, "Patterns of Scottish Emigration to Canada, 1750-1870," *Journal of Historical Geography* 18 (1992), 398.

[43] Meek, "Independent and Baptist Churches," 277-78.

[44] John Dempsey ("Late Rev. W. Fraser," 8, "William Fraser," 245) and Donald Meek give 1831 as the date of Fraser's emigration to Canada ("Evangelicalism and Emigration," 31; "Fraser, William," 336). Stuart Ivison and Fred Rosser [*The Baptists in Upper and Lower Canada before 1820* (Toronto: University of Toronto Press, 1956), 95] place his emigration in 1830. The *Report of the Baptist Home Missionary Society for Scotland, chiefly for the Highlands and the Islands,* (1831), 6 seems to indicate that Fraser sailed for British North America in the summer of 1830.

Breadalbane Baptist Church, 1831-1850

Among the Gaelic-speaking Highlanders who landed in Canada after the close of the Napoleonic Wars were a group from the Baptist causes in Killin and Lawers on Loch Tay, Perthshire. The roots of these two churches went back to a large-scale awakening in the Loch Tay district in 1801 and 1802, in which the preaching of a Haldane-trained evangelist named John Farquharson (fl. 1800-1810) was instrumental.[45] Sailing from Greenock on the *Dorothy* on July 12, 1815, only a few weeks after the Battle of Waterloo, these Baptists landed at Montreal after a lengthy voyage. That year they wintered in the southern portion of Glengarry County in Upper Canada (Ontario). The following spring they made their way north to Breadalbane, not far from present-day Dalkeith. A Baptist church was formally organized a year later, on August 2, 1817, with thirteen members and two elders, Allan McDiarmid and Peter McDougall.[46]

By 1829 church membership had grown to about sixty, yet the church lacked a pastor who could devote himself fully to ministering to its needs and reaching out into the surrounding communities with the gospel. The Breadalbane Baptists discovered that John Edwards (1779-1842), a Scotsman from Morayshire who had been converted through James Haldane's ministry and had had the oversight of a Baptist work at Clarence on the Ottawa River since the early 1820s,[47] was preparing to sail back to Scotland with the aim of encouraging pastors there to emigrate to eastern Ontario because of the region's great spiritual needs. They asked him to seek out a suitable pastor for their congregation. Edwards sailed for Britain in the autumn of 1829. Two pastors responded positively to his invitation to emigrate: John Gilmour (1792-1869), who came to

---

[45] Meek, "Independent and Baptist Churches," 278-79. For Farquharson, see D. E. Meek, "Farquharson, John," in De S. Cameron, Wright, Lachman, and Meek, eds., *Dictionary of Scottish Church History and Theology*, 316.

[46] Daniel McPhail, *Circular Letter of the Ottawa Baptist Association* (Montreal: J. Starke & Co., 1865), 13. For the history of this congregation, see *Breadalbane Baptist Church History 1816-1991* ([Dalkeith: Breadalbane Baptist Church], 1991).

[47] For Edwards, see "Biography: Mrs. John Edwards," [Montreal] *Register* 2, No. 2 (January 12, 1843), 5-6.

Montreal in 1830 and organized the first Baptist work there,[48] and William Fraser, who settled as the pastor of the Breadalbane church.

Fraser arrived at Breadalbane in the summer of 1831 and preached his first sermon from the phrase "Escape for thy life" in Genesis 19:17, where Lot and his family are told to flee the city of Sodom and not to look back.[49] Though he was well received by the congregation, the early years of his ministry were not easy. Since the congregation was unable to pay him an adequate salary, Fraser had to teach school for a year or so. He purchased a farm, on which the present church building stands, but since it took some time to clear the land the farm was of little value for a number of years. Thus, Fraser was forced to seek assistance from the New York Baptist Missionary Society.

These financial difficulties were not the worst of his problems, however. What Fraser felt most keenly was that his ministerial labours seemed to be bearing little fruit. Converts were few and the spiritual life of the church seemed to be ebbing away. In Fraser's own words, "the congregation appeared in a most careless, hardened, and desperate stage."[50] He supposed, he wrote many years later, that "probably all the election of grace were found" in the Breadalbane area and that he "might as well go and seek them on other mountains."[51] In this frame of mind he actually left Breadalbane for a period of time, traveling close to a thousand miles over to Lake Huron and back.[52] By the time that he returned he was convinced he was where God wanted him to be, but this conviction appears to have done little to alleviate his state of despondency.

---

[48] On Gilmour, see Paul R. Dekar, "The Gilmours: Four Generations of Baptist Service," in his and Murray J. S. Ford, eds., *Celebrating the Canadian Baptist Heritage: Three Hundred Years of God's Providence* (Hamilton, Ontario: McMaster University Divinity College, [1985]), 42-46; *idem*, "Gilmour, John," in Lewis, ed., *Blackwell Dictionary of Evangelical Biography*, I, 444.

[49] *Breadalbane Baptist Church History*, 6.

[50] Letter, October 24, 1834 [cited in *The Baptist Magazine*, 27 (1835), 147]. Although this letter is said to be from a "Mr. John Fraser," everything in it indicates that William Fraser is its author.

[51] "Sketches of Canadian Baptist Churches. II," *Scottish Baptist Magazine*, 4 (1878), 28.

[52] Ibid.

John Gilmour visited him in the summer of 1834 and sought to encourage his fellow Scotsman. He soon became cognizant, however, that Fraser seemed to have imbibed the notion that praying and preaching for spiritual renewal were utterly useless since this was a sovereign work of God. There must be fire in the pulpit, Gilmour admonished his friend, before there will be a blaze among the congregation. Fraser evidently took this admonition to heart. In his words:

> I betook myself to humiliation, prayer, and fasting; and by solemn inquiry, was astonished to find how full the whole Bible made success depend on God's grace. But not as Antinomian would have it, and go *to rest*; but would have the true labourer go to work, depending on the Master and His promise for success, as any farmer ever did in his own field, and much more. . . . How evident that God is the life and working power of all the great men of antiquity — Abraham, Isaac, and Jacob; Moses and Joshua; David, and all the prophets; and surely the Apostles, under a far more favourable ministration of the Spirit . . . . Now, all this saving power and converting power of God's Spirit is placed in Christ Jesus, as a granary for the supply of the life and labour of the church, and will be given to every sincere seeker; and surely His own faithful ministers will not seek it in vain, while they are eminently "co-workers with God" in the work of saving souls: — a work which never was meant to be begun or carried on by mere human power.[53]

This text reflects strongly the standpoint of evangelical Calvinism, which had been diffused throughout the nineteenth-century transatlantic Baptist community by the writings of the English Baptist theologian Andrew Fuller (1754-1815).[54] From the vantage point of this theological system,

---

[53] *Ibid.*

[54] On Fuller's life, the classic study is John Ryland, *The Work of Faith, the Labour of Love, and the Patience of Hope Illustrated; in the Life and Death of the Reverend Andrew Fuller* (London: Button & Son, 1816). A second edition of this biography appeared in 1818. For more recent studies, see E. F. Clipsham, "Andrew Fuller and

there are two major errors to be avoided with regard to the Christian life. The first is that of antinomianism, in which divine grace and Christian freedom are so emphasized that the need for the Christian to follow earnestly after sanctification and to be engaged heartily in evangelism is neglected. The other is moralism, in which the Christian life is viewed primarily as a matter of human will power and obedience. Rather, Fraser asserts, God's Spirit works in and with Christians, not without them, and thus makes them willing to be his co-workers."

Equipped with "these keenly felt convictions" Fraser threw himself back into the work at Breadalbane. His sermons to the unconverted, undergirded by the prayers of his congregation, now "fell on their ears and on their hearts with life and power."[55] That fall and winter there was a large-scale awakening throughout the region around Breadalbane. Similar to the revivals that had swept transatlantic British society in the previous century, the central vehicle in this awakening in the Ottawa Valley was the pulpit. Those who were as "hardened as the flinty rock," to quote what Fraser wrote at the time,

> were made to weep over their sins as little children; almost every house [in the community] has one or more in distress, or rejoicing in the cross of Christ, and the people seem to be smitten with a kind of holy awe, and a respect for divine things. The Lord God of Jacob have all the glory![56]

Between August and December 1834, Fraser baptized fifty-eight new converts.[57] By the fall of 1835 over one hundred had been converted and

Fullerism: A Study in Evangelical Calvinism," *The Baptist Quarterly* 20 (1963-64), 99-114, 146-54, 214-25, 268-76; Phil Roberts, "Andrew Fuller," in Timothy George and David S. Dockery, eds., *Baptist Theologians* (Nashville: Broadman Press, 1990), 121-39. For a good analysis of evangelical Calvinism, see L. G. Champion, "Evangelical Calvinism and the Structures of Baptist Church Life," *The Baptist Quarterly* 28 (1979-80), 196-208.

[55] "William Fraser," 245-46.

[56] Letter, October 24, 1834 (cited in *The Baptist Magazine*, 148)

[57] John Edwards, Letter, January 5, 1835 [cited in *The Baptist Magazine*, 27 (1835), 233].

brought into the membership of the Breadalbane church.[58] It should be noted that the Breadalbane revival was part of a larger work of the Spirit in the Ottawa Valley. All told, some 365 individuals were added to the six Baptist churches of this area of Ontario between August 1834 and December 1835.[59]

In addition to his ministry in Breadalbane, Fraser took an active role in the Ottawa Baptist Association, which was constituted in 1836 and consisted of the six churches in the Ottawa Valley and one in Montreal. This Association was intimately connected with the formation of the first Baptist Educational Institution in central Canada, namely, Canada Baptist College.[60] Throughout its eleven years in Montreal, from 1838 to 1849, the Baptist College struggled with numerous liabilities, not the least of which was the distrust that many Baptists had for "man-made ministers."[61] In an attempt to drum up support for the College, the Ottawa Association devoted its annual circular letter of 1840 to the issue of "Ministerial Education." Written by the College's first principal, Benjamin Davies (1814-1875),[62] and signed by Fraser as the moderator of the Association's annual meeting, the letter recognized that there were a number of influential ministers of the gospel who had had no formal theological education, among them "some of the very Fathers" of the transatlantic Baptist community. For instance, there was John Bunyan (1628-1688), "whose natural powers of mind made the untutored Tinker, a mighty

[58] John Edwards, Letter to J. Neave, January 3, 1836 [cited in *The Baptist Magazine*, 28 (1836), 403]; Fraser, "Sketches of Canadian Baptist Churches," 28.

[59] *Ibid. (Baptist Magazine*, 403).

[60] For a brief history of the College, see Charles M. Johnston, *McMaster University, Volume 1: The Toronto Years* (Toronto/Buffalo: University of Toronto Press, 1976), 3-10.

[61] *Ibid.,*9-10. This distrust has a long pedigree in Baptist circles. In the eighteenth century, for instance, the deacons of Westbury Leigh Baptist Church, Wiltshire, had such a strong aversion to the only Baptist seminary in England, Bristol Baptist Academy, that they regarded any who went there as going "down to Egypt for help"! [John Clark Marshman, *The Life and Times of Carey, Marshman and Ward* (London: Longman, Brown, Green, Longmans, & Roberts, 1859), I, 105-106].

[62] On Davies, see J.H.Y. Briggs, "Davies, Benjamin," in Lewis, ed., *Blackwell Dictionary of Evangelical Biography*, I, 295.

preacher and an immortal author."[63] Yet, the letter went on to assert, the majority of budding ministers need formal education to help them understand the Scriptures and to enable them to pass on their knowledge to others. Davies, Fraser, and their peers in the Ottawa Association thus closed the letter with a rousing appeal to the voluntaristic spirit of their fellow Baptists: "Will you permit [the College] to decline and fall, by withholding from it your prayers and contributions? Will those who have the means to provide education for pious and gifted young men, who thirst for improvement, deny them any assistance?"[64] The appeal, though, fell on deaf ears, and the school closed its doors nine years later.

Fraser also took extensive preaching tours throughout the Ottawa Valley, often preaching in Gaelic since many of the settlers in this region were from the Highlands. In the Breadalbane church itself Sunday services were held in both Gaelic and English, the services following each other with only a few minutes' interval. According to accounts it was not infrequent for many who heard Fraser preach during this period to be reduced to tears as he warned them of what it meant to be outside of Christ.[65] Many years later E. R. Fitch would recall Fraser as "a powerful evangelist," whose preaching centred "upon the exceeding sinfulness of sin, the judgements of God and the terrors of the law."[66] For an evangelical Calvinist like Fraser, however, such themes were not an end in themselves. Rather, to quote remarks made recently about that quintessential evangelical Calvinist, Jonathan Edwards, preaching on these topics was "part of a larger campaign to turn sinners from their disastrous path and to the rightful object of their affections, Jesus Christ."[67]

[63] "Ministerial Education," *The Canada Baptist Magazine, and Missionary Register* 3, No. 9 (March 1840), 194-95.

[64] *Ibid.,* 200.

[65] See, for example, *The Canada Baptist Magazine and Missionary Register* 2, No. 10 (March 1839), 223; 3, No. 8 (February 1840), 188.

[66] *The Baptists of Canada: A History of their Progress and Achievements* (Toronto: The Standard Publishing Co., Ltd., 1911), 105, 171.

[67] "Editor's Introduction," John E. Smith, Harry S. Stout, and Kenneth P. Minkema, eds., in *A Jonathan Edwards Reader* (New Haven/London: Yale University Press, 1995), xviii.

It was also during Fraser's sojourn at Breadalbane that he began to be known in Baptist circles as "the ablest controversialist among his brethren."[68] A. H. Newman (1852-1933), a leading nineteenth-century Baptist historian, made this comment about Fraser and mentioned particularly two pieces by him: "one against the Irvingites and the one against a rabid opponent of ministerial education."[69] Fraser was also involved in a small controversy with William McKillican (1776-1849), a Scottish Congregationalist minister, over the issue of believer's baptism. Before he emigrated to Canada McKillican had pastored the Congregationalist church at Tuar and Acharn, Perthshire, the very locale from which the founders of Breadalbane Baptist church had come.[70] Settling at Breadalbane in 1816, McKillican was soon preaching throughout Glengarry County in both Gaelic and English. In 1838, he clashed with Fraser over the issue of believer's baptism and accused the Baptist of being in "a feverish heat about an ordinance, which, however important in its place, is so distinct from real religion, that a *Sorcerer* may submit to it, as well as a *Paul*."[71] Fraser's reply to McKillican was not slow in coming. He denied being consumed with a "feverish heat" with regard to baptism, but did emphasize that McKillican's remark that

> baptism is so distinct from real religion that a sorcerer may submit to it as well as a Paul, is unsound in theology and evil

---

[68] "Sketch of the Baptists of Ontario and Quebec to 1851" in D.M. Mihell, ed., *The Baptist Year Book (Historical Number) for Ontario, Quebec, Manitoba and the North-West Territories and British Columbia* (London, Ontario: The Baptist Convention of Ontario and Quebec, 1900), 77.

[69] *Ibid.,* 77. The piece against the doctrines of the Scottish preacher Edward Irving (1792-1834) may be found in the "Letter from Mr. Fraser to a Preacher of Irvingism," *The Canada Baptist Magazine, and Missionary Register* 1, No. 5 (October 1837), 97-101. The other piece mentioned by Newman has to be Davies's "Ministerial Education," discussed above, which Fraser signed as the moderator of the Association meeting that published it.

[70] Meek, "Independent and Baptist Churches," 279-80, 323. For an account of McKillican's ministry in Glengarry County, see Donald Neil MacMillan, *The Kirk in Glengarry* (N.P.:n.p.,1985), 204-08.

[71] "[Letter] To the Editor," *The Canada Baptist Magazine, and Missionary Register* 2 (1838-39), 10. This letter is in reply to a piece by Fraser: "Mr. Fraser's Visit to Osgood," *The Canada Baptist Magazine, and Missionary Register,* 1 (1837-38), 258-60.

in tendency. It must . . . be a part of *real* or of *false* religion; for my part I take it to be a part of the religion of Jesus Christ, as laid down in the New Testament, for our faith and obedience; and Christ crucified is the sum and substance of the ordinance.[72]

In the final remark about the nature of baptism one sees clearly Fraser's voluntarist understanding of Christianity. Only those who can put their trust in the death of Christ for their sins should be baptized.

Despite the fruitfulness of his ministry in the Ottawa Valley, by the end of the 1840s Fraser had come to the conviction that his career in Glengarry County was drawing to a close. The membership of the Breadalbane church had declined from 184 in 1838 to 118 in 1849,[73] despite at least one other season of revival in 1840.[74] The decline appears mainly due to many of the members re-locating in other parts of Ontario, in particular Bruce County, which was opened up for settlement in the late 1840s.

Tiverton Baptist Church, 1855-1875

Ever the pioneer church planter, Fraser made the decision to leave Breadalbane in 1850 and head west to Illinois.[75] But he reached no further than Bruce County. Initially, he lived on a farm adjoining Kincardine, where he held services in his own home in Gaelic and English. By the spring of the following year he was restless. He wrote to John Winterbotham, pastor of the Baptist church in Woodstock, that he was thinking of leaving Kincardine for a place "more eligible for gospel

---

[72] "[Letter] To Mr. McKillican," *The Canada Baptist Magazine, and Missionary Register* 2 (1838-39), 62.

[73] *The Canada Baptist Magazine, and Missionary Register* 1, No. 10 (March 1838), 232; *The Register*, 8, No. 9 (March 1, 1849), [3].

[74] *The Canada Baptist Magazine, and Missionary Register* 4, No. 4 (October 1840), 150.

[75] Dempsey, "William Fraser," 246.

usefulness." Winterbotham suggested he try Owen Sound, where he had just conducted a successful preaching mission.[76]

As it turned out, Fraser moved to what would become Lorne, a hamlet only a few miles to the north of Kindardine along the Lake Huron shoreline. Once settled he erected a sawmill, followed by a grist mill three years later in 1854. Apparently neither of these ventures turned out to be a success.[77] But if he failed in business, the same cannot be said of his preaching and pastoral ministry.

He continued to hold services in Kincardine till 1863, but from the time that he moved to Lorne, he also began to hold services in the home of a fellow Highlander, John Paterson (1805-1833), in the village of Tiverton. Paterson was originally from Tobermory on the Inner Hebridean island of Mull. He had come to Canada in 1831 and settled on a farm in Mariposa township, north of Toronto. In 1851 he had re-located to a farm in what would become the village of Tiverton. On Sundays Fraser would walk the five or so miles from his home to that of Paterson, knocking on the doors of all the homes in between, regardless of whether or not they were Baptists. Fraser, said to have "a herculean physical frame,"[78] was probably not an easy man to refuse. Thus he gathered his congregation as he went!

Tiverton Baptist Church, first known as the Regular Baptist Church of Kincardine and Bruce, was formally constituted with twenty-four members on June 4, 1855. They held their first communion services a few weeks later, on July 1, in the Paterson barn. Over twenty years of ministry, the Tiverton work flourished. Just as Fraser had widely itinerated in the Ottawa Valley, so he did in Bruce County. Often he had to blaze a trail through the woods as he went to preach in towns and villages like Port Elgin, Glammis, and North Bruce.[79] When Fraser resigned the pastorate due to age and infirmity in October 1875, the church membership stood at 354, a figure which would not have included

---

[76] John Winterbotham, "Mission at Owen Sound," *Christian Observer* 1, No. 5 (May 1851), 74-75. The clause in quotation marks is that of Winterbotham, but he is quoting Fraser.

[77] Dempsey, "William Fraser," 246-47.

[78] *Ibid.*, 248.

[79] *Tiverton Baptist Church. 1855-1905* (Tiverton: Tiverton Baptist Church, 1905), 5.

members dismissed to form other Baptist churches in the area or those who might either have died or moved away from the district altogether. While there were a few periods of revival during his ministry at Tiverton – though none it would appear on the scale of that which took place in Breadalbane – much of this growth resulted from Fraser's labours, year in, year out.[80]

After retiring from the ministry at Tiverton, Fraser went to live with his daughter, Mary Ann Coutts (1839-1881), whose husband, James Coutts, was the pastor of the Baptist church in Collingwood. Coutts would later move to Georgetown, where Fraser died on August 30, 1883.

Three years before he left the Tiverton pastorate, Fraser found himself embroiled in what may well have been the fiercest controversy of his life. Five years after the formal organization of the Baptist church in Tiverton, the Presbyterians in the town had called their first full-time minister, Alexander Mackay (1833-1904), a recent graduate of Knox College, Toronto.[81] Mackay demitted this charge in 1869 to take up a ministry in Illinois. His successor was John Anderson (1823-1908), a native of Strathspey like Fraser. It would appear that during the course of 1872 the former minister was asked to return to Tiverton to deliver two long lectures on the subject of baptism. Peter Cameron, one of the Tiverton Baptist deacons, attended the lectures, which were quite polemical in tone.[82] Apparently, Mackay not only attacked the Baptists as a

---

[80] For a mention of one such revival, see *ibid.,* 5. Throughout this period Ontario Baptists generally continued to be very interested in revival, unlike other denominations such as the Methodists. See M. Richard Mitchel, "A Study of Change Among Ontario's Wesleyans and Baptists, 1840-1900" (Unpublished M. A. Thesis, Laurentian University, 1987), 65-76.

[81] On Mackay, see *Knox Church, Tiverton, Ontario: One Hundred Years of Presbyterianism 1859-1959* (Tiverton: Knox Church, Tiverton, 1959), 8; Kenneth Barker, "Presbyterianism in Grey and Bruce Counties: The Presbyterian Church of Canada (Free) Experience," *Presbyterian History* 38, No. 2 (October 1991), 4-5; *idem, Response to Challenge: Presbyterianism in Grey and Bruce* (Owen Sound: n.p., 1995), 10, 25.

[82] Peter Cameron, *The Subject of Baptism. A Reply to the Rev. A. McKay's Lectures at Tiverton, Bruce* (Toronto: Dudley & Burns, 1872), 15. This pamphlet by Cameron was printed together with one by Fraser: *A Historical Sketch of The Baptist Body all the way down from the Apostolic Age* (Toronto: Dudley & Burns, 1872).

denomination but even hurled abuse at Fraser by name.[83] Mackay lumped the Baptists together with various groups which many in the nineteenth century, including Baptists, regarded as heterodox, the followers of the German Anabaptist Thomas Müntzer (c. 1490-1512), the Mormons, and the Campbellites.[84] Mackay further suggested that Baptist views about the ordinance of believer's baptism were tantamount to worship of the water and their actual practice of immersing believers quite "indecent"![85] Apart from these inflammatory remarks Mackay spent most of his lectures seeking to demonstrate that baptism in the New Testament era was by "pouring or sprinkling," while baptism by immersion actually could not be found prior to the third century.[86] There appears to have been little substantial argument regarding the subject of baptism, though Mackay did declare his willingness to "die for infant baptism."[87]

Fraser's reply was two-fold. First, on November 24 he preached a closely-argued sermon on Galatians 3:16 ["Now to Abraham and his seed were the promises made. He saith not, And to seeds, as of many; but as of one, And to thy seed, which is Christ"], in which he rejected the common paedobaptist argument that infant baptism is the New Testament counterpart to circumcision, and that the natural offspring of believers who were so baptized could be assured of salvation. Such a doctrine, he strongly maintained, "has chloroformed millions to live without God, and die in their sins."[88] His argument as a whole is shaped by the voluntarism of the Baptist tradition, though a few of his remarks are particularly noteworthy.

Though there has been ultimately only one way of salvation, Fraser believed God has carried it out in "three successive, and very different administrations of grace." The first took place during the days of the Patriarchs, when a saving relationship with God was not possible apart from belonging to the extended family of Abraham, Isaac, and Jacob, et

---

[83] Cameron, *Subject of Baptism*, 15.

[84] *Ibid.*, 15.

[85] *Ibid.*, 17, 18.

[86] *Ibid.*, 18-20.

[87] *Ibid.*, 21.

[88] *The Covenant of Circumcision as the Ground of Infant Baptism* ([Tiverton: n.p., 1872]); 1-2.

al. The second had a national dimension: instituted at Mount Sinai under Moses, salvation was now linked to one's ethnic status. The final "dispensation," Fraser held, was that of the New Testament, in which people entered into the experience of salvation "as individuals through faith." Only an individual who has personally and sincerely believed in the gospel can have any assurance of salvation. In Fraser's words: "the door of the church is not wide enough on earth or in heaven for couples, families, or nations, but [only for] individuals."[89] To believe differently from this, in particular to be convinced of the salvific effects of infant baptism, was, from his standpoint, "pure popery." To Fraser it seemed as if the Baptists had been specially raised up to demolish what he termed the "Romish pyramid" of infant baptism.[90]

The second item Fraser prepared in response to Mackay was *A Historical Sketch of the Baptist Body all the way down from the Apostolic Age* (1872). Its basic argument is that the Baptist cause has enjoyed an uninterrupted chronological succession since the Apostolic era. John the Baptist was "the first Baptist" and, according to Fraser, "a people rejecting infant baptism, and holding the immersion of believers in water for baptism" can be traced in the historical record ever since that time.[91] To substantiate this claim he cited a wide variety of groups and individuals. For example, there were the Donatists, who professed "fine Baptist doctrine," [92] Peter de Bruys (d. *c.* 1140), Peter Valdes (d. *c.* 1205-1218), Henry of Lausanne (d. after 1145), Arnold of Brescia (d. 1155), and Berangar of Tours (*c.* 1010-1088), all of them Baptists whose "followers had the same faith;"[93] there was even William Tyndale (*c.* 1494-1536), who should be recognized as an important Baptist leader.[94] This misreading of the historical evidence was, of course, not unique to Fraser. Known as Baptist successionism, it was particularly popular among nineteenth-century North American Baptists. Fraser, it seems,

---

[89] *Ibid.*, 5-6.

[90] *Ibid.*, 8.

[91] *Historical Sketch*, 1.

[92] *Ibid.*, 3-4.

[93] *Ibid.*, 10.

[94] *Ibid.*, 11-12.

learned it from G. H. Orchard (1796-1861), an English Baptist minister, whose *A Concise History of Foreign Baptists* (1838) and *A History of the Baptists in England* (1859), proved to be among the most influential successionist sources in the nineteenth century.[95]

What is unique about Fraser's *Historical Sketch* is the lengthy section devoted to showing that the Celtic Church in Britain was actually a Baptist body.[96] This interest was obviously linked to Fraser's background. The Celtic Church, the writer asserted, had "no connections with the state, therefore it was more simple, pure and scriptural in faith and practice." No pastor claimed lordship over another, "for they were all brethren." They rejected infant baptism, a claim Fraser based on his own observation of a baptistery on the island of Iona. Moreover, the Celts' long isolation from ecclesial developments on the European continent "naturally served to strengthen and confirm in them the spirit of ecclesiastical freedom."[97] Although this idealized portrait of the Celtic Church distorted somewhat the real nature of Celtic Christianity, it does provide insights into Fraser's own convictions late in his life. His voluntaristic vision of the Baptist life, learned first in the Strathspey, then tested and refined in the crucible of ministry in the Scottish Highlands and in the Ottawa Valley, appears to have diminished little during his days in Tiverton.

Fraser was buried in Tiverton Cemetery, surrounded by many of his flock. A granite obelisk erected to his memory in 1907 can be found immediately in front of the original tombstone. On the obelisk is carved the following epitaph about him: "Pioneer and Father of his people in Ontario, both east and west. Wise for this life and the next. He allured to brighter worlds, and led the way."[98] One suspects that if Fraser had been able to choose his epitaph he would have chosen something simpler than this

---

[95] See *Ibid.*, where Fraser explicitly cites Orchard.

[96] *Ibid.*, 6-9. These four pages amount to nearly a quarter of the pamphlet. For two excellent rebuttals of successionism, see W. Morgan Patterson, *Baptist Successionism. A Critical View* (Valley Forge: The Judson Press, 1969), 19-20 and James Edward McGoldrick, *Baptist Successionism. A Crucial Question in Baptist History* (Metuchen, New Jersey/London: The American Theological Library Association/The Scarecrow Press, Inc., 1994).

[97] *Historical Sketch*, 6, 8.

[98] Ruth Dimmick, *Tiverton Baptist Church, Tiverton, Ontario 1855-1995* (Tiverton: n.p., 1995), 4.

flowery Edwardian prose. He often likened his ministry to that of the biblical voluntarist, John the Baptist,[99] in view of which, the following, said by our Lord about his cousin in John 5:35, might be a better way to remember the ministry of William Fraser: "He was a burning and a shining light."

---

[99] Dempsey, "William Fraser," 247.

3
The Catholic Voluntary

Brian Hogan·

Introduction

This excursus into Roman Catholic variations on voluntary themes considers organizational and thematic developments in the twentieth century, with particular reference to Canadian experience. The focus of this paper is voluntary associations with a Church base that clearly distinguished between clerical and lay roles at the beginning of the century, and that moved towards a more complex theological understanding of what constitutes Christian service, ministry, and participation in the works of the Church as the century progressed.

With regard to the question of "voluntarism," if defined as opposition to state establishment or recognition of a particular religious body, the Christian church has embraced, tolerated, or endured a wide variety of experiences. These include the pre- and post-Constantinian periods in the Roman Empire and the extended univocal experience of "Christendom," dating from at least the time of Charlemagne to the age of the Reformation. The papacy, in the early nineteenth century, had the power to appoint only a few dozen bishops in the world without the approval of the secular power. Concordats, and other diplomatic instruments governing the church-state relationship, continued to be popular in certain regions, as for example Latin America, well into the present century. Even the lapse of such legal arrangements has not guaranteed complete religious independence. The case of France serves as an interesting example. While no longer required by concordat, custom demands consultation with the government by the Vatican in matters of episcopal appointments down to the present time.

In his chapter on the "Enlightenment: Secular and Christian, 1600-1800," in *The Oxford Illustrated History of Christianity*, John McManners comments that with regard to social questions Christianity was non-revolutionary during this period. The establishment of a vast network of charitable institutions was intended to balance any lacunae in these areas:

Brian Hogan is dean of theology at the University of St. Michael's College and teaches church history in the Toronto School of Theology.

From huge institutions like the Albergo dei Poveri at Genoa and the Hotel de Dieu at Paris down to tiny three-bed hospitals in villages, from orders expert in surgery to others specializing in ransoming slaves from the Barbary Corsairs, Catholic Europe was covered with a network of organizations to help the poor and sick, with parish priests and committees of devout ladies organizing outdoor relief. . . . In Protestant Europe, voluntary societies arose to fill the gap left by the abolition of the religious orders. Pious laymen, reinforced towards the end of the eighteenth century by some of the less pious who were afraid of revolution, were astonishingly active. The list of societies something like a hundred – to which Wilberforce subscribed indicates the scope of the movement. . . .[1]

In the same volume, Bryan Wilson, treating "New Images of Christian Community" in the contemporary period writes of the adaptations being made by Christian churches with the increasing hegemony of the secular nation-state by the late nineteenth century. In Belgium, for example, the Roman Catholic Church, in response to the excoriating condemnations of liberalism by Pope Pius IX,

. . . sought by 'pillarization' to embrace its members in what almost amounted to an alternative Christian society, rejecting civil provision, almost like a state within a state. It created (as elsewhere in Europe) its own political party to promote its interests and the moral philosophy that lay behind them.
. . . Those who accepted the embrace of the Catholic subculture of the newly emerging 'pillarized' institutions did so as a matter of personal choice. The principle of voluntarism was apparent, and the church was now tacitly acknowledging

[1] John McManners, "Enlightenment: Secular and Christian 1600-1800," *The Oxford Illustrated History of Christianity*, ed. John McManners (Oxford: Oxford University Press, 1990), 299.

the growing strength of the organized secular civil alternative to church organization and Christian culture.[2]

"Pillarization" represents a useful descriptor and transitional stage for tracing a continuum from the establishment to the voluntary form of church life. Depending on the jurisdiction, along this continuum might be several phases or transitional periods, including that of quasi- or semi-establishment, when *de jure* arrangements may be abrogated but many *de facto* recognitions remain for a variety of cultural or political reasons. Quebec, for example, succeeded in resisting the significant accommodations accompanying modernity for a remarkably long time. When it did change, beginning in the post-Second World War period, it did so with a vengeance, with mediate ecclesial control of health, educational, and social welfare functions passing to a rapidly secularizing state and society in very short order. In the decades leading up to this transitional period beginning in mid-century, a plethora of voluntary societies identified under the generic title of "Catholic Action" flourished both in Quebec and in other parts of the Canadian Catholic Church. Depending on time and place they might be said to be in aid of a society supporting many vestiges of an established state church, as in Quebec, or to represent a more-or-less "pillarized" response, or to depict a shrewd expression, along voluntary lines, of pastoral adaptation to an increasingly secular society.[3]

---

[2] Bryan Wilson, "New Images of Christian Community," *The Oxford Illustrated History of Christianity*, ed. John McManners, 574. McManners notes that there was a tri-partite "pillarization" of Belgium society at the time, including the Catholic, liberal, and socialist variants.

[3] Lines are not cut-and-dried as to just where a particular society is at a given time. Sidney Ahlstrom writes of a new American Protestant ascendancy early in the last century that ". . . the revivals of the early nineteenth century brought to the churches a greatly increased measure of influence. Evangelical attitudes and assumptions very nearly became constituent elements of Americanism. Because many of the customary ties between religion and government had not been severed, moreover, evangelical Protestants were able to create a new sort of "quasi-establishment." *A Religious History of the American People* (New Haven and London: Yale University Press, 1972), 382-83.

As suggested above, within the Catholic Church, voluntary societies[4] are hardly new to this century. Almost from the beginning of Christianity there were efforts to develop organizations to respond to perceived needs beyond the immediately spiritual or religious as expressed in liturgical worship. While leadership in these latter activities was restricted to clerics, both clerical and lay members of the church might assume direction and other functional roles in other undertakings. Such efforts were seen in a sacral light themselves as serving essential local and larger communal needs.[5] Therefore, while different in kind from sacramental functions, they were considered to be immediately related to the primary injunction that Christians express love of God and of neighbour, and in concrete ways. With the centuries, according to time and place, these efforts have stemmed from perceived lacunae in a wide variety of areas, including those of health, education, commerce, hostel, and security needs. At times such voluntary agencies have metamorphosed into formal religious orders of men or women who dedicated their lives totally to the service of God and their fellows in order to answer pressing need. More frequently they have maintained their lay and secular character intact, while clearly accomplishing an expression and integration of spiritual intent, regardless of the particular content of their activity. A variety of brotherhoods, sisterhoods, and lay organizations can be easily identified such as the Knights of Malta, the Order of Jerusalem, the Guild societies of the Middle Ages, the Knights of Columbus, the St. Vincent de Paul Society, or such contemporary expressions as hospices for the dying and "street people."

In his monumental history of Christianity, Kenneth S. Latourette postulated that for Roman Catholics "the twentieth century could be

---

[4] While the concept is familiar the term "voluntary organization" or "voluntary society" is not favoured in Roman Catholic conversation. There are no references to such a term in the *New Catholic Encyclopedia* (1967) index, *The New Dictionary of Catholic Social Thought* (1994), or the *Harper Collins Encyclopedia of Catholicism* (1995). There are references to "voluntarism."

[5] See, for example, reference to the extensive network of institutions created by Basil of Caesarea in the fourth century in M. Scaduto, "Charity, Works of," *The New Catholic Encyclopedia*, vol. 3, 485.

known as the century of the laity."[6] Interestingly, Latourette's judgement preceded the theological developments attending the Second Council of the Vatican, based on his observation of the plethora and prominence of the organizations loosely identified under the umbrella term "Catholic Action." These organizations were well developed in Europe by the end of the First World War and were ubiquitous by the end of World War II. At times they had a recognizable "spiritual" cast, as with certain "sodality" societies, at others a more immediately secular identity. They involved every level of life from agricultural pursuits to purchasing, producing and marketing co-operatives, credit unions, political parties, and a wide variety of organizations representing specific professional interests.

Catholic Action was defined as "the participation of the laity in the apostolic works of the hierarchy." The undergirding watchwords of Catholic action societies, "See, Judge, Act," bespoke a pedagogy aimed at encouraging an activist faith commitment in everyday social life. The growth of Young Catholic Worker, Young Catholic Student, and a host of other organizations, meant that committed Catholics had support vehicles for the activation of their faith life in their social, political, economic, and cultural milieux. The definition illustrates that these initiatives were at the instance of the Church hierarchy and subject to oversight by the clergy. The "participation" was thus understood as derivative and delegated at the discretion of the hierarchy. These types of organizations and the activities they promoted were championed by popes, bishops, and church leaders at every level from early in the century.

While the definition implies a clear intention of clerical direction and control, organizations tend to take on a life of their own. Catholic Action organizations were no exception, although the question of clerical control, or over-control, remains a hotly debated topic in many countries and regions where these societies suffered a steep decline after the 1960s. Paradoxically, this decline followed closely the legitimating theological advances and definitions of Vatican II, a Council thoroughly supportive of these agencies' interventionist agenda. Nevertheless, the organizations succeeded in developing several generations of lay leaders with wide

---

[6] Kenneth S. Latourette, *The Twentieth Century in Europe: The Roman Catholic, Protestant and Eastern Churches,* Vol. 4: Christianity in a Revolutionary Age. (New York: Harper Brothers, 1961), 67-68.

influence in both Church and society. They also played a great role on the development of novel approaches to missionary efforts in distant lands and determinedly engaged totalitarian regimes of both the right and the left.

The Young Christian Workers (YCW) movement enjoyed a prominent role in Quebec society over several decades and a more modest but significant role in other areas of Canada, notably Ontario. Montreal native Romeo Maione, who did his organizing work for the YCW in the Toronto area, became the first elected leader of the international YCW movement in the late 1950s. The YCW movement had played a crucial part in European labour and political life in the decades following the First World War. Because of this, and due to its influence among workers generally, it was targeted for suppression by Nazi and Fascist organizations in occupied countries. The movement's founder and leader, Canon (later Cardinal) Cardijn of Belgium, took refuge in Montreal during the war and moved the international headquarters to that city, where the YCW was well established. In Quebec local, regional, diocesan, and provincial assemblies were regular features of the social landscape. Canadian missionaries brought this form of organization to two dozen Latin American countries after World War II, providing workers with some of their initial experiences in organization activity. In some of these countries the organization was suppressed by governments fearing the revolutionary implications of an organized workers movement trained in activating the watchwords of "See, Judge, Act." Under Canadian missionary guidance the YCW organizations in Santiago, Chile prepared a one-hundred page study of the organizational and methodological patterns of the Montreal YCW to illustrate what could be done for Chilean workers.

Activities in Ottawa, 1940s-'50s

Catholic and social action activities at the University of Ottawa and St. Patrick's College in Ottawa during the 1940s and 1950s illustrate the range and significance of Catholic voluntary undertakings in the Canadian context.[7] Some of these activities, such as the YCW, are clearly identified

---

[7] The material in the following section is drawn from Chapter 4 of Brian Hogan, "Salted with Fire: Studies in Catholic Social Thought and Action in Ontario, 1931-1961" (Ph.D. dissertation, University of Toronto, 1986).

as Catholic Action organizations. A host of other ventures involving such social and economic activities as credit unions, labour unions and cooperatives do not easily fit into this category. They do, however, fall within the context of voluntary organizations. While they might have a distinctly social complexion, these groupings often employed the organizational techniques and the methodologies of the more strictly defined Catholic Action programs.

In 1935, in conjunction with Fr. André Guay, OMI, the founder of the University of Ottawa's Centre Catholique, Fr. Gustave Sauvé, OMI, began a series of courses on Catholic Action. These initial talks were attended by some three hundred persons and led to the formation of L'école d'Action catholique de l'université d'Ottawa, of which he was director from 1936 until 1938 and again from 1940 to 1946. In March 1940 Fr. Sauvé was instrumental in founding Centre social/The Social Centre of the University of Ottawa, a centre which actively developed Catholic social programs for the next fifteen years. The Centre came to involve faculty and students and operated a successful outreach program to communities throughout Quebec and Ontario. It undertook the development, printing, and dissemination of materials dealing with social and economic themes. Publications and activities included brochures, conferences, films, development of study clubs, and establishment of correspondence courses.

These courses achieved considerable success. The concern for practical application led to the development of work with co-operatives, particularly among French-Canadian communities throughout Ontario, and a detailed submission to the Royal Commission on Co-operatives in 1945. From this emerged an involvement with the Caisses populaires movement and the development of an umbrella organization for the Ontario Caisses. Under the direction of the Centre Catholique, a marriage preparation course of significant impact was developed in response to a request from the Jeunesse ouvrière catholique du Canada.

Many faculty members and students were directly or indirectly involved in the activities of the Centre. Among faculty members, none was more prominent than Dr. P. Hubert Casselman. Casselman became senior statistician in the Department of Labour in 1943, but remained active in the work of the Centre for some time afterwards. Later he became chief of the specialized manpower resources section in the economics and research branch.

To accomplish their intention of serving as a university of the people, Fr. Sauvé and the directors of the Centre turned towards co-operative techniques. In 1941 Sauvé published a study booklet entitled "Savoir pour agir: La reconstruction économique du demain et à base de corporatisme et co-operatisme." This exploration into the teaching of co-operative techniques enabled the Oblate to review the history and methodologies of co-operatism around the world and to introduce the basic technique of study clubs, particularly as developed by St. Francis Xavier University in Antigonish, Nova Scotia.[8]

This initial foray into the work of correspondence courses was quickly followed by the development of seven formal courses of twelve lessons each.[9] At least three of the courses were being distributed by 1943-44 and the remainder were in operation during the next four years. At the end of a course, an examination was held. If the course were successfully completed, the student received a certificate. This entitled him or her to become the leader of a study circle in that area of study.

The correspondence courses were offered under the general title of "Les cours de reconstruction sociale." The course on syndicalism, developed for the Centre social in 1945, began with a review of the history and necessity of unions, pointing out their legitimacy and noting the long history of opposition to them. The Rapport Annuel, 1948-49, charted statistics for each of the courses from 1943 through 1949. Altogether some 6,057 individuals had registered for courses, of whom 1,922 were awarded certificates. Supporting the several thousand students, the Centre had several hundred study groups affiliated with its various programs.[10]

The Centre social began during World War II, and as the war continued concern grew for social reconstruction at home. Looking to the end of hostilities, Centre personnel predicted considerable social stress, and even chaos, if proper preparations were not made. In order to prepare

---

[8] The St. Francis Xavier Movement, initiated by pioneers Fr. Moses Coady and Fr. Jimmy Tompkins, represents the premier accomplishment of Canadian social Catholicism in this century.

[9] Annual Report, University of Ottawa, 1948-49, 71.

[10] Rapport Annuel, Université d'Ottawa, 1947-48, 66.

for the post-war period and to avoid great social or political upheaval, the Centre insisted on the need for developing a serious program of social reconstruction.

In the Centre's view strong emphasis on the development of cooperative institutions for the stability of the country and the service of the people was needed. Centre leaders believed that consumers had to regain control of credit,[11] consumption, and production if they were to have economic independence.[12] In order to achieve this end, the Centre provided not only formal study courses but adult education materials and propaganda advancing the cooperative ideology. These included brochures, novelettes with co-operative themes, films, lectures, and a library.

On another front, the Jeunesse ouvrière catholique made ready for celebrating its fifteenth anniversary in Canada by studying the papal encyclical Casti connubii of 1930 (on Christian marriage) and by preparing a study of marriage and family conditions among working people. The investigation revealed an appalling lack of knowledge and preparation for marriage. Following their conference, responsibility for developing a complete program for marriage preparation was given to Fr. Guay of the Centre Catholique. The resulting course proved popular beyond the wildest imagination. By late 1944 it was available in French, and the publication of an article on the Centre by the U.S. National Catholic Welfare Conference News Service led to an immense demand for the Centre's services: "About four thousand persons in one month have asked for further information on the fifteen-lesson correspondence course,

---

[11] Between the late 1940s and the early 1950s the caisse populaire and credit union movement saw a dramatic upsurge in which hundreds of small credit unions were opened across the country. A surprisingly high number were either attached to a Roman Catholic church initially or strongly supported if not initiated by a local pastor. They may not have had any official church connection, such as bearing the name of the parish, but many credit unions used church facilities for their business, and even the gathering day of worship as the best time for providing for financial needs of members. While support of the credit union movement was not restricted to the Roman Catholic Church, this Church clearly provided a great deal of support and stimulation for it.

[12] "La reconstruction sociale y croyez-vous? Pour Rebattir," Undated. No. 1. Centre social de l'Université d'Ottawa,. Mimeograph, p. 115. Archdiocese of Ottawa Archives, File: University of Ottawa, 1943-1946.

which discusses with frankness all phases of marriage – spiritual, physical, legal and economic."[13] Some forty U.S. bishops had written to Fr. Guay expressing their appreciation for the Centre's work, and inquiries had been received from Ireland, the Philippines, and other countries. By this time about 1800 clerics were using the course in Canada, and it had been translated into English. By 1954, it was available in twenty-one countries, and had been translated into the world's major languages, as well as many minor languages, for distribution throughout Europe, the Americas, and many eastern and Asian countries. The course enlisted the aid of doctors, nurses, accountants, lawyers, priests, and married couples to present the very best preparation for marriage.

From marriage preparation as an attempt to solidify family life to cooperative undertakings intended to undergird the economic stability of families and communities, these programs developed from theologies which insisted on the basic bonding of human peoples, and a common humanity under one God. The programs influenced thousands of families. In many ways they bridged private and public spheres, religious and secular, and enabled participants to escape a dualistic separation of religious beliefs from life activities. In this manner, the Catholic voluntary contributed to a commonwealth more truly Christian than jurisdictions where the Church may have been established but where the engagement of Christian citizens was considerably less exacting.

In 1943 the Canadian Catholic hierarchy formed a national secretariat in Ottawa. For the first time the Canadian Church had an ongoing representative body aimed at developing and expressing a consensus on a variety of theological and social questions, in a manner which was simply not possible previously, given the infrequent meetings of the bishops. Similarly, in 1948, with the inauguration of the office of the Social Action Department (SAD), the Church possessed for the first time a national focal point for the explication of social teaching. The bond between the Social Action Department and the Institute of Social Action (ISA) founded

---

[13] "Thousands Apply for Instruction course on Marriage," *Record* (London, Ontario), 8 June 1946, 1; "JOC Initiators of Marriage Preparation Service," *Register* (Toronto, Ontario), 12 July 1947, 2.

at St. Patrick's College in Ottawa led to advances for voluntary Catholicism in the capital.[14]

Institute of Social Action

The development of the Institute of Social Action was fostered by Oblate priests at the College and came fully alive with the enthusiastic participation of Fr. Francis Marrocco, the first Director of the Social Action Department in 1948. The Institute was formally founded in 1951, but classes pre-dated the foundation by at least two years. The ISA's annual activities began with a Social Action Rally at St. Patrick's College in late September. Here a distinguished speaker introduced the several hundred people in attendance to the ISA activities for the year. In 1951 Peterborough's Bishop Joseph G. Berry, "a nationally known social worker," advised an audience of five hundred that courses offered by the ISA were designed to "get the principles of religion soundly back into Canadian business, education and family life."[15]

The Institute worked from the premise that "many Catholics are too silent or too negative in their social thinking"[16] and attempted to develop a lay leadership educated to accept the responsibility of translating thought into action at the local, provincial, and national levels of Canadian life. Members understood that:

> The object of social action is the 'Salvation and Christianizing' of social institutions. The human person is part of, and influenced by, his culture, neighbourhood, occupation, leisure time pursuits, social status, the theatre, the press, and government. It is the aim of social action to humanize and Christianize these institutions.[17]

---

[14] This material is derived from Chapter 7 of Brian Hogan, "Salted with Fire."

[15] "Social Action Study Course Takes Practical Turn at Ottawa School," *Register*, 29 September 1951, 1.

[16] *Ibid.*

[17] "Object of Social Action," Social Action Newsletter, Vol. 1 (15 January 1995), Ottawa: Institute of Social Action, St. Patrick's College, File PC101, Archives Deschatelets.

To accomplish this educational goal the ISA offered five courses during 1951-52: the Mystical Body of Christ; Introduction to Social Action; Objectives of Social Action Training; Christian Family Life; and Lay Leadership. Each course sought to integrate theological and sociological insights in a manner designed to stimulate efforts to correct social abuses and to encourage active participation by Catholics in everyday problems.

The following year Fr. Marrocco secured the services of Msgr. Moses Coady of St. Francis Xavier University as rally speaker.[18] The Nova Scotian spoke of the importance of adult education. He saw commitment as a second significant ingredient in any formula for change, commenting that the real test lay in the response to the question: "Have you the courage to come out with a social program that will incur the odium of the great and powerful interests of society?"[19] Coady's challenge corresponded exactly with the Institute's purposes and he saw in such agencies the real hope for introducing social reform into the body politic. For the next dozen years the Institute's courses, lectures, and field work programs involved men and women in developing and implementing solutions to a multitude of problems. The first years of the decade witnessed the conjunction of more than a dozen young people, most of whom remained to form the core of the ISA for more than a decade.

George Wicks, formerly with the British army and sent to Ottawa from Geneva to serve as the Resettlement Officer for the UN's International Refugee Organization, was in charge of Canadian immigration for a time, and in that capacity worked with Fr. Marrocco, who was also director of Catholic Immigration Aid.[20] Another central figure among ISA staff was Mary Kehoe, an Ottawa University alumna who had received her initial training in Catholic Action with the YCW between 1948 and 1950, while clerking at External Affairs. Her contact with the ISA came through a course offered in 1949-50, shortly prior to beginning work in the Public Relations Department of the Canadian

[18] Rev. F.A. Marrocco to Msgr. M. Coady, 9 July 1952. St. Francis Xavier Archives.

[19] "Need Adult Education to Reconstruct World," *Ensign*, 11 October 1952, 3.

[20] Under Wicks's direction the office processed more than 100,000 applications. Interview, Mr. George Wicks, Malignant Cove, N.S., 18 July 1980.

Congress of Labour.[21] She interrupted her work with the ISA in the mid-1950s but returned in 1961 in time to do much of the revision of the ISA course on Labour Unions and to launch St. Patrick's successful Credit Union Administration courses. She coordinated these courses for the nine years after 1962. As much as anyone, and far more than most, Mary Kehoe pioneered women's initiatives in church and marketplace.

Another member of the volunteer band was Gerald E. Clarke, an RCAF veteran who attended St. Patrick's College until 1949, then lectured at St. Dunstan's University, where he received a B.A. in 1951.[22] On his return to Ottawa in 1951 he became involved in the ISA, eventually heading the Co-operative Housing section and co-authoring the housing manual. Along with many others, Clarke, Kehoe, and Wicks developed a structured organization for the Institute of Social Action under its Director, the Rev. L. K. Poupore, OMI.

Co-operative home building

In Ontario the demographic shift to the cities increased through the Depression and the war years, adding considerable strain to the housing market. The stream of immigrants in the post-war period continued the trend and added further stress. In response to this general need and to their own need for housing, a number of ISA members undertook a co-operative housing program near Ottawa. Subsequent demand led to the development of courses and manuals for similar groups elsewhere in the province. As a result, promoting, educating, and supporting such groups became one of the ISA's most successful undertakings during the next decade.

In May 1952, with Fr. Marrocco's encouragement, a co-operative housing research project was launched. Some sixty volunteers participated over the summer under the chairmanship of George Wicks. The group studied Canadian, American, Swedish, and other approaches to co-

---

[21] Interview, Mary Kehoe, Ottawa, 7 March 1980; "Mary Kehoe—Trade Union Pilgrim," Presentation to the Canadian Religious Conference—Ontario Region, Toronto, 3 October 1981, 15.

[22] Interview, Prof. Gerald E. Clarke, Ottawa, 31 January 1980; Profile, program booklet, Ninth Catholic Social Life Conference, Halifax, N.S. October 1961. Courtesy of Mr. R. E. Walsh, Grimsby, Ontario.

operative building.[23] At the end of the summer, eight of the researchers formed a co-operative home building study group. By December sufficient interest had been aroused to initiate three study groups in the Ottawa area. Another group had begun in Lindsay, Ontario in October. Early enthusiasm for the housing co-operative work led to the development of an Ottawa regional Central Administrative Board (CAB) in December.[24]

In February 1953 the Institute published a Guide to Co-operative Housing, its eight booklets totalling 190 pages detailing the results of the summer research and laying down the principles for developing a homebuilding study group. The researchers investigated federal legislation requirements and established a working arrangement with the Central Mortgage and Housing Corporation (CMHC) permitting the application of the co-operators' physical labour on the project to the total value of the home and allowing that labour as the downpayment required by CMHC rules.[25] The publication of the Guide attracted much media attention, and the *Ensign* launched a six-part series on co-operative housing in the spring of 1953. At the annual meeting of the Canadian Trades and Labour Congress in Ottawa, Fr. Marrocco's speech on co-operative housing won enthusiastic applause.[26] Later, at the September gathering of the Canadian Congress of Labour in Montreal, the Social Action Director made a similar appeal, urging the 800 delegates to develop a method for easier access to "starter funds" for home-building societies.[27]

---

[23] Interview, George Wicks, Malignant Cove, Nova Scotia, 18 July 1980.

[24] G.E. Clarke, "Co-operative Homebuilding in Ontario, 1953-1957" (M.A. thesis, University of Ottawa, 1959), 3. The ISA group was not the first in the area to follow the co-operative building route. Across the river, in Wrightville, Quebec, a small group of men had begun a co-operative housing venture in the autumn of 1948. With study course plans from the Ligue ouvrière catholique, and financial support from Hull's Notre Dame Caisse Populaire and the Union St. Joseph, this group had completed fifteen homes and was working on ten others in December 1952. "Half Price Houses, but Not by Magic," *Ensign*, 6 December 1952, 3.

[25] "Heritage Series Tells Co-op Story," *Register*, 30 January 1960, 1.

[26] "Co-operative Building Urged to Combat Shortage of Housing," *Ensign*, 22 August 1953. Premier Leslie Frost, also appearing at the convention, and impressed by the rapid development of the co-operative society in his home town of Lindsay, promised provincial government support to aid the development of the new program.

[27] "Urges CCL Support for Co-op Housing," *Register*, 26 September 1953.

Between 1953 and 1963 ISA-associated groups built more than one thousand homes. In the case of the first 512 houses, the typical builder was 29 years of age when he began building and had two children. As for finances, the typical member "earned an income of $3,700, made a down payment of $860, moved into a house costing $10,630 and undertook to repay a mortgage debt of $9,750."[28] In any comparative test co-operative homes were found to be either average or above average in size and appearance. The ISA co-operators earned salaries only two-thirds as high as the average income of all National Housing Association (NHA) borrowers, indicating that rather more Canadians were potential home owners than was currently thought possible.[29] In terms of work time the average co-operator invested 1,470 hours of manual labour onsite. The average estimated saving of $2,110 thus suggests an hourly wage of $1.44. This, of course, does not account for the dozens of hours spent in study and committee work. However, when it is considered that the savings was not subject to income tax, and was also applicable, through the principle of "sweat-equity," to the downpayment, the significance of the savings appreciates considerably.

The ISA program illustrated the potential strengths of the ordinary citizen joined with others to fulfil a common need. The ISA staff were volunteers and few people associated with the homebuilding program derived any renumeration from it. The experience stands as an excellent example of clergy and Church drawing people together in communal support and service for mutual benefit. However, if begun by priests, it was the men and women of the ISA who provided the materials and who invested hopes, money, and time in carrying the projects to completion. As is evident from the testimony of participants, the projects were ultimately as much involved with building people as with building homes. Along the way the enterprise served as an initiation into ecumenism for priests and people. The building groups were broadly ecumenical, providing many of the participants with their first experience of working closely with those of other faiths.

For all participants the study and work experience taught the possibility of some added control over the direction of their lives. All were

[28] G. Clarke, M.A. thesis, 13.
[29] *Ibid.*, 37.

exposed to democratic involvement at its most basic level, all developed social skills and, for the first time, many learned to express their concerns and ideas. Experience generated an expertise, and later groups benefitted from the building pains of the pioneers.

The examples of community outreach represented in the work of the Centre social and Institute of Social Action illustrate two of the most dynamic initiatives expressed by Catholic Action and like structures in Canada outside of Antigonish. The political success of these small efforts in achieving the necessary legislative adjustments to assist their work helped to establish a more positive view of the secular societies in which they lived. Such practical experiences here, and in other countries, prepared for a more positive interpretation of the possibility of influencing increasingly secularized environments, but only through very considerable levels of commitment.

Second Vatican Council

In most national jurisdictions the establishment experience of the churches has fast been fading with the centuries and the advances of modernity. Within the Roman Catholic Church, adjustment to a more voluntary world has been most particularly provided for in two documents of the Second Vatican Council. The first, Gaudium et Spes, generally known as "The Pastoral Constitution on the Modern World," established principles for engaging the world in a proactive and positive dialogue and pastoral. This posture starkly contrasts to the reactive and judgmental approach characterizing the official pastoral in the generations following the Enlightenment. The specification of five areas of concern gives the document its unique appellation of "Pastoral" Constitution. A strange hybrid, it is the only such document in conciliar history. These five areas – marriage and family, the development of culture, socio-economic life, the life of the political community, and the promotion of peace and harmonious world relations, encompass a very broad range of extra-liturgical activities indeed.

The second document, a "declaration," enjoys a conciliar status less than that of "constitution." In spite of this, it has already proved an essential vehicle for the practical implementation of such a pastoral in the pluralist mix of cultural and religious realities governing our global village. Dignitatis Humanae (The Declaration on Religious Freedom), with its insistence on the right of the person to religious freedom in thought and practice, provides a necessary condition for the efficacious mix of religious and cultural convictions in contemporary society.

Structurally, advances in theology and accompanying developments in ecumenics, strongly buttressed by biblical, anthropological, and sociological studies, give evidence of signal advances along the lines proposed by Gaudium et Spes and Dignitatis Humanae. These developments have been in sympathetic harmony with several general theological progressions. These include a shift towards the subject, a move away from a classicist and towards an historical understanding of person and community, and a renewed emphasis on pastoral theology, with all that this implies. The accompanying focus on social justice issues of the last generation has been strengthened not only by a general focus on doing theology from the "bottom up" and by the categories of liberation theology, but also by papal encyclicals. The 1971 Synod of Bishops statement, Justice in the World, provided a solid foundation for such emphases, with its insistence that social justice issues are "a constitutive dimension of the preaching of the Gospel. . . ."[30] These theological realities are further supported by Vatican II initiatives at the personal level expressed in the understanding that through baptism the believer is consecrated into the priesthood of Jesus Christ and, whether lay or clerical, is expected to exercise an appropriate level of ministry in his or her life, both within Church and within society. Following Vatican II, therefore, one no longer speaks of "participation in the apostolic works of the hierarchy" as in some derivative manner. Rather there is a clear acknowledgement and expectation of the immediate commission and responsibility of all the faithful for furthering Gospel teachings and enacting the implications of these teachings in their daily lives.[31]

Similarly, the large numbers of Catholic lay students pursuing advanced theological degrees and deeply involved in a wide variety of

---

[30] "Action on behalf of justice and participation in the transformation of the world fully appear to us as a constitutive dimension of the preaching of the Gospel, or, in other words, of the Church's mission for the redemption of the human race and its liberation from every oppressive situation." "Justice in the World," in The Gospel of Peace and Justice, ed. Joseph Gremillion (Maryknoll, NY: Orbis Books, 1976), 514.

[31] Juridical structural foundations for such an interpretation can be found in Canons 215ff., The Code of Canon Law, 1983.

social and cultural issues suggests a vibrant response to a more voluntary environment. In the 1950s Jacques Maritain warned against an over-emphasis on "Catholic Action" as tending towards isolation, one possible consequence of the "pillarization" approach. Rather he insisted on "action by Catholics," presuming their ability to mix in their secular environments and successfully influence virtue and religious values in their respective societies. He was probably not contemplating the degree of pluralism the Western churches have come to know, and would undoubtedly be distressed by a number of features of the secular world. Neither was he naive, however, and his admonition would no doubt remain – Christians must cooperate in a broad range of activities in order to give structural reality and vitality to Gospel values.

Conclusion

This essay has focused on programs and organizations of a social and economic variety in an attempt to trace the projection of voluntary activities well beyond the normal parameters of the local church. This is not to deny the impact of such organizations as the Catholic Women's League, the Knights of Columbus, and the Saint Vincent de Paul Society on their larger social environments. It is, however, to suggest that this new range of activities definitely intended to engage the community at deeper levels, to support members in a wider variety of activities, and to welcome collaborative efforts with those of other faith convictions. Further, it is to note that the Canadian Church, faced with an expanding voluntary environment, has amassed a precious store of experience and dynamic expression in its positive response to a radically altered milieu. The interaction of clerics and lay persons through various social and economic programs in an earlier period represents a tradition on which to build for the challenges of the new millennium.

A definition of voluntary associations in the *Dictionary of Sociology* stresses their double usefulness in drawing the marginalized into the mainstream and serving as bridges between the private and public spheres.[32] The argument advanced in this essay is really twofold. For the

[32] "Participation in voluntary associations such as political parties, churches, trade unions, and professional bodies has been regarded as integrating marginal groups such

internal world of Church life these associations have fulfilled the purposes of the definition in drawing clergy and laity into common mission beyond the sanctuary. These tasks have provided opportunity for a reciprocal bonding movement between clergy and laity. Secondly, for the external world of Church and society, such undertakings have assisted in overcoming a dualism common to modernity where faith tends to be relegated to increasingly more discrete and remote locales of life. Again, a double movement is obvious, for by bridging this gap and expanding the perceived topography of faith and expression, these efforts have likewise helped to establish the continuity of faith and life and, reciprocally, to extend and to animate the experience of worship.

At this point, so goes the argument, the reality exceeds the limits of the definition, for the voluntary agencies serve as quite more than bridges or transitional conduits. They are, in fact, transformative vehicles, influencing not only participants but the environments within which they live and move and have their being.

---

as immigrants and ethnic minorities into society. In America, voluntary associations are regarded as important elements in participatory democracy. As secondary groups they bridge the gulf between the individual or family and the wider society." Nicholas Abercrombie, Stephen Hill, and Bryan S. Turner, *The Penguin Dictionary of Sociology* (London: Penguin Books, 1988), 265.

4

Individualism Shaping
Mennonite Community

Leo Driedger

Emphases on normative theology and cohesive community in the "voluntary" believers church have been so strong in Anabaptist writings that writers have tended to neglect the values of individualism which increasingly shape postmodern society (Holland, 1995). Indeed, in many conservative traditions, there has been much suspicion about the dangers of individualism, so that it has been suppressed to the point of interfering with the mission of the church. This paper examines the strengths and liabilities of individualism, and shows that it is an essential ingredient of strong leadership, and important to a creative and plausible Anabaptist presence in constantly changing postmodern contexts.

Conceptual bases

Alexis de Tocqueville coined the term "individualism," which has been followed by Reisman's, Simmel's, and Park's personality types and Bellah's (1985) four individual types. In *Democracy in America* Tocqueville claimed that it is the "chaotic but creative moment of transition from aristocracy to democracy that makes the best form of society possible":

> At that moment the repressive and conservative features of the old society are broken through so that new ideas can come forth, but there is still enough social solidarity left that initiative from popular leaders can mobilize support for significant reform"[1] (Bellah, et al., 1985:3).

Leo Driedger is professor of sociology at the University of Manitoba in Winnipeg, Manitoba.

[1] Alexis de Tocqueville, *Democracy In America*, trans. George Lawrence (New York: Doubleday, 1996), 29; Robert N. Bellah, Richard Madsen, William M. Sullivan, Ann Stevens and Stephen Tipton, eds., *Individualism and Commitment to American Life: Readings in the Themes of Habits of the Heart* (New York: Harper and Row, 1985), 3.

That sounds like the situation Anabaptist forebears were facing during the Reformation as well as the postmodern situation today. When tradition and hierarchies are strong, there is little room for discussion and experimentation, but when social structures are changed through immigration, mobility, and revolution, there is again room for individual initiative. In old structures, bureaucrats put their energies into maintaining their own power, not conducive to new initiatives. Democracy, Tocqueville suggested, is the way to cultivate and prolong creative voluntary periods of excitement and growth. It is like the surfer who rides the crest between the old receding and the newly forming waves, who is at the top of creative heights which require all the voluntary individual resources of freedom, independence, balance, judgment, anticipation, selection, and finesse to survive. Alvin and Heidi Toffler's recent work (1995) on the politics of the third wave is instructive here.

It was the Puritans, Quakers, Amish, Mennonites, and others who left the old feudal states and ecclesiastical structures to find new freedoms in North America, creating homesteads on virgin soil and unleashing the pent-up creative energies smouldering in the hearts of the oppressed. Thrown together with many languages, cultures, and religions, they along with the aboriginals who welcomed them nurtured their freedom while creating new communities, churches, cultures, and societies. It was a plural setting which those of Anabaptist ancestry had experienced again and again in the Reformation, in Switzerland, the Netherlands, Ukraine and finally America and Canada. These persecutions, migrations, and multiple pioneer settlements helped to create individualism, in the context of the *Gemeinschaft*.

Changing personality types
Tocqueville's thesis requires further analysis of transitional types of individuals who either stay in the traditional culture, or as newly-arrived immigrants and persons who have just moved into city life, launch into strange new cultures and environments. Such newcomers (who often included Mennonites who moved every several generations) are faced with alternatives such as 1) segregating and isolating themselves again, 2) assimilating into the host society and losing their identity, or 3) adopting some modified version of being a stranger or middle person, like a broker seeking to balance the pulls and pushes of both ingroup and host cultures.

In *The Lonely Crowd*, David Riesman (1950) developed "tradition-directed," "inner-directed," and "other-directed" types. The tradition-directed person is typical in non-industrial non-urban societies where birth and death rates are high and where spatial and social mobility is low. As these people are introduced to the industrial environment, they move through an inner-directed phase in which they become conscious of their traditional state and begin to become aware of other non-traditional options. Their rising awareness creates much evaluation and inner turmoil. Riesman's other-directed third type is one who has become urbanized, lives in an industrial environment, and is oriented toward secondary others who have entered his social arena and influenced his values.

The ingroup culture in the traditional-directed controls behaviour minutely: there is intensive socialization and a careful and fairly rigid etiquette. Little energy is directed towards finding new solutions for age-old problems or towards developing new agricultural techniques or the like. Usually the traditional-directed ethnic is found in a rural, agricultural, or food-gathering society, although these values are also brought to the city by ethnic villagers.

A broker or middleperson is one who enters the urban, industrial fray seeking to remain an integral part of both worlds. Pierre Van den Berghe claims that every country has its middlemen: "Turkey has Armenians and Greeks; West Africa has Lebanese; East Africa has Indians and Pakistanis; Egypt has Copts; Indonesia, the Philippines, Malaysia, Vietnam and Thailand have the Chinese."[2] These are minorities who compete well and are also fairly well-to-do socio-economically. When they compete in the melting pot, they seem able to separate their economic and social lives, and to retain their separate ethnic identity. Van den Berghe suggests there is a cluster of characteristics of middlemen minorities (MM) which are remarkably uniform from society to society.[3] MMs usually maintain strong extended families, perpetuate endogamy, and try to perpetuate their own cultural, institutional, and spatial identity so that they acculturate more slowly than most other groups. Van den Berghe also classifies MMs as an urban petty bourgeoisie social class, better off than the majority of the population but often far from wealthy. This status often

---

[2] Pierre L. Van den Berghe, *The Ethnic Phenomenon* (New York: Elsevier, 1981), 137.
[3] *Ibid.*, 138.

provides them with many advantages in competition with their neighbours. MMs often hold ethnic values such as thrift, frugality, lack of ostentation, and postponement of gratification. Jews, Chinese, Japanese, East Indians, and Mennonites come readily to mind, and most of these can be recognized by their distinctive religion or visibility.

George Simmel's "stranger" is similar to the middleperson. The concept of the stranger unifies the two characteristics of fixity and transience.[4] Simmel thought that the stranger could retain a separate identity by controlling his behaviour with others, often by being physically near them to perform economic functions, for example, but distant with respect to their values. On the other hand, the stranger could often be far away from his reference ingroup when performing his duties in urban society, but could still retain a symbolic feeling of nearness and belonging to it. We would expect that when the stranger or middleperson enters the strange environment of others, he/she is secure only if grounded in a reference group, or socially and psychologically motivated by the norms and networks of such a group.

For many migrants, however, retaining a stable secure base is difficult. Robert Park's ideal marginal person is typical of another type to which many Blacks from the rural American tenant farms of the south belonged, when they moved into northern cities. This change of residence, typical of new migrants and the concomitant breaking of home ties with traditional rural values and norms, resulted in great cultural upheavals which led to change and sometimes to disorganization and conflict.

Park thinks of the marginal person as a racial or cultural hybrid: one who lives in two worlds, in both of which he is more or less a stranger; one who aspires to, but is excluded from, full membership in a new group. The marginal person is between two cultures and not fully a part of either. "Park's excluded marginal man was depicted as suffering from spiritual instability, intensified self-consciousness, restlessness, and in a state of malaise"[5] (Levine, et al., 1976:830). This person could not cope in the new situation and was a potential deviant who might look for outlets of expression in unacceptable ways. This type is becoming more evident as

[4] George Simmel, *The Sociology of George Simmel* (Glencoe: Free Press, 1950), 402.
[5] N. Levine, Ellwood B. Carter, and Eleanor Miller Garman, "Simmel's Influence on American Sociology," *American Journal of Sociology* 81(1976):830.

Mennonites increasingly seek to survive in the city for several generations. Anabaptists began as surfers seeking to live between two waves (worlds), but soon opted for more tranquil shores where they lost their surfing skills. Today, as new Anabaptists enter cities like a surfer who mounts an emerging wave, their surfing skills are quite undeveloped. However, individual aptitudes can go a long way towards learning to survive and compete.

Bellah's four individual types
"In 1985, Robert Bellah and his co-authors (Richard Madsen, William Sullivan, Ann Swidler and Steven Tipton) published their best-selling book *Habits of the Heart* and, almost overnight, restored the interest of sociologists in the concept of individualism"[6] (Ainlay, 1990:135). Bellah et al. define individualism as "a belief in the inherent dignity and . . . sacredness of the human person," and "a belief that the individual is a primary reality whereas society is a second-order, derived or artificial construct. . . ."[7] They devote their entire book (1985), and a reader which followed (1987), to constructing four types of individualism (biblical, civic, utilitarian, expressive). They claim that "individualism lies at the very core of American culture," and this sacredness of the individual involves the "right to think for ourselves, judge ourselves, make our own decisions, and live lives as we see fit."[8] The same could be said for Anabaptists and their ancestors. All four types of individualism assume these rights, but the deepest problems are also linked to individualism.

Some dimensions of individualism can be plotted along polarities of commitment and local or public arenas. "Expressive individualism holds that each person has a unique core of feeling and intuition that should unfold or be expressed if individuality is to be realized."[9] Expressive individualism is related to the phenomenon of romanticism in eighteenth and nineteenth-century European and American culture. Today it may be expressed most clearly by the artistic communities in creative writing and

[6] Stephen C. Ainley, "Communal Commitment and Individualism" in Leo Driedger and Leland Harder, eds., *Anabaptist-Mennonite Identities in Ferment* (Elkhart, IN: Institute of Mennonite Studies, 1990), 135.

[7] Bellah, *Habits of the Heart,* 334.

[8] Bellah, *Individualism and Commitment,* 143.

[9] Bellah, *Habits of the Heart,* 334.

the arts (painting, sculpting, etc.). The self is the primary focus of commitment in a "local village" arena. The downside of expressive individualism is that it can be too focused on self and its limited locale, while the opportunities lie in expressing most deeply individual psychological and creative feelings, motives, and desires.

Utilitarian individualism is usually traced to John Locke, who held that the individual was prior to society and that the individual's self-interest should be maximized. For Thomas Hobbes the desire for power over others and the fear that others wish you ill was clearly present, suggesting that the individual needs to be wary of social commitments. Bellah et al. (1985:145) suggest that "America is also the inventor of the most mythic individual hero, the cowboy, who again and again saves a society he can never completely fit into," because he can shoot straighter and faster than others. The other American hero is the hard-boiled detective, a loner, whose marginality is his strength. Society in each case is corrupt to the core. In the case of Locke and Hobbes and their utilitarian individualism the question arises, Can such individualism, where the self has become the main focus of reality, be sustained? In the case of the cowboy and detective, are such individuals real and plausible? The utilitarian as the self-contained individual who may express individualism in a more public arena is understood in this way. Some individuals enter into a contract with society in order to advance their self-interest. For Bellah et al., both the expressive and utilitarian forms of individualism are considered impoverished because they focus on immediate payoff, rather than on the traditions which have formed us, or society's larger problems and needs.[10] Television and the mass media, they claim, are couched largely in utilitarian and expressive forms, playing to emotions, wants, and desires of the self.

In contrast, the biblical and civic forms of individualism are private and public expressions and action directed toward others. Bellah's Republican tradition, which Ainlay (1990) has renamed "civic individualism," originated in classical Greece and Roman traditions, was expressed later in the civic humanism of late medieval and early modern Europe, and contributed to the formation of modern western democracies. It presupposes that citizens are motivated by civic virtue as well as self-

---

[10] Bellah, *Individualism and Commitment*, 4.

interest, for moral purposes such as justice and the public good. In the United States the biblical and civic forms of individualism seem to have agreed on common purposes of justice.

The tradition that originates in biblical religion, widely diffused in American and Canadian culture, is carried primarily by Jewish and Christian religious communities (Bellah, et al., 1985). Numerous versions, including the Puritan and Protestant sects which promoted voluntarism, were refugees from European state church regions. They sought religious freedom from the establishment and were willing to live with religious diversity. These groups inspired a notion of government based on the voluntary participation of individuals.

The biblical record is laced with, indeed is dominated by, individuals, so it should not be surprising when individualism and Christianity highly correlate, as Max Weber suggested in his *Protestant Ethic and the Spirit of Capitalism*. What was more individual than Abraham leaving the first great urban civilization of Mesopotamia and starting a new religion in the wilderness, Jacob snitching a blessing from Esau, and his grandson Joseph, becoming a major minister in Pharaoh's cabinet in charge of famine relief in the second great urban civilization of Egypt? Moses learned independence in Pharaoh's court to challenge Pharaoh himself and led the children of Israel into the desert, while Joshua set out to conquer Palestine. The prophets receive ample attention – consider the individual courage of Jeremiah, the commitment of Ruth the immigrant, Esther the leader, Hosea the deviant, Jonah the coward, and Amos the shepherd railing at the city folks. The New Testament is dominated by two individuals, Jesus who defied traditions all around him, and Paul who travelled all over the urban mediterranean world from Jerusalem to Rome challenging politicians, entrepreneurs, and religious and political leaders where he could find them.

Mennonites especially have a community tradition which has obscured the importance of individualism, placing leadership drive under the shroud that it is only God doing all this. When leaders lead another schism, setting themselves apart in the name of Christ, Christians act surprised and puzzled. That should not be, because the *Martyrs Mirror* clearly shows a history of individualism. Currently there is a reluctance to acknowledge individualism, although C.J. Dyck's *Twelve Becoming* is a good beginning in that direction.

Although religious groups vary, both biblical and civic individualism places the person in the context of a larger whole, a community and a tradition capable of sustaining a genuine individuality nurturing both private and public life.[11] However, expressive and utilitarian forms of individualism today seem to be growing at the expense of biblical and civic individualism. Biblical and civic individualism are committed to others in their major focus; it is doubtful that expressive and utilitarian forms of individualism focused on the self can be sustained for long. While biblical individualism in the private-other cell has been plotted, such individualism also involves important public commitments to action. However, Mennonite biblical individualism has been formed largely in the context of the private local village community, and only for some have their religious sights begun to include the larger arenas of the public global village, to which this discussion turns next.

Empirical findings

To see whether the above discussion has some confirmation in fact, several examples will be used below to show how individualism has played an important role in leadership training, especially in times of transition as Tocqueville predicted. Then the 1989 Church Membership Profile (CMP II) data will be compared to see whether the four individual types of Bellah et al. can be documented.

"Deviant" individualism
While *The Martyrs Mirror* is a monument to the lives of biblical individualism, Mennonites soon retreated toward the periphery of societies, isolating themselves in local segregated ingroup communities, where individualism became taboo, shrouded in the mystery of God and community. A brief illustration can be found in the experiences of my grandfather in the Old Colony Mennonite community, and historical events such as the scattering in alternative service, the development of Mennonite Central Committee, and the flowering of the creative arts.

---

[11] Bellah, *Habits of the Heart*, 143.

My grandfather, Johann Driedger, migrated as a 14-year-old from the Ukraine to help found the village of Blumenthal, Manitoba in 1875. As an adult he became the village Schultze (mayor) and started a small store in his house before he migrated to Saskatchewan in 1904. This time the family settled at Clark's Crossing on the edge of the solid Mennonite Hague-Osler block reserve settlement north of Saskatoon.[12] Here Johann built a store on the railroad line and operated a post office while farming his land. A photograph taken in 1906 shows a traditional Old Colony Mennonite Driedger family dressed in dark colours – women with traditional head coverings, men without ties, although Johann was testing the boundaries by wearing a white handkerchief in his coat pocket. Taking a photo itself was taboo.

Settling outside the Mennonite reserve and setting up a store raised suspicions, but to move three years later into the small hamlet of Osler in 1907 as storekeeper again soon raised troubles. The new store in Osler burned down in 1907 before Johann had entirely moved in, raising suspicions of arson; and it was insured with the Old Colony Mennonite fire insurance, which created a serious dilemma for the Ohms (elders). Should the policy of Driedger, who first settled outside the Mennonite village reserve, had become a storekeeper, and had moved into town (all of which were taboo), be recognized and honoured? The elders waffled, Driedger insisted on insurance payments, and by 1908, he found himself excommunicated. His individual initiative had gone too far.

But Johann refused to be excommunicated, and continued to come to church – not by buggy as the rest did, but in his new car. The 100 letters of correspondence we have between Driedger and the church elders tell of members holding the church door shut when he arrived, or the entire congregation running out when he did get in, to the point where Mr. Fischer, an English farmer nearby, was deputized by the RCMP to keep Driedger from coming to church. Driedger's several stores were boycotted with almost complete effectiveness in the Mennonite community, so he had to move his business to other non-Mennonite towns.

---

[12] Leo Driedger, "Individual Freedom vs. Community Control: An Adaptation of Erickson's Ontogeny of Ritualization," *Journal for the Scientific Study of Religion* 21 (1982): 226-42.

In 1919, eleven years after excommunication, Johann sent a letter with a $1,000 cheque asking for forgiveness. He was reinstated, and the elders conducted his funeral a year later. Had he lived only eight years longer, he would have seen the newly-built General Conference Mennonite Church, three blocks from his former Osler store. Three of his sons were on the building committee and the church executive. I was present at the dedication in 1928 (I was three months old), I grew up there, and I was elected at age twenty-one as an assistant minister by the congregation. Can you imagine the individual stamina required by my grandmother Katerina, a member of the quiet, shy Martens family, who was expected not to share the same bed with Johann but did, who was shunned by relatives and the Old Colony community like Johann, and who remained a member of the Old Colony church until she died?

In the terminology of David Reisman, Johann and Katerina Driedger came from a deeply conservative village background to which Katerina remained committed in a "tradition-directed" way. Johann tested the boundaries of tradition and was excommunicated, becoming very much a marginal man as Park predicted. While three of their ten children remained Old Colony tradition-directed members, four others – in line with Reisman's inner-directed way – joined a more liberal General Conference Mennonite church open to other-directed individual opportunities. The remaining three youngest children did not commit themselves to any church, were marginalized by the church, and were assimilated into the larger society.

Alternative service as individualism

While examples of Mennonite individualism could be found by the bushel, larger historical phenomena have also shaped modern Anabaptist individualism. Involuntary alternative service during World War II created an enormous reservoir of individual church leaders some fifty years ago. These men who resisted military service and entered alternative service to work in forestry projects, mental hospitals, and the like were forced out of their enclavic rural community cocoons to try their wings.[13] From this tragic blessing poured out tried-in-the-fire leaders who are just now

---

[13] Lawrence Klippenstein, ed., *That There Be Peace: Mennonites in Canada and World War II* (Winnipeg: Manitoba C.O. Reunion Committee, 1979).

moving out of the leadership core of the Mennonite church. A recent photo in *Mennonite Life* showing Kansas men who served included Maynard Shelly, Robert Kreider, Gordon Kaufman, Don Smucker, and Verney Unruh, who were the driving force of the Board of Christian Service and MCC in the 1950s and '60s, which included at least four college presidents, several General Conference presidents, and many prominent Mennonite Church pastors. In Canada it was David Schroeder, Gerhard Ens, and many others who likewise became stalwarts in our Mennonite schools, churches, and institutions. All of this illustrates well the connection between individual courage and commitment to alternative service, which developed leaders for the church.

World War II and the opportunity for alternative service created the foment which pushed Mennonite youth into the world. They saw opportunities for service in the larger society, and for much needed experience and practice in surfing the tide between their traditional community and newly forming waves outside. As Tocqueville predicted, this creative newfound individualism, still anchored in social ingroup solidarity, changed and launched a new phase in the Mennonite Central Committee, which had formed in 1920. MCC was originally set up to help Russian Mennonites and remained largely a relief agency to serve ingroup needs for the first twenty-five years. However, after the war, the creative forces of Mennonite alternative service released hundreds of the most able, committed Mennonite youth to help serve the needs which they had found outside their Mennonite enclaves.

MCC outreach and individual leadership
Similar to what Tocqueville saw in the new American democracy, Mennonite youth were propelled out of their traditional segregated environs to where new ideas were found, and they returned to launch a variety of MCC programs of voluntary service, PAX, relief work, Mennonite Disaster Service, and Mutual Aid. During the past fifty years this activity has grown to an other-directed MCC with 1,000 workers in fifty countries supported by an annual budget of $30 million. Alternative service forced youth into the larger arena, the old traditional ingroup structures had to give way to new ideas, and the old patterns of leadership were broken and gave way to refreshed ideas from youth and their experiences. For fifty years MCC has been able to extend these renewed

democratic forms of leadership training, which are now widely recognized in North America generally.

MCC has been especially successful in sending out what Simmel would call "strangers," who have their roots deeply lodged in the sending churches, clearly focused and directed by a committed agency, where youth are able to surf successfully on the crest between the new challenges and the traditional ingroup values and communities from which they come. Such biblical individualists with MCC experience return home with new leadership potential.

Mennonite urban professional individualism
Anabaptists in the sixteenth century were heavily engaged in the craft industry, which provided more mobility than those who were confined to the land as serfs. As Mennonites increasingly urbanize and change their occupations from being farmers to professionals, Mennonite urban professionals (Muppies) are again forced to surf, this time on the waves of urbanism and professionalism. While before 1940 most Mennonites farmed, by 1989 only seven percent did so. The largest number, twenty-eight percent, are now in the professions. Mennonites no longer are segregated spatially, nor are their patterns of making a living segmented. This Muppie revolution, where half who are now urban are surfing the metropolitan crest, will require all the voluntary individual resources of balance, judgment, anticipation, selection, and finesse that they can muster. There are both hopeful and discouraging signs.

Urbanization has again launched Mennonites into the cities, which provide more ready-made natural individual opportunities for influence and service. By 1989 half had attained at least some college and one in five had at least a year of graduate school, similar to the general population, a development which provides the resources for independent competition for jobs and income. Mennonites' socio-economic status has increased considerably since 1972, and they have become more independent, self-reliant, and free to make their own decisions than ever before. Opportunities for Muppies, especially, to engage in all forms biblical, civic, utilitarian, and expressive individualism are amply available to many, as illustrated in recent forms of individualism in their creative, artistic community.

Individualism in the creative arts
The creative arts such as music, writing, and art seem to be the new frontier for individualistic Mennonite expression today. The musical tradition began early in Amsterdam in the Dutch tradition and was carried eastward into Russia and then to North America. Choirs were especially well integrated into church and community institutions. In Canada this tradition was continued by 1920s Russian Mennonites such as K.H. Neufeld, H. Neufeld, John Konrad, David Paetkau, and Ben Horsch. These choral leaders constantly extended the traditional choral boundaries into classical arenas, but not without considerable resistance. Institutions such as Mennonite schools became favourable grounds on which to further the musical cause. A second cycle of musical creativity was amply spearheaded by George and Esther Wiebe, William and Irmgard Baerg, and John Martens at the Winnipeg Mennonite colleges. Helen Martens at Conrad Grebel College in Waterloo, Ontario and Henry Engebrecht at the University of Manitoba extended individual creativity into the outside worlds of concert halls, universities, television, and the media. Hundreds of choir directors, soloists, and instrumentalists were able to express their individualism largely within and with the blessing of their churches.

Creative writers had a much harder time surfing on the new waves of creative writing, as Arnold Dyck of Steinbach (and later, Winnipeg) could well attest. Trained in Europe, Dyck found little interest in his plays, novels, pamphlets, and art, until more recently when urban Mennonites like Al Reimer, Harry Loewen, Victor Doerksen, and Elizabeth Peters resurrected his works in a four-volume publication. Rudy Wiebe, a Mennonite college graduate also experienced a rude jolt when his first of many novels, *Peace Shall Destroy Many*, got him into trouble in his Mennonite Brethren community, and he was let go from his editorship of the *Mennonite Brethren Herald*. Fortunately, he found a welcome hearing at the University of Alberta, where his novels and creative works have continued to win national prizes.

While Arnold Dyck and Rudy Wiebe were marginalized individuals still related to the Mennonite church, most younger Mennonite creative writers have voluntarily left the church. Winnipeg is a hotbed of such a colony of 1870s-heritage Mennonite writers who began writing about their frustrations in the traditional family and community. Included are Patrick Friesen, Di Brandt, Sandra Birdsell, Armin Wiebe, Sarah Klassen, Audrey

Poetker-Thiessen, David Waltner-Toews, Diane Driedger, John Weier, and many more. Some of these expressive individual younger writers usually begin by processing their local traditional past, after which some have turned to the larger scene for their inspiration. Many of these are Mennonite marginals, seemingly unable to turn their creativity into biblical individual inspiration, or unaccepted by their churches, or both.

While the visual artistic Mennonite community is not nearly as expanded and developed, it too is emerging as a creative expressive individual influence whose members are increasingly exhibiting paintings, sketches, and sculptures in public displays in both Mennonite schools and elsewhere. Here fraktur traditional art, well-developed in the Swiss Mennonite wing, grew out of accepted community patterns like music did. It is well accepted because it uses visual forms of birds, animals, and plants that are close to and dear to the conservative rural Mennonite past. Les Brandt, Dale Boldt, Margaret Doell, Aganetha Dyck, Helene Dyck, Leonard Giesbrecht, Lois Klassen, Ernie Kroeger, Grace Nickel, Susan Shantz, Jean Smallwood, Al Toews, and Erma Martin Yost are but a few recently presented in *Mennonite Artist: Insider as Outsider*. As the title of this recent book suggests, they too feel like "strangers," riding the crest between their traditional and newly expanded worlds.

Finding Bellah's individual types
Using Kauffman and Driedger's (1991) four personal independence indicators to measure expressive individualism, Table 1 shows that a majority of the sample of over 3,000 North American Mennonites and Brethren in Christ thought that making your own decisions, and being self-reliant, being independent, being free to do what you want were important. Four out of five wanted to make their own decisions and be self-reliant, and one-fourth thought this was very important. Two out of three wanted to take care of their own needs, and one-third thought it important to be free to do what one wants. It is quite clear that Mennonites are strongly independent.

TABLE 1

Indicators of Mennonite Personal Independence and Expressive Individualism

Values that guide life and thought	No Importance	Not Very Important	Somewhat Important	Important	Very Important
	(Percentages)				
Being able to make *own decision*	0	2	16	56	26
Being *self-reliant*	0	3	20	51	27
Taking care of my own needs — being *independent*	1	5	29	49	16
Being *free* to do what I want to do	2	19	45	27	7

These four indicators have not been linked to any utilitarian, civic, or biblical commitments, so there is as objective a measure of independent expressive individualism as possible. These individual expressions of self-reliance, independence, and freedom can be used for selfish as well as service-to-others ends.

While expressive individualism portrays private values of the self, utilitarian individualism represents values that guide the individual in public life and thought, which is measured in Table 2 by using six indicators of security, getting ahead, saving, earning, and aspirations toward fashions and home furnishings. Six of ten respondents thought it important to earn enough money to be secure in old age so they would not be dependent on others. One-third thought it important to work hard to get ahead financially, while one-fourth did not consider this important. So there is a range of values, with almost half in the middle. The profile for saving as much money as possible is very similar to getting ahead; respondents seem torn between getting ahead for themselves and caring about other values. Once earning as much money as possible is the goal, the numbers begin to skew toward less importance. When the emphasis turns clearly on stylish dressing and personal home furnishings, almost two-thirds no longer think it important, and very few admit to personal dress and home comfort as being important. Mennonites seem to favour utilitarian individualism for the purpose of responsible security and caring for self, but as the focus turns to optional needs of money, dress and home comfort, very few give it high priority.

TABLE 2

Indicators of Utilitarian Individualism and Values
Which Guide Mennonite Life and Thought

Values that guide life and thought	No Importance	Not Very Important	Somewhat Important	Important	Very Important
			(Percentages)		
Earning enough money to be *secure* in old age	1	6	33	47	13
Working hard so as to *get ahead* financially	3	19	45	29	5
Saving as much money as possible	3	22	48	23	4
Earning as much money as possible	4	33	44	17	2
Being *dressed* in the latest styles and fashions	14	49	29	7	1
Getting the nicest *home* and furnishings I can afford	10	49	33	7	1

While expressive and utilitarian individualism focus on the private and public self, civic and biblical individualism focus on others, as is indicated in Table 3. Using five indicators for civic individualism, all Mennonites in our sample wish to be at peace with others and treat others properly, and four out of five also want to use their resources for the good of others. These Mennonites are strongly motivated toward the welfare of others, and three-fourths actually volunteered to work for church and community agencies, and visited non-relatives when they were sick or shut-in.

TABLE 3

Indicators of Mennonite Civic Individualism

Values that guide life and thought (actually were active)	No Importance	Not Very Important (Never)	Somewhat Important (Few Times)	Important (Occasionally)	Very Important (Frequently)
			(Percentages)		
Being at *Peace* with other persons	0	0	2	28	70
Making sure I *treat* others properly	0	1	1	37	61
Using my *resources* for good of others	0	2	18	57	23
Volunteered work for church or community agencies	0	5	18	43	34
Visited a non-relative who was sick, shut-in	0	4	48	48	24

The strong independence found in Mennonite expressive individualism does not seem to be a deterrent to help others. This seems to confirm the findings in Table 2, that while Mennonites want to be secure, get ahead, save, and earn, they do wish to do so not exclusively for their own ends but for the welfare of others also.

Biblical individualism illustrates the tension between the self and others as well as the private-public dilemma. Three out of four Mennonites agree that church membership means that the individual should both be willing to give admonition and receive it. This involves the courage both to restrict the individualism of others and also to be restricted by others for the sake of the church. One-half think of their religion as being a more personal choice, while one-third lean toward directions by church doctrine, which illustrates the self-other dilemma. When faith is pushed as a private matter, one-third agree, but well over half then opt for less privacy in their decisions and practice. The strongest statement saying that it is not the business of the church to be directly involved in personal affairs, is too much individual privacy for six out of ten, with only one out of four agreeing. The largest majority clearly feel most at ease with admonition which involves restrictions of give-and-take, and a strong majority agree that the church does have a right to be involved in personal affairs.

TABLE 4

Indicators of Mennonite Biblical Individualism

Values that guide life and thought	Strongly Disagree	Disagree	Uncertain	Agree	Strongly Agree
	(Percentages)				
Church membership means to give and receive mutual *admonition*	1	9	15	65	10
Religion should be a more *personal choice* than church-doctrine-directed	5	29	14	40	12
Faith is a *private* matter for each to decide and practice	8	47	11	29	5
Not business of church to be directly involved in my *personal affairs*	7	52	17	22	2

In Table 5, on the following page, the correlations between the four individualism scales are presented. The first three expressive, utilitarian, and biblical scales were designed to focus on the independence of the self, correlated negatively with outreach to others, especially associationalism, Anabaptism, religious life, stewardship and the like. These associations clearly show that focus on the self is an independent phenomenon, quite different than a focus on others, as suggested in our model in Figure 1.

The civic individualism scale shows that when items are designed to show outreach to others, then these correlations are all positive. While the correlations of expressive individualism and utilitarian individualism are somewhat lower than the biblical and civic ones, they are all in the same direction. This again shows the independence of individualism from focus on the Self compared to focus on others.

The intercorrelations between the four expressive, utilitarian, biblical, and civic scales are also strong, which suggests that they all measure a similar phenomenon no matter what type of individualism we are focusing on. These findings show the basic differences between focus on the self and concern for others which also act as a dialectic in religious faith and action.

The Believers Church

TABLE 5

Correlations Between Expressive, Utilitarian, Biblical, and Civic Individualism (Pearson's rs)

	Expressive Individualism (Independence)	Utilitarian Individualism (Materialism)	Biblical Individualism (Individualism)	Civic Individualism (Self/Others)
Independence	-	.49	.33	-.01
Materialism	.49	-	.28	-.18
Individualism	.33	.28	-	-.31
Civic, Self/others	-.01	.18	.31	-
Secularsim	.20	.23	.54	-.35
Media Use	.11	.15	.17	-.11
Political Participation	.10	.05	-.02	.10
Age	.08	.01	-.02	.22
Role of Women	.06	.01	-.06	.02
Memberships	.06	.08	-.06	.02
Ethnicity	.01	.02	-.10	.13
Communalism	-.02	.00	-.13	.15
Socioeconomic Status	-.02	-.04	-.17	.16
Fundamentalism	-.04	.06	-.14	.07
Welfare Attitudes	-.05	-.08	-.21	.20
Education	-.06	-.13	-.21	.14
Pacifism	-.08	-.27	-.15	.17
Race Relations	-.08	-.17	-.23	.14
General Orthodoxy	-.10	-.04	-.23	.07
Evangelism	-.11	-.18	-.31	.43
Charity	-.12	-.08	-.15	.16
Charismatics	-.12	-.12	-.18	.20
Moral Behaviour	-.13	-.07	-.19	.15
Moral Attitudes	-.14	-.10	-.29	.21
Separatism	-.14	-.16	-.31	.24
Stewardship Attitudes	-.16	-.07	-.33	.22
Devotionalism	-.16	-.18	-.38	.45
Religious Life	-.17	-.21	-.43	.51
Anabaptism	-.19	-.23	-.42	.29
Aspirationalism	-.24	-.21	-.47	.42

Conclusions

Alexis de Tocqueville concluded that creative changes in society occur at special revolutionary times like waves, where new ideas can be introduced when the old society structures are weakened or broken down, and popular leaders can then initiate and mobilize significant reform. The Reformation was such a time when the Anabaptists emerged, and Mennonites are again in such a revolutionary time, when urbanization, professionalization, modernization, and individualism enhanced by the electronic media are shaping postmodern Mennonite identity.

Individualism and types, such as Reisman's tradition-directed, inner-directed, and other-directed personality types, have been examined. Simmel's "stranger," and Van den Berghe's "brokers" acted as positive individual leaders in such times, bridging the old and the new, while Park's "marginal" person is an example of negative breakdown of identity. The empirical evidence of these types, using Johann Driedger as a "deviant" individual type creating problems in the tradition-directed community, has been demonstrated. Alternative service during World War II resulted in renewed leadership, MCC outreach acted as a training ground for leadership, and Muppies and creative artists are two good examples of postmodern, 1990s' forms of individualism at work. These forms of individualism are strongly shaping Mennonites today, as increasingly Mennonite individuals are "surfing on the crest" between tradition and renewal.

Bellah and his associates introduced four types of individualism, two of which focused on the self and two on others. All four forms of individualism are very much present among Mennonites today. Expressive individualism in the private-self corner, emphasizing self-reliance, independence, free expression, freedom and making your own decisions, was found to be very strong among most Mennonites. Utilitarian individualism representing the public-self was strong on security, getting ahead and saving, but was less supported when the focus was only on personal dress and a comfortable home. Civic individualism in the public-others corner was also well supported, and focused on being at peace with others and treating others well, using resources for others, volunteering, and visiting others. Biblical individualism, representing acceptance and giving of mutual admonition, was strong, but there was a considerable range on how far faith should be a private matter, how far the church could direct individuals, and how far the church should be involved in personal affairs. To conclude, individualism has been and is still strong among Mennonites, and they use such initiative and assertiveness extensively for the service of others.

References

Ainlay, Stephen C. (1990) "Communal Commitment and Individualism." In Leo Driedger and Leland Harder (eds.), *Anabaptist-Mennonite Identities in Ferment*. Elkhart, IN: Institute of Mennonite Studies.

Bellah, Robert N. Richard Madsen, William M. Sullivan, Ann Swidler and Steven M. Tipton, eds. (1987) *Individualism and Commitment to American Life: Readings on the Themes of Habits of the Heart*. New York: Harper and Row.

Brandt, Di (1996) *Dancing Naked: Narrative Strategies for Writing Across Centuries*. Stratford, ON: Mercury Press.

Doerksen, Victor G., George H. Epp, Harry Loewen, Elizabeth Peters, and Al Reimer, eds. (1985-90) *Collected Works of Arnold Dyck*. Volumes I-IV. Winnipeg: Manitoba Historical Society.

Driedger, Leo (1982) "Individual Freedom vs. Community Control: An Adaptation of Erikson's Ontogeny of Ritualization." *Journal for the Scientific Study of Religion* 21:226-242.

Driedger, Leo (1996) *Multi-Ethnic Canada: Identities and Inequalities*. Toronto: Oxford University Press.

Driedger, Leo and Donald B. Kraybill (1994) *Mennonite Peacemaking: From Quietism to Activism*. Scottdale, PA: Herald Press.

Driedger, Leo and Paul Redekop (1996) "Testing the Innis and McLuhan Theses: Mennonite Media Access and TV Use." Paper presented at the Canadian Ethnic Studies Association conference in Gimli, Manitoba, 1996.

Gans, Herbert (1962) *The Urban Villagers*. Glencoe, IL: Free Press.

Holland, Scott (1995) "Communal Hermeneutics as Body Politics or Disembodied Theology?" *Brethren Life and Thought* 40:94-110.

Kauffman, J. Howard and Leo Driedger (1991) *The Mennonite Mosaic: Identity and Modernization*. Scottdale, PA: Herald Press.

Klippenstein, Lawrence, (ed.) (1979) *That There Be Peace: Mennonites in Canada and World War II.* Winnipeg: Manitoba Conscientious Objectors Reunion Committee.

Kreider, Robert and Rachel Waltner Goossen (1988) *Hungry, Thirsty, A Stranger: The MCC Experience.* Scottdale, PA: Herald Press.

Levine, N., Ellwood B. Carter and Eleanor Miller Gorman (1976) "Simmel's Influence on American Sociology." *American Journal of Sociology* 81:813-45.

Redekop, Calvin, Stephen C. Ainlay and Robert Siemens (1995) *Mennonite Entrepreneurs.* Baltimore: Johns Hopkins University Press.

Reid, Angus (1996) *Shakedown: How the New Economy is Changing Our Times.* Toronto: Doubleday Canada.

Reisman, David (1950) *The Lonely Crowd.* New Haven, CT: Yale University Press.

Reimer, Priscilla B. (1990) *Mennonite Artist: Insider as Outsider.* Winnipeg: Main/Access Gallery.

Simmel, George (1950) *The Sociology of George Simmel.* Kurt Wolff (ed.). Glencoe, IL: Free Press.

Tocqueville, Alexis de (1996) *Democracy in America.* Trans. George Lawrence. New York: Doubleday.

Toffler, Alvin and Heidi Toffler (1995) *Creating a New Civilization: The Politics of the Third Wave.* Atlanta: Turner Publishing.

Van den Berghe, Pierre L. (1981) *The Ethnic Phenomenon.* New York: Elsevier.

Wiebe, Rudy H. (1962) *Peace Shall Destroy Many.* Toronto: McClelland and Stewart.

5
The Voluntary Impulse
Among Canadian Evangelicals

Brian C. Stiller

My first serious experience as a volunteer – apart from selling hot dogs for my Cub pack – was as a highschool student when I was asked to direct the Youth for Christ Saturday night rally in my home town of Saskatoon. Some years later, after graduating from university, I was invited to join that youth organization as a staff member in Montreal. Only then did I realize that a volunteer could get a salary for doing what I had enjoyed doing without pay.

When asked some time ago to address the annual dinner meeting of the Women's Christian Temperance Union, I was forced to examine more carefully the benefit that this group of women volunteers has been to Canada. My generation has tended to view the WCTUers' kind of social control with a liberal groan: "How can they be so intrusive, preventing people from living as they choose?" But I recall the devastation alcohol had on families we knew while growing up on the prairies. Often farmers – isolated, working alone, anxious about the weather, crop rust or drought, grasshoppers, or the wheat pool price for grain – would take their grain cheque and stop in at a beer parlour in the local hotel, then hours later, broke and drunk, stagger home. In the end, wives and children would bear – if not the brutal attack of a man out of control – the next month with an empty wallet. It was in part members of this volunteer Christian movement, led by women – and this it was in the days before Gloria Steinem – who faced these social realities and fought the status quo. As I stood before those blue-haired grandmothers that evening, I knew a spirit of humility was appropriate: I recalled that Christian volunteers, in their sacrifice, had suffered the barbs of ridicule because they refused to do nothing and to allow this social scourge to ruin family, home, and enterprise.

Brian C. Stiller is executive director of the Evangelical Fellowship of Canada. Since 1996 he has served as president of Ontario Theological Seminary in Willowdale, Ontario.

Christian voluntarism is essential to ministry and one of the most telling theological impulses of evangelicals. Even though the spirit and activity of voluntarism are so essential to bearing witness of Christ in our society, that is not something we often consider. Yet voluntarism within the Canadian evangelical community is alive and well. Because my task is to reflect on voluntarism within the evangelical community, let us first recall who makes up this Canadian group called "evangelicals."

Who are Canadian evangelicals?

Canadian sociologist Reginald Bibby, beginning with *Fragmented Gods* in 1987, was one of the first to document carefully the religious scene in Canada. Up to that time, most of our reading came from the analysis done each decade by Statistics Canada, or from an extrapolation of the Gallup figures for the United States. Given that Canadians live alongside Americans with a one-to-ten ratio of population, there has been an inclination to apply that same ratio to social, religious, and political analysis: wrong of course, but quick and cheap. Along with Bibby, the Angus Reid Group provides a more reliable analysis of the importance and role of faith among Canadians. This study is headed by Andrew Grenville, son-in-law of the late George Rawlyk (1935-1995), who for years was professor of history at Queen's University and championed serious historical research on Canadian evangelicalism.

Canadian evangelicals are inheritors of the European and American religious traditions. Protestant denominations in these traditions were evangelical in theology up to the beginning of the twentieth century, if we use David Bebbington's fourfold definition of evangelicals as: being Christ-centred; considering the Bible to be God's word; experiencing conversion; and witnessing for Christ. Many of the branches of the contemporary evangelical community developed following the "modernist" controversy of the early years in this century.

If one moves to Canada from the United States, you find here much the same sort of religious smorgasbord among evangelicals as there; minus, of course, the many megachurches which increasingly characterize the American scene. But one thing that is very different is the actual percentage of evangelicals in the total population. The ratio of one Canadian to 10 Americans – in population terms 28 million Canadians to 280 million Americans – doesn't work in this examination of the number and relationship of evangelicals in each country. In the U.S., some 30 percent identify themselves as evangelicals. In Canada, that number drops to slightly more than 12 percent. On critical mass, that translates into almost 90 million evangelicals in the U.S. and some 3 million in Canada. So for every one evangelical in Canada you have not 10, but 30 evangelicals in America. And that can make a world of difference. Of course, an important element in both the perentages and regional realities is that Quebec, which makes up 25 percent of our population, is almost completely affiliated with the Roman Catholic Church.

A word on the actual numbers. The Angus Reid poll of 1993 – again using Bebbington's fourfold definition – showed that 15 percent of Canadians would be considered evangelical. (This includes 15 percent of Roman Catholics who qualify under this definition to be evangelical. For the purposes of this address, I am referring to only Protestants who are evangelical, which is around 12 percent).

This evangelical community is primarily a function of the last one hundred years of newly formed or merged church and parachurch groups. In Canada in 1925, several old-line Protestant churches made a decided shift theologically and formed the United Church of Canada by the joining of the Methodist, Congregational, and two-thirds of the Presbyterian churches. What they eventually tended to lose and what the twentieth century evangelicals picked up was an evangelical orthodoxy as noted in Michael Gauvreau's *The Evangelical Century: College and Creed in English Canada from the Great Revival to the Great Depression* (1991) and David Marshall's *Secularizing the Faith: Canadian Protestant Clergy and the Crisis of Belief 1850-1940* (1992).

Voluntarism

Dr. William Brackney, in his defining work on voluntarism – the 1990 Hayward Lectures – provides an understanding of the cyclical nature of organizations and movements as they come and go. This understanding is especially important for evangelicals in Canada as the end of a century approaches and many wonder what will become of evangelicals in the coming century. Brackney concludes the lectures with this:

> The cycle of voluntarism is thus complete. In the first stage, religious organizations are called into being by theological, social and political factors. Gradually, these structures and

organizations achieve a permanent existence of their own and maintenance becomes a primary function. As this becomes more difficult in a voluntary social context, these organizations assume a status which is frequently self-protective, lacking in creativity and openness to change. In response, a new set of voluntarist forces sets in, calling for appropriate modification: renewal, critique or change, greater co-operation, empowerment, or service. In the final stage of the voluntarist cycle, the religious structures are modified and/or the voluntary associations assume a role as part of the mainstream itself.[1]

Where are evangelicals in this cycle? Do we have what is needed to resist being encrusted within the self-interests of organizations, overcome by entropy? It reminds me of the adage from Will Durant: it is the tragedy of things spiritual that we languish when disorganized: but we are destroyed by the material means of our organization. Will the evangelical community retain that creative, open, voluntaristic spirit, or will it too get trapped in the old ways and serve out its existence only with an eye to self? What gives me hope that this community will continue to grow and serve with strength beyond social or economic factors is our theology. I believe it will lose its vitality of faith, however, if it loses its theology. Along with our theology, there are six other reasons why I expect evangelicals to retain a high commitment to the voluntary spirit, as follows.

1. *The meaning of evangelical theology*
Evangelical theology speaks to the nature of inner conversion and transformation. Not only do we have significance by creation in God's image, but we also become temples in which the Holy Spirit of God chooses to live. This is pivotal, for as we recognize the strategic importance of God living within us, our sense of mission and responsibility is sharpened. To lose that theological understanding which defines the nature of fallenness ("I am guilty and am in need of a

---

[1] One could say the cycle continues. See William H. Brackney, *Voluntarism: The Dynamic Principle of the Free Church* (The Hayward Lectures at Acadia University, 1992), 2.

Saviour") and empowerment ("you shall be filled with the Holy Spirit") would be to lose identity and motivation.

The closest historical shift in our time away from this basic ingredient of faith was the Social Gospel movement in its theological drift from orthodox Protestantism. This was a distinct move away from a belief that the person is a sinner in need of a Saviour, to a view that at the heart of our problem is a corrupt society in need of salvation. What this theological move did was to lift the focus of God from the person over to social and political life. (Parenthetically, the resulting tragedy is that evangelicals over-reacted and tended to ignore the social dimension of salvation.)

2. *Congregational ecclesiology*
Voluntarism rises naturally out of our ecclesiology: congregationalism. Although within the charismatic and holiness communities there is a rather wide spectrum of definition of congregationalism and the authority of leadership – as some churches seem functionally more episcopal than congregational – the role of the congregation is affirmed. This ecclesiology not only provides opportunity for initiative to set up a church or ministry, but its leaders and members are motivated to be personally responsible. The option of calling a bishop to intervene is not as strong. As well, in a day when baby boomers call for a stake in their associations, such a form of church government will only extend the force of the voluntary spirit within the church community.

On this issue of ecclesiology, there is a very important subsection often referred to as the "parachurch." For some denominations, parachurch groups have been merely tolerated, but they have been, and continue to be, a vital element in our community. Linked to the Catholic orders of the European experience, and more importantly to the Anabaptist groups of the early 1500s, there are today multiple groups and quasi-congregations springing up across Canada in response to issues ranging from evangelism to unmarried mothers, relief and development, aboriginals and hockey schools, to name just a few. A few years ago, *Faith Today*, the evangelical magazine, did a study on the giving patterns of the evangelical. We learned that for every six dollars given to a congregation – including the denomination, four dollars were given to a parachurch agency. That is, forty percent of our charitable dollars went to fund groups apart from congregations. To understand evangelicals in this century, one cannot leave out this vibrant and dynamic part of our community.

3. *Evangelical marginalization*

We live with a sense of being marginalized. Though Canadians have a proclivity for feeling marginalized, this is also a sensitive issue within much of the evangelical movement. I say this because of where we are today: McMaster Divinity College, which enjoys intellectual, social, and cultural acceptance, is not all that typical of the general experience of most evangelicals throughout much of this century. The history of a large part of the evangelical Canadian community in this century shows how sectarian evangelicals became, withdrawn from the wider culture. This has been felt here in Canada more than in the U.S., where larger segments of the Protestant church retained an orthodoxy, stayed self-consciously within the evangelical community, providing leadership and funding, and by so doing gave respectability to the evangelical church.

The sense of marginalization in Canada has continued even though evangelicals are no longer economically marginalized. Though evangelicals are mainstream, most of their cultural gatekeepers continue to regard faith as illegitimate as an informer of public policy. This is especially true among journalists who like to link evangelicals to the American religious right or, worse yet, with American fundamentalism. Marginalization presses members of the community in one of two directions: to ignore the rest of society and get on with one's own agenda, or to fight the good fight and resist the sense of being marginalized. Either case requires the spirit of voluntarism.

4. *The lasting impact of Dispensationalism*

Dispensationalism, the biblical theory of John N. Darby, made popular by the *Scofield Reference Bible* (1909, 1967), affected a large part of our community and served to drive missionary enterprises, both within denominations and within independent missionary agencies. While as a theory, Dispensationalism no longer is as distinguished as it once was, still within many evangelical churches there is a strong belief that history is at its conclusion, and with the soon return of Christ it is incumbent upon believers to give faithful witness of Christ.

There are two competing forces in this religious impulse. One is the expectation that arises at the turn of a century. This is further extended by the turn into a new millennium. The flurry of books, spinning their interpretations, highlight this very important element of our theology – the physical return of Jesus Christ. On the other side, diluting this enthusiasm and blurring this focus, is good old-fashioned materialism. When life wasn't so good and when the Communists were really about to take over, Christ's return was very inviting doctrine. But now as evangelicals climb the ladder of social and economic respectability, the delay of Christ's return a few years doesn't seem like such a bad idea after all.

Even with these competing realities, I see the teaching of Christ's return continuing to shape evangelical theology. Its effect is to press personal witness, by giving of one's own time and money to support missions at home and abroad, and to work with groups involved in evangelism.

5. *Relationship with American evangelicals*
In general, within our culture, Canadian heroes, publishers, films, and media are largely American. A recent set of questions was asked of Canadian teenagers, one of which was, Who is your favourite sports hero? I expected the hero would be a Canadian, and even hoped that person was continuing to play his or her sport in Canada. But I knew that was asking too much. I was sure they would choose Wayne Gretzky. Wrong. Even those interviewed in Inuvik said their sports hero was Michael Jordan.

That is the cultural reality of Canada. The same applies to evangelicals. Until recently, Canadian evangelicals would commonly attend graduate school in the U.S., not in Canada. We still have no Canadian evangelical publisher. Most new church models are American, whether the Willowcreek model out of Chicago or the Saddleback model from Colorado. Moreover, we have known for a long time that in planning a conference, American leadership is useful.

So why does this influence voluntarism? American sociologist Seymour M. Lipset says Canada was "Tory and conservative in the British and European sense – accepting of the need for a strong state, for respect for authority, for deference – and endorsed by hierarchically organized religions that supported and were supported by the state." About the Americans Lipset argues that the U.S. was Whig and "classically liberal or libertarian," subscribing to egalitarianism and populism – doctrines that emphasize distrust of the state – "reinforced by a voluntaristic and congregational religious tradition." I think he is right.

Within Canada, where much of the old-line religious community was more British in its orientation, the twentieth-century evangelical community, in finding its models in the United States, is infused with that spirit of being a volunteer. Like it or not, Canadian evangelicals are infected with the American voluntaristic spirit.

6. *The influence of western Canada*
An important factor which keeps voluntarism alive is the influence of western Canada. Though the percentage of evangelicals is the same there as in the East – (British Columbia 12%; Alberta 15%; Saskatchewan and Manitoba 16%; Ontario 12%, Quebec 2%; Atlantic Provinces 16%) – there is an economic and social factor which gives substance to ministries, especially those funded by non-church support.

Canadian evangelicals had virtually no continuing wealth surviving from the nineteenth century. The Protestant churches which moved to unity in 1925 to become the United Church of Canada took with them families with pools of capital. The pools of wealth within the evangelical community have emerged after the 1940s. In central and eastern Canada, there was a tendency for people to work for major organizations or labour groups. In the west, there was little of that available. As a result, entrepreneurial activity there was alive and well, especially among evangelicals. Over the past couple of decades, this has grown to the point that the support of national evangelical agencies depends significantly on funds from western Canada. As well, their support base tends not to be directed to the old organizational machinery but towards newer and more innovative forms of ministry.

Conclusion

Though these six factors may not be so surprising and may not distinguish Canadian evangelicals that much from their American counterparts, there are significant nuances. It is important that Canadians know who they are and how evangelicals can encourage the understanding of their calling, so that by increased voluntary effort they can carry out the work of Jesus Christ.

A recent study by the Angus Reid Group on urbanization and Christianity sought to discover if there is any data to suggest that the social capital of Canada is being reduced. The authors studied involvement with volunteer organizations and volunteer donations to charitable causes. They found that of those who attend church weekly, 76 percent are members of a volunteer organization and 59 percent donate to overseas organizations. Of those who attend church occasionally, 45 percent are members of a volunteer organization, and 28 percent donate to overseas work. Of those who never attend church, 35 percent are members of a volunteer organization, and 23 percent donate to overseas work.[2]

One might assume that people who go to church more often, because of the amount of time spent in such activities, would have less time for community work, compared to those who don't attend church or do so only occasionally. The studies point otherwise: the more one attends church, the more likely that person will be involved in community volunteer work and the more likely will their volunteer funds go to overseas work. St. Augustine was right when he said, "Where there are good Christians, there are good citizens."

[2] Andrew Grenville and Donald Posterski, "Urbanization, Christianity and Contributions to Social Capital: Can Committed Christians Be in the City but Not of the City?" Unpublished paper delivered at the annual meeting of the American Scientific Affiliation in Toronto, Ontario, May 1996.

6

The Toronto Blessing
as a Voluntary Phenomenon

James A. Beverley

Whatever one might say ultimately about the Toronto Blessing, it serves as a great case study for thinking about a voluntary movement.[1] At an initial glance the famous and controversial renewal seems the epitome of voluntarism.

First, the Blessing has brought a couple of million people to Ontario's capital city, and this at their own discretion, under no formal ecclesiastical direction. In this vein, *Toronto Life* magazine dubbed the Toronto Blessing one of the city's top tourist attractions. Second, renewal leaders like John Arnott have placed emphasis on lay ministry teams and tried to downplay the importance of a clergy class. From the outset, the Toronto Blessing has been designated a "nameless and faceless" revival.[2] John Arnott (1940-), senior pastor of the Toronto Airport Christian Fellowship (the Blessing's home site) has repeatedly stressed the humble origins of the Blessing. Third, the renewal has been managed to a large degree by unpaid volunteers. Hundreds of Christians have kept it alive through voluntary service ranging from chair stacking to tape editing to being a "catcher" for those who are "slain in the Spirit." The church staff receive very modest salaries, a fact that deserves serious notice in an age when church leaders are often expected to be in ministry for the money. In this regard, Arnott deserves strong commendation for how he has resisted the temptation to raise his salary in direct proportion to the size of the crowds and the fame of the renewal.

James A. Beverley is professor of theology and ethics at Ontario Theological Seminary in Willowdale, Ontario.

[1] This essay is an expanded and updated version of remarks I made on a panel with Ronald Kydd on the Toronto Blessing at the Believers Church conference. I am grateful to Professor Kydd and to panel moderator Clark Pinnock for providing stimulating analysis that led to open and gracious dialogue. I also thank Dr. William Brackney for encouraging me to prepare this essay for the conference volume.

[2] Blessing leaders like Arnott, Guy Chevreau, Ken Gott, and others have become rather well known, written books, and travelled the world. Thus, early claims about the faceless revival need some modification.

On another level, the worldwide sweep of the Toronto Blessing has led to a large army of volunteers who have embraced this renewal as the way to "do church" and as a model for experiencing the power of the Holy Spirit in our time. With little help from creed or official church policy, millions of Christians from a hundred nations have come to believe that the Toronto Blessing represents a fresh anointing from God, an outpouring of the Spirit on the level of Pentecost or Azusa Street. This army of volunteers is not easily affected by the concerns of critics or by the changing moods of denominational life.

These points about voluntarism emphasize the human element. Enthusiasts of the Blessing would be expressly concerned about any analysis that failed to explain the renewal on divine terms. After all, God is at work, the public is told. Critics are dismissed on the grounds that one should not question "what God is doing." The human volunteers are following the Holy Spirit, not human leaders. This is from God, not "man." Those who doubt God's role at the root of the Blessing could be in more danger on Judgment Day than the cynics of Sodom and Gomorrah, according to one word of prophecy. I will return to this specific issue later.

As a regular observer of the Blessing and the Vineyard movement, I continue to be amazed at the ways in which many enthusiasts for the Blessing want only a one-dimensional response and approach to the renewal.[3] Hence, we must note at the outset the tensions created by focusing on the voluntary element. A stress on the human dimension is viewed as a betrayal of the alleged divine source. However, a study of the voluntary aspect does not demand an automatic dismissal of the alleged divine element. God, after all, was not only pleased to dwell incarnate in Jesus but also often works through his human volunteers.[4]

---

[3] Many critics will allow only negative data about the Toronto Blessing to be shared. Hank Hanegraaff consistently avoids discussion of the positive aspects of the renewal. In fact, his recent work *Counterfeit Revival* has no positive comment about John Wimber, John Arnott, James Ryle, and every other charismatic leader mentioned in the book.

[4] In this regard, Mark Noll's lecture "The Christ of the Academic Road" offers a wonderful analysis of Christ's incarnation as a way to celebrate the working of God in our humanity. Noll's lecture was given at a conference at Wheaton College on "Renewing the Christian Mind" (April 1997).

There is a paradox in criticism of too much focus on the voluntary side of the Blessing, since the voluntary component has served as a powerful factor in the renewal's apologetic. That several million people have come to Toronto on their own free will is powerful proof, advocates say, that the Blessing is from God. What else can explain this pilgrimage except the drawing power of the Holy Spirit? Further, the Blessing has spread around the world as pilgrims return to their home bases and their fellow believers experience the same power released in Toronto, all in a voluntary human response to God's obvious work.[5]

I continue to assert the absolute importance of free enquiry and testing of this or any other alleged renewal. In principle a study of the voluntary dimension needs no apology, as long as it is carried out with care and integrity. This applies to study of every aspect of this or any renewal. Intellectual examination of the multi-faceted dimensions of the Toronto Blessing can be readily defended from Scripture and does not violate any principles about being open to the Spirit. In fact, an openness to the Spirit demands a testing of the spirits. Any voice to the contrary is rooted more in cultic ideology than Christian, though renewal apologists have every right to warn against a blind and mean-spirited criticism that is tone deaf to the leading of God's Spirit and the teaching of Scripture.[6]

With these preliminary points in mind, we can now reflect more fully on the nature of the voluntaristic impulse in the Toronto Blessing. My study suggests that both subtle and transparent factors in the renewal mitigate against making too much of the voluntary component. While the Blessing appears to be everything one would expect a voluntary movement to be, there are very serious reasons to be somewhat sceptical of many interpretations of the renewal that are rooted in a simplistic understanding of the voluntary human component. That is, voluntarism is subject to very strong pressures that make the human the target of forces which call into question the reality of the alleged "voluntary" human dimension.

This point does not suggest there is no voluntary nature to the Toronto Blessing. I remain convinced that this renewal is a voluntary phenomenon – but it is not simply that. Rather, as one would expect in something

---

[5] For defence of the Blessing see Arnott, *The Father's Blessing* (Orlando: Creation House, 1995) and Guy Chevreau, *Catch the Fire* (London: Marshall Pickering, 1994).
[6] On these matters see my *Holy Laughter and The Toronto Blessing* (Grand Rapids: Zondervan, 1995), 25-36.

involving a religious story, particularly one dominated by controversy, the issue of voluntarism opens up a window to explore very significant and difficult issues. We can explore such issues on seven different fronts.

1. Claims of divine origin

The claim that the Toronto Blessing is from God mitigates against focus on the voluntary human component, as noted above. Though the renewal has an Arminian base to it, Blessing defenders say so often and so strongly that God is behind them that their emphasis suggests a rather Calvinistic view of the human agent. It takes a strong will to face the human dimension honestly when renewal preachers are so certain of the divine dimension. The human dimension must be faced, however, especially because there is a *human* dimension. If only the renewal were as divine as enthusiasts suggest! It is its "human" aspects that demand constant monitoring. The Toronto Blessing has not been distinguished by careful boundaries. This has led to statements, actions, and emphases that call into question the Divine so easily referenced in the renewal's defensive reaction to criticism.[7]

The antipathy to open critique is particularly ironic in a movement that seems so self-assured of God's hand upon it. Jarold K. Zeman made a similar point about Baptist hostility to ecumenism and diverse viewpoints. He said that one might expect and hope that Baptist self-confidence would lead Baptists to have greater serenity in the mix with other Christians and in the dance of various theologies.[8] One can make the same argument about apologists for the Toronto Blessing.

The invocation of divine endorsement for the Blessing should not distract us from necessary focus on the human component, voluntary and otherwise. Lines must be drawn against statements, actions, and emphases that run counter to plain biblical teaching. The strong anti-intellectual ethos of the Blessing must be questioned, given the command of Jesus to love God with our minds. The focus on "what God is doing" must not quench the need to look very carefully at what humans are doing. John

---

[7] See the very instructive warnings in Richard Lovelace, "The Surprising Works of God," *Christianity Today* (September 11, 1995), 32.

[8] See my agreement with Zeman in "Tensions in Canadian Baptist Theology, 1975-1987," in Jarold K. Zeman, ed., *Costly Vision* (Burlington: G.R. Welch, 1988), 228f.

Wimber said in one of his early assessments of the Toronto Blessing that it was not God's involvement that worried him![9]

2. Claims of Satanic and occult influence

The voluntary human component also becomes problematic in the face of claims that the Toronto Blessing is largely the product of Satan or, at best, is an intentional imitation of the hypnotic tactics of occult gurus like Rajneesh, the infamous Hindu swami. In an array of articles one finds the renewal dismissed as being largely a narcissistic exercise in "spiritual masturbation" or a case of the "anoinking," not the Anointing. Even these charges pale in contrast to overt claims that the Blessing leaders intentionally deceive their followers by engaging in pagan spirituality and bring Christian believers under occult power.

This latter critique is now chiefly associated with the work of Hank Hanegraaff, president of the Christian Research Institute, one of the most influential anti-cult organizations among evangelicals. Hanegraaff has been attacking the Blessing since its inception through his radio program "The Bible Answer Man" and has recently formalized his critique in *Counterfeit Revival*.[10] For him, the voluntary nature of the Toronto Blessing is insignificant since the renewal leaders are consciously manipulating "devotees" through very clear hynoptic, occult, and pagan procedures. Hanegraaff heaps scorn on renewal leaders by arguing that they represent APES who use (to follow his loaded acronym) altered states of consciousness, peer pressure, expectations, and suggestibility to control the vast crowds in a way ultimately rooted in Satanic deception.

If Hanegraaff's interpretation is correct, the voluntarism of the Blessing is a mere surface appearance. In the view of Blessing apologists, God is drawing pilgrims to Toronto. For Hanegraaff these deceived believers are pawns of Satan, whom he calls "a master counterfeiter" whose "ultimate deception is a counterfeit revival."[11]

---

[9] Wimber, *Vineyard Reflections* (July-August 1994), 2.
[10] I was so disappointed by the extreme and careless charges in *Counterfeit Revival* that I wrote a book-length reply under the title *Revival Wars*. It is available from Evangelical Research Ministries, 1550 Kingston Road, Suite 1009, Pickering, Ontario L1V 6W9.
[11] See Hanegraaff, *Counterfeit Revival* (Dallas: Word, 1997), back cover.

3. Pressures of the crowd

Though Hanegraaff overstates the socio-psychological forces at work in the Blessing and too readily advances a demonic explanation, he correctly notes the power of group psychology. In mass movements, the whole is greater than the sum of the parts. When the renewal first started, the attraction revolved around the strange manifestations (holy laughter, animal noises, shaking, jerking, etc.) accompanying the nightly meetings. While the manifestations continued as the main attraction, by mid-1994 there was enormous pressure in the charismatic world to follow the crowds as they made their way to Toronto.

In both of my books on the Toronto Blessing I have drawn attention to the wariness that Jesus showed to crowds. He was willing to speak to them but he understood their fickle nature. He was not overly impressed by the adulation of the throngs of people who followed him, a view that finds validation in the group hysteria that formed part of his death. Crowd pressure is not evil per se, but such power of the masses is a force to reckon with in religious movements.

The worldwide flow of pilgrims to Toronto creates a force that also mitigates against understanding the renewal as an example of pure and simple voluntarism. It is very difficult for individuals to resist "group think" in moments of mass religious mobilization. One of my friends was warned that he dare not miss the Toronto Blessing since it was the last train out of town. Likewise, the pressure to duplicate the desired manifestations is strong as thousands of worshippers succumb to the rhythms of holy laughter and the other alleged signs of God's presence. The lonely volunteer who resists the pressures of the crowd has to know something about inner strength or a perverse love to be different from everyone else.

4. Church politics and the power of fame

The voluntaristic component of the Blessing is also made more problematic by the reality of the politics of church life and the influence of famous leaders in renewal movements. Todd Hunter, the current National Coordinator of the Vineyard, said that the Blessing owed much of its impact to the influence and fame of John Wimber, the Vineyard's International Director. When news spread about the Blessing, John Arnott's church was a part of the Association of Vineyard Churches. The renewal spread in part because of the blessing of Wimber, the healing pastor from Anaheim and one-time adjunct professor at Fuller Theological Seminary. Hunter has a valid point: the credibility of the Toronto renewal rested in large part on the implicit endorsement that came through Arnott's association with Wimber. This suggests, then, that the voluntaristic realities have to be noted in conjunction with the forces at work when powerful church leaders give their endorsement to a renewal. It is not simply a case of an army of volunteers on their own free will hearing the call of the divine or the demonic to Toronto. Mixed in with these possible realities is the fact of blessing from powerful church leaders.

Wimber monitored the Toronto renewal from the beginning, spoke at the Airport Vineyard Church in June 1994, and gave his endorsement in Vineyard publications. If he had chosen, he could have shut the renewal down in the early months of 1994, and Arnott and others on his staff would have obeyed him. Nevertheless, Wimber gave it his approval and though he had some serious reservations, his name gave credibility to what was going on at the meetings.

By the first anniversary of the renewal there was no end to charismatic leaders rushing to embrace the Toronto experience. *Charisma* magazine did a very positive cover story. This meant that the magazine's owner-editor Stephen Strang had given it his support. Soon there were positive reports on Pat Robertson's 700 Club. Pentecostal healers Charles and Frances Hunter were enthusiastic. Kansas City pastor Mike Bickle was supportive. Benny Hinn was a friend of John Arnott, and Hinn's name was invoked in the earliest writings on the renewal.[12] Jack Deere, well-known charismatic Bible scholar, was in favour. Likewise, the renewal had received enthusiastic praise from top charismatic leaders in Britain, and soon there was endorsement from Pentecostal and charismatic leaders throughout the world.

From one angle, church politics play a large part in stories like the Toronto Blessing. Does a given event, practice, or idea get approved by the powers that be? If yes, the way ahead is much easier for the volunteers eager to be swept along in the developing drama. If not, the voluntarism

---

[12] Though Hinn expressed some disagreement with aspects of the Toronto Blessing at one of his healing crusades in Halifax (Summer 1996), his wife visited the Toronto Airport Christian Fellowship when he held a crusade at Maple Leaf Gardens in the fall of the same year.

becomes much more complicated, as people are forced to take sides. When most of the prominent leaders in a given religion are united in favor of some new "move" of God, the transition to a new mode of worship or religious experience runs smoothly. Once dissent is voiced by a powerful person within the respective tradition, the political factors get complicated. Church politics came into full display when John Wimber removed the Toronto Airport church from the Vineyard in December 1995. This created a storm in the Vineyard in particular and in the charismatic world in general. By that time the Blessing had been endorsed by so many prominent charismatics that it was impossible to do a complete turnaround on the renewal. Yet Wimber said he could no longer let his name be connected with the Blessing's ongoing realities. The voluntary dynamism at work in the renewal suffered a serious setback.

5. The prophetic factor

Related to the alleged divine endorsement of the renewal is the claim that the Blessing has been predicted by those who have prophetic gifting. The Vineyard movement specifically and many in the charismatic and Pentecostal world have adopted Wayne Grudem's understanding of prophecy.

Grudem, a professor of theology at Trinity Evangelical Divinity School, has argued that (a) the Old Testament prophetic books are inspired by God and inerrant, (b) the New Testament is also inspired by God and inerrant, and is the final authority in all matters, (c) the gift of prophecy to the New Testament church is not an infallible charism, and (d) the gift of prophecy mentioned in Acts and in Paul's writings is for the church today.[13]

John Arnott and Guy Chevreau (former Convention Baptist pastor and major apologist for the Toronto Blessing) have both argued that the renewal was predicted ahead of time by several prophets. For example, Marc Dupont (currently prophet in residence at the Toronto Airport Christian Fellowship) claims to have received a word from God in 1993 about a forthcoming outpouring of the Spirit in the ministry of John and

---

[13] See Wayne Grudem, *The Gift of Prophecy in the New Testament and Today* (Westchester: Crossway, 1988).

Carol Arnott. Prophetic words about Toronto have also been given by Paul Cain, Bob Jones, Larry Randolph, Stacey Campbell, and Jill Foster, among others. Their prophetic utterances involve both endorsements of the renewal, predictions of changing developments, and warnings against critics and those who remain indifferent to this new "river of God's anointing." On the latter, prophetic wrath has often been quite explicit.

I mentioned earlier the judgment against those who resist the blessing and cause division over it. This prophecy was given in the fall of 1994 by Stacey Campbell at the first "Catch the Fire" conference. Allegedly under a direct prophetic word from God, Stacey (with head shaking back and forth in rapid motion) announced that it would be better for Sodom and Gomorrah on the Day of Judgment than for those who strongly oppose this work of God. Her prophecy has been the subject of significant debate since 1994. Her husband Wesley Campbell gives a passionate defense of the accuracy of this prophecy in his recent book *Welcoming a Visitation of the Holy Spirit*.[14]

Whether or not the gift of prophecy is valid for today, the exercise of prophecy carries enormous weight in churches and movements which readily believe in a prophetic word from God through a human agent. Several Vineyard ministers have told me of the incredible expectancy in prophetic conferences when thousands waited for a "fresh word" from Bob Jones or Paul Cain. Cain, a former Southern Baptist from Garland, Texas, is viewed as the most anointed prophet by many charismatics. I argue in *Holy Laughter and The Toronto Blessing* that this adulation is all out of proportion, since Cain has made significant blunders in prophecy and brought much division to the Vineyard movement from 1988 to 1991. In interviews with Cain and in one social engagement, I found him to be warm and pleasant, and I believe that he has sometimes given wonderful words of wisdom to people that points to a divine reality in his ministry. However, I cannot share the high estimate given to him among his followers. Likewise, I would not share Hanegraaff's assessment that Cain, Bob Jones, and Rick Joyner are all "slaves of depravity."[15]

---

[14] See Campbell, *Welcoming a Visitation of the Holy Spirit* (Orlando: Creation House, 1996), 204-207.

[15] *Counterfeit Revival*, 160.

For those who are considering joining the millions who have embraced the Toronto Blessing, the prophetic component would add pressure on any volunteer easily persuaded by the rhetoric about prophetic gifting available today, a charism that is said to point to the Toronto renewal as a sign that God's endtime work is nearing the return of the Lord Jesus Christ.

6. The power of ideas

Volunteers are subject also to the influence of ideas. With regard to the Toronto Blessing, these ideas form a powerful framework to draw and hold people to the important task of furthering the spread of the renewal. These ideas are presented in formal, academic mode and in off-hand comments that express the core ideology of the movement. On the former, Guy Chevreau enlists the powerful voice of Jonathan Edwards. Chevreau interprets him in a way that suggests the famous revivalist would want believers today to be open to this latest fresh move of the Spirit. The interpretation of Edwards continues to be a matter of significant debate.[16]

In terms of popular sentiments among renewal enthusiasts, a host of comments would constrain volunteers to remain faithful: "If you leave because you are tired, perhaps the Spirit will decide to shut down the renewal." And, "Who are we to question God?" Or, "If we miss this anointing, who is to say we will get another chance?" "Jesus had opposition too." "Those who resist the Holy Spirit are Pharisees." "God is willing to offend the mind to reveal the heart."

These statements are not often the subject of contextual care. Rather, they are given as holy mantras to allay doubts and criticisms. In the process, it is very difficult for legitimate objections to be raised. It has amazed me how unwilling renewal leaders have been to embrace criticism in a positive way or to bring immediate correction to grievous weaknesses. These failings should have been corrected in the early months of the renewal. If this had been done in 1994, the critics of the Blessing would have found it a far more difficult target.

Of course, the power of ideas can be used in an opposite way to lead uninformed Chrsitians to believe that the Toronto Blessing is a force from Hell. A web site against the renewal begins with the sound of someone

---

[16] See the interviews with leading Edwards scholars in my *Revival Wars*, 28-37.

vomiting. Hanegraaff's book contains a whole arsenal of ideas that would lead the unsuspecting person to believe that Toronto or the revival in Brownsville, Florida are both products of Hell. Advertising for Hanegraaff's *Counterfeit Revival* compares Toronto and Brownsville to the tragedies of the cultic events of the Branch Davidians and Heaven's Gate.

The voluntary impulse in Toronto runs on the power of an ideology that brings apologetical endorsement to the renewal. Volunteers must also face equally passionate ideologies that bring the renewal under scorn and sarcasm. This does not mean that participation in the Toronto renewal is involuntary but rather that volunteers are subject to formidable pressures in the realm of ideas.

7. Forces of institutionalization

Cambridge University sociologist of religion Martyn Percy has done significant study of the Vineyard and the Toronto Blessing.[17] In his doctoral dissertation and in several articles, he has carefully explored the process of institutionalization in a church not predisposed to being a denomination and a renewal not wanting to give into the routinization of ritual. Percy contends no renewal can maintain the spontaneity and freedom that dominates the earliest days of its birthing. The "new" sooner or later becomes the standard, and when it becomes the predictable routine, it loses the creativity and uniqueness that made it an attraction in the first place. The fires of charismatic life cannot burn forever. Here Percy is not making a theological point against the abiding presence of the Spirit but a sociological observation about the human dimensions to renewal.

In the case of the Toronto renewal, crowds were drawn to the strange manifestations. There had to be something unique going on at the Toronto Airport Vineyard to draw them. In January 1994 Vineyard members would have been inclined to make a trip only to Anaheim (Vineyard Church headquarters) as a form of pilgrimage. John Arnott was not a well-

---

[17] On the Vineyard in particular see his *Words, Wonders and Power* (London: SPCK, 1996). Percy uses "fundamentalist" in a British context, where it carries the meaning of "evangelical" in North American audiences.

known Vineyard pastor, nor was Randy Clark, the visiting Vineyard pastor who brought the "signs and wonders" to Toronto. Once Toronto became a famous revival site, questions arose about the proper control of manifestations. Should people be allowed to act like animals? How much attention should be given to manifestations? Behind these questions were far more disturbing issues to face: What happens when the number of pilgrims starts to drop? Does declining attendance suggest that the Spirit power is gone? How do we maintain and control the renewal?

Percy suggests that it is virtually impossible to keep a renewal like the Toronto Blessing going at the same pace and with the same interest among both fans and critics. After a reasonable period of time, enthusiasts no longer feel the need to come back to Toronto. Or, the Blessing can be imported back home, and there is no need to make the long trek to Canada. Even the dynamic of criticism is subject to routinization as people get used to the warnings of those who are deeply distressed by the alleged renewal. Hanegraaff's wrath against Toronto and Pensacola is the subject of increasing concern, since even some of his loyal supporters are starting to worry about the level and persistence of his criticism.

Since the late fall of 1995 average weekly attendance at the Toronto renewal has dropped significantly. Blessing leaders realized early on that a day would come when the number of people coming to the Toronto base site would diminish. They prepared for this financially and had to think about what this means for them as a church and as a renewal centre. On a fundamental level, they realized that the fires of the Holy Spirit would have to be reconfigured in creative and unique ways to have any hope of maintaining the same level of interest in 1997 and beyond as was seen in the early days.

In the summer and fall of 1996 there were prophetic words from both Paul Cain and Marc Dupont that God would raise the Blessing to a new level in the spring of 1997. Cain predicted a level of Spirit anointing such that there would be a working of miracles unlike anything previously seen. From even the most optimistic angle, that prophecy has not been accurate. In the end, it looks more like a desperate wish for something new to happen that would assure the Blessing continued on par with the enthusiasm at its inception and in the early months when it was announced that "Revival ignites Toronto."

Conclusion

It is a truism that volunteers deserve praise for their service, especially in a materialistic age. The work of the volunteer is often unnoticed and undervalued. This holds true as well in the world of faith. In the Toronto Blessing the voluntarist impulse is strong and clear but, as noted, it is a complicated reality given the enormous theological, social, and ecclesiastical forces at work. The volunteer is easily lost sight of in the overwhelming issues at stake in response to this renewal.

My hope is that this study provides a stimulus to careful consideration of these forces and issues, without losing sight of the decency and good faith of the many volunteers who have genuinely helped spread the true fires of God's spirit through the Toronto Blessing and in all the diverse ways that God brings people the gospel of Jesus.

7

The Resurrection of the Soul
in the Anabaptist Body:
A Postmodern Pietist Meditation

A. Scott Holland

Many artists, preachers, historians, theologians, and intellectuals from the believers church tradition now recognize that Anabaptism is an imaginary homeland. Anabaptism is not a place; it is in fact many places and thus provides many possibilities for the composition of a spiritual life in creative conversation with the heritage.[1] In recent years the genealogy of Anabaptism has moved from monogenesis to polygenesis in the historical discussion of Anabaptist origins. Polygenesis reminds the contemporary, pluralistic believers church that there is no pure, unified, originating, sixteenth-century narrative for the church at the end of the twentieth century to recover and mimic. There is no Anabaptism; there are in fact many anabaptisms. The Anabaptists were pacifists and violent revolutionaries, evangelical pietists and bold sexual libertines, communitarians and free spirits, biblicists and mystics, prophets and pragmatists, holy martyrs and reckless merrimen, saints and sinners. They are all our kin.

Yet some members of this diverse faith family with the surname Anabaptist have been an embarrassment to those of us seeking a more responsible or respectable place in Christendom. In a recent issue of a

Scott Holland is pastor at Monroeville Church of the Brethren in Monroeville, Pennsylvania.

[1] Here I am of course suggesting that the "theological" appropriation of any historical movement or heritage is always an act of imaginative construction. For a discussion of doing theology as imaginative construction see my "*Einbildungskraft*: 1. Imagination 2. The Power to Form Into One," in Alain Epp Weaver, ed., *Mennonite Theology in Face of Modernity: Essays in Honor of Gordon D. Kaufman* (North Newton, Kansas: Bethel College, 1996), 244-54. Paul Ricoeur understands the theological and philosophical encounter with historical narratives as a process of figuration and reconfiguration. Paul Ricoeur, *Figuring the Sacred: Religion, Narrative, and Imagination* (Minneapolis: Fortress Press, 1995).

literary journal, poet John Burt presented the following reading of the Radical Reformation:

(Muenster, 12 August 1534)
The Anabaptists have the city now:
One night a defrocked priest, one "Bread Bernard,"
Ran naked through the streets crying aloud
That all alone he'd wrestled many nights
With evil spirits (as I well believe)
And God Himself had told him to go forth
Into the public ways to choose the saved.
So out they came, tangled in their sheets
No less than their bad consciences, and said
The day of woe will come upon them soon
(Which, no doubt, it will), and beat their heads
Upon the paving stones, tore their hair,
And showed other ways their perfect faith.
Just after that we brought our armies in.

A certain tailor they have made their king.
He also talks with God, calling himself
The death-angel, and well makes good his boast.
Just bread, says Juvenal, and circuses
Can rule an Empire, but this tailor does
One better: short of bread, thanks to us,
He rules the town with circuses alone.
He parodies the Mass, devises hats,
And with great ceremony disembowels
The luckless wretches he's suspicious of,
He's saved the city from the curse of gold,
I've heard, by taking all of it himself,
And many saintly women came to sing
Hosannas in the highest to his name.
Atop the walls are angels militant
Like none that heaven ever saw.

How strange...
(From *Viglius Zuichemus*, by John Burt, *Salmagundi*, Summer 1996)

De-frocked priests running naked through the streets, true believers mocking the Mass, militant prophets bringing in the kingdom with the sword, and a tailor king seducing sweet sisters with the word of God and holy kisses. Little wonder why Mennonite historian H.S. Bender, in a skillful rhetorical move called "The Anabaptist Vision,"[2] brought a bishop's soul to discipline the unruly body of Anabaptist historiography and theology. With political and pastoral brilliance, Bender rescued Anabaptism from the trash bin of history as he excommunicated many rebels and redefined normative Anabaptism as an evangelical commitment to Christ through community, discipleship, and nonresistance. Through Bender's historical theology, Anabaptism even won the respect of the reserved suit-and-tie scholars of the American Society of Church History.

Bender's reconfiguration of Anabaptism[3] has been very useful for the believers church, giving it a normative narrative and moving it from sect to church status in modern Christendom, while retaining some of its original oppositional and counter-cultural impulses: communal solidarity over the autonomy of the soul, discipleship or ethics over mere orthodoxy, and peace over all holy crusades and politically just wars. For at least some contemporary Anabaptist faith communities, the old era of the bishops has been replaced with the new era of Anabaptist scholars.

Yet Bender's almost exclusive attention to Swiss Anabaptism in the composition of his Vision, and his suspicion of other Free Church radicals who failed to neatly embody the evangelical ideals of community, discipleship, and peace, has cut some of our most interesting ancestors from the family tree. Further, the strength of soul that gave rise to Hans

---

[2] See J.M. Stayer, W.O. Packull, and K. Deppermann, "From Monogenesis to Polygenesis: The Historical Discussion of Anabaptist Origins," *Mennonite Quarterly Review* 49 (April 1975): 83-121. For an analysis and criticism of "normative Anabaptism" see Rodney Sawatsky, "The Quest for a Mennonite Hermeneutic," *Conrad Grebel Review* 11 (Winter 1993): 1-21. Mennonite historian Arnold Snyder has recently published an introduction to Anabaptist history and theology, which unlike many earlier works in the field, struggles seriously with the reality of polygenesis, yet in an imaginative search for a "theological core," demonstrates significant areas of consensus in the midst of conflict: C. Arnold Snyder, *An Introduction to Anabaptist History and Theology* (Kitchener, ON: Pandora Press, 1995).

[3] H.S. Bender, "The Anabaptist Vision," *Mennonite Quarterly Review* 16 (April 1944): 67-88. This version of Bender's classic reconfiguration of Anabaptism was reprinted with minor revisions from *Church History* (March 1944), 3-24.

Denck's mysticism, Gottfried Arnold's radical pietism, and Balthasar Hubmaier's baptist faith must become disappointingly nonresistant and yielding before the bounded body of Bender's normative Anabaptism.

Indeed, the central categories of Anabaptist Vision theology or neo-Anabaptism assume a rather submissive soul: Gelassenheit, Nachfolge, and Gemeinde. The nonresistant body and soul yield to God through the community (Gelassenheit). The individual will submits to the communal demands of discipleship (Nachfolge). The self is absorbed into the collective identity (Gemeinde).[4] The communitarianism of neo-Anabaptist theology has placed a collective moral character over personal conscience and communal conformity over self-consciousness. Stanley Hauerwas, a guru to many neo-Anabaptists, gleefully declares: "The Mennonite farmer in central Indiana may be quite happy in his community and strikingly 'unaware' of himself, but that in no way disqualifies him from being a person of character."[5]

Perhaps, but I know that farmer. I was his pastor. Some days he is depressed, anxious, and confused about his personal meaning on the planet. Other days, trying desperately to believe that his community can name his soul and define the whole wide world, he becomes strident, intolerant, even bigoted in the face of modernity's cultural pluralism and religious diversity.

Mennonite theologian Steven Dintaman also knows that farmer and worries about his soul in light of what he calls "The Spiritual Poverty of the Anabaptist Vision."[6] While Dintaman's criticisms of neo-Anabaptism seek to recover a "heartfelt religion" through the classical doctrine of justification by faith, which has been eclipsed by an ethos of justification

---

[4] A more complete discussion of my concern that the communal formalism of neo-Anabaptism or Anabaptist Vision theology can become a totalitarianism of community can be found in my essay, "Communal Hermeneutics as Body Politics or Disembodied Theology?" *Brethren Life and Thought* XL (Spring 1995): 94-110.

[5] Stanley Hauerwas, *Character and the Christian Life: A Study in Theological Ethics* (San Antonio: Trinity University Press, 1975) third printing, with a new introduction by the author, 1985), xxii.

[6] Steven Dintaman, "The Spiritual Poverty of the Anabaptist Vision," *Conrad Grebel Review* 10 (Spring 1992): 205-208. The many enthusiastic and angry responses to Dintaman's essay signal the great conflicts contemporary Anabaptists experience around not only the question of spirituality but individual and communal identities.

by belief and behaviour in modern Anabaptism, he is also searching for a spiritual sense of "self" somewhere between the drives of the libido and the demands of the super-ego. Dintaman contends that there has been a terrible "trivialization of subjectivity" in modern Anabaptism in which the collective body almost erases the personal soul. Dintaman offers this insightful analysis of the individual and the community in current Radical Reformation religion:

> Though neo-Anabaptism appears to be a radical break in Mennonite history, I believe it is part of a deeper continuity that ties the new radicals to the old conservatives. I would call this the continuity of superego religion in Anabaptism. In a superego religion the needs and interests of the individual are regarded as inimical or threatening to the community. In a superego religion the individual's agenda is always wrong, and obedience means the interests of the community win while those of the individual lose. For both traditional Mennonites and neo-Anabaptist forms of thought and life, obedience involves the needs and priorities of the individual being overridden or denied for the sake of the externally imposed church order (Ordnung).[7]

If Dintaman's reading of this religion of the superego is correct, and I believe it is, then we must seek to resurrect the category of the soul from the bounded body of Anabaptism. A believers church theological heritage which values religious voluntarism must have a stronger anthropology and theology of individual agency, the self, and the soul. In short, we need a more profound sense of individualism, because too many faithful disciples have surrendered their souls not to the Pope's Inquisitors nor to the Emperor's Anabaptist catchers but to their own brethren, bishops, and theologians.

---

[7] Dintaman continues the criticism of neo-Anabaptism he began in his "Spiritual Poverty" piece in "The Pastoral Significance of the Anabaptist Vision" in John D. Roth, ed., *Refocusing a Vision: Shaping Anabaptist Character in the 21st Century* (Goshen, IN: Mennonite Historical Society, 1995), 35-50.

Such an individualism will of course recognize that self-creation can never be pried apart from communal participation. Behavioural and social scientists have taught us that the romantic ideal of the solitary soul is an unhelpful fiction, for we come to consciousness only in the company of others. Indeed, if New Age spirituality or pop psychology ever finally succeed in finding that insufferable inner child, it will find him mute if he has been nurtured only in the wilderness of psychic space, void of tradition and communities of memory.

Our Anabaptist heritage has also given us a some understanding of the social construction of reality, yet it has been less helpful in encouraging the individual believer to develop a sense of owning himself or herself while in conversation and communion with one's own cultural-linguistic community. Instead, it has urged us to shun individualism, for the personal and political problems of our age are believed to be related to individualism and the answers are thought to be found in community.

In recent years many intellectuals and social critics have likewise warned against the morally and socially corrosive potential latent in modern individualism. Sociologist Robert Bellah and his circle are perhaps best known for leading this charge against "expressive individualism." Bellah and his colleagues are careful to point out that they are not opposed to *individuality* as such, but that their argument is with *individualism*. For Bellah, the "church idea" – the view that the church as community has ontological priority over the individual – affirms individuality while denouncing individualism.[8] Thus Bellah champions what he terms biblical and civic forms of individualism, which are always directed toward others, and opposes utilitarianism and expressive forms of individualism which, he claims, are too funded by the self and its desires.

Although Bellah and his colleagues title their first collaborative book *Habits of the Heart*,[9] their rage against ontological individualism in favour of a "social realism" in service of *The Good Society* has led pastoral psychologists Donald Capps and Richard Penn to warn of the serious loss of heart, self, and soul in modern academic culture. They caution against the sociologizing of the self, where the individual is seen as a phenomenon

[8] Robert N. Bellah et al., *Habits of the Heart: Individualism and Commitment in American Life* (Berkeley: University of California Press, 1985), 334.

[9] Robert N. Bellah et al., *The Good Society* (New York: Knopf, 1991).

that is wholly contained and explained in terms of sociological dynamics.[10] They further challenge Bellah's assumptions that an expressive individualism emerging from the id of desire cannot contribute powerfully to a complicated common good. Do not strong, expressive souls build strong societies? Do not repressed and passive souls produce pathological communities?

Even though both neo-Anabaptism and much of our modern academic culture share a suspicion about the soul, those of us who study social and intellectual history recognize that prophets, pietists, and mystics, to say nothing of poets, artists, and intellectuals, must have strong and creative souls. Can the contemporary Anabaptist community greet the prophet and embrace the poet? Can it welcome both the intellectual and mystic to the communion table? Can the artist's imagination and the pietist's heart aflame be celebrated in the *Gemeinschaft*? Only by the resurrection of the soul in the Anabaptist body. I would suggest that our communities will become more soulful and satisfying if we again invite to the Lord's Table the mystic's imagination, the Pietist's heart, and the poet's gift.

The mystic's imagination

The mystic teaches us that in the cosmos there is a structural relationship of God-world-soul-body. While proclaiming the reckless grace of God, the mystic celebrates the connections between God and world, self and other, word and image, spirit and flesh, mind and body, reason and revelation, similar and different. The mystical imagination gives us a profound awareness of similarity-in-difference as it identifies points of connection or common ground, and uncovers the common dimensions of our diverse human languages, experiences, and dreams. The mystic talks to us about the interdependence of life. He or she reminds us that the sacred rhythms of the cosmos are wonderfully alive in our bellies and bones. The mystic discloses that God is revealed not only in the rhetoric of proclamation, but also in the mystery of manifestation. In creative tension with the

---

[10] Donald Capps and Richard Penn, *Individualism Reconsidered: Readings Bearing on the Endangered Self in Modern Society* (Princeton: Centre for Religion, Self and Society, Princeton Theological Seminary, Monograph Series, No. 1, 1992). For a more focused critique of Bellah and the problem of the self see Capps, "Expressive Individualism as Scapegoat" in his *The Depleted Self* (Minneapolis: Fortress Press, 1993), 101-125.

thundering "No" of the dialectical imaginations of the prophet and Pietist, the analogical imagination of the mystic whispers, "Yes, Yes, Yes![11]

Our Anabaptist tradition has given itself much to decision and discipleship and little to mystery and grace. We have created a rule-based morality and an often graceless uniformity that mocks and betrays our nonconformist roots. So what does the normative Anabaptist theologian say when a member of the community sneezes out of turn? *Gelassenheit!*[12] In our usage of this German term, we risk making an idol out of the rule of community by teaching that one can yield or submit oneself to God only in and through the disciplined community.

The fascinating medieval poet-preacher-mystic, Meister Eckhart (1260-1329), first coined the term *Gelassenheit* for spiritual discourse. Eckhart is of course the towering figure of German mysticism. His theology of divine immanence asserted that "every creature is a word of God." His *Gelassenheit* was an "abandonment" or "letting go" to God, not a narrow "yieldedness" to God's community. It was an abandonment to the God beyond the sovereign self, an abandonment to the God beyond the sovereign community, an abandonment to the God beyond the static letter of the Word of God. It was a passionate, ecstatic letting go to the God beyond the God we name. Eckhart's God-intoxicated vision of eros toward the world undermined the sacramental offices and rites of the official medieval church. His lyrical sermons were thus viewed as politically subversive documents, and he was condemned by a papal decree after his death.[13]

---

[11] A more complete treatment of the vision and voice of the mystic in the Anabaptist heritage is found in my "Preaching with Prophets, Musing with Mystics, Dancing with Strangers: Anabaptism as Public Theology," *Brethren Life and Thought* 39 (Summer 1994): 167-79.

[12] A standard study of Anabaptist *Gelassenheit* is Sandra Crock's Ph.D. dissertation, "*Gelassenheit*: The Rites and Redemptive Process in Old Order Amish and Old Order Mennonite Communities," (University of Chicago, 1977). Also see her article by the same title in *Mennonite Quarterly Review* 60 (January 1981): 5-54. This term has had an interesting pilgrimage in German thought from Eckhart's mystical "letting go or letting be," through Anabaptist "communal yieldedness," to Heidegger's existential-phenomenological "abandonment."

[13] Matthew Fox, *Breakthrough: Meister Eckhart's Spirituality in New Translation* (New York: Image Books, 1980). It is interesting to consider how important mysticism is becoming for postmodern thought. Consider, for example, Lacan on the jouissance of

Hans Denck, our South German Anabaptist spiritual father, was influenced by Eckhart and other mystics such as Tauler and the anonymous author of the *German Theology*. Denck does not fit neatly into the mold of normative, Swiss-inspired, Schleitheim Anabaptism. He is clearly not an Anabaptist Vision Anabaptist, yet he is our kin. Referred to by various scholars as a humanist, an ecumenist, and a mystic, he was not dominated by the "Anabaptist" preoccupations of biblicism, community, and discipleship. He was quite interested in the largeness of the *communio sanctorum* and suspicious of the petite righteousness of the *Gemeinde* (the believers church of Swiss Brethren and latter Hutterites).[14]

Denck's mystic gaze, his universalism, and his individualism have led some historians to label him as a *Halbtaufer*: only a semi-Anabaptist, not representative of the real faith of our fathers and mothers. Yet for many believers on the margins of the community he is becoming one of the most attractive figures of the Radical Reformation heritage. H.S. Bender doubted that Denck was an "authentic" Anabaptist. Ecumenical mystics like Eckhart and Denck can in fact be threatening to leaders of the institutional church and guardians of conventional morality, for their free souls are not easily tamed and tutored by those who might place communal discipline over the heart's desire.

The Pietist's heart

Older members of my Church of the Brethren congregation in Pittsburgh remind me that in their earliest spiritual formation they understood their faith in the language of Pietism, not Anabaptism. They report that in

Teresa of Avila, Kristeva on Bernard of Clairvaux, Certeau on the excessive language of mysticism, and Irigaray on the love mystics. A consideration of the links between mystics and postmodern literary critics is found in David Tracy's "Literary Theory and the Return of Forms for Naming and Thinking God in Theology," *Journal of Religion* 74 (July 1994): 302-19.

[14] Clarence Bauman, ed. and trans., *The Spiritual Legacy of Hans Denck: Interpretation and Translation of Key Texts* (Leiden: E.J. Brill, 1991). Daniel Leighty has recently edited, translated, and introduced a collection of Anabaptist writings on spirituality. Note especially his translations of South German and Austrian Anabaptists in *Early Anabaptist Spirituality: Selected Writings* (New York: Paulist Press, 1994). My evolving work suggests these mystics had a more independent "Christomorphic" spirituality in contrast to the more communal "Christocentrism" of the Swiss evangelicals.

recent decades it seems that the communal and ethical discourse of Anabaptism has overtaken the personal and experiential language of Pietism. It is probably accurate to say that in terms of theological models, the paradigm of Anabaptism is in fact now privileged over the less manageable model of Pietism in the teaching coming from contemporary Church of the Brethren pulpits and lecterns.

Consider this warning against personalism and individualism from a Church of the Brethren Conference paper: "Our Anabaptist heritage teaches that no one enters the kingdom of God apart from one's brothers and sisters. It is within the community of believers and for their sake that the Spirit is given. . . ."[15] *Extra ecclesiam nulla salus?* There is no salvation outside of the community? Anabaptism has triumphed!

Yet happily, at least from my perspective, several of my brother and sister preachers have been reaching for Dale Brown's revised and newly released little book, *Understanding Pietism*.[16] It is my sense that a new hunger for true spirituality and the resurrection of the soul in the believers church will lead to a revival of Pietism as we prepare to enter a new century. Further, Brown's assertion that "from the beginning Brethren imbibed a love theology that was destined to soften and erode church discipline"[17] speaks gently yet so clearly to many of us who are alarmed by an insanely moralistic and judgmental call by Anabaptist zealots for a return to a more rigorous church discipline, all in the name of community, discipleship, and peace. It is a peace that has destroyed many.

The contrasting principles of Anabaptism and Pietism are quite familiar and perhaps even too reified. Anabaptism focuses on the outer Word of Scripture while Pietism is more attentive to the inner Word of Spirit. Anabaptist obedience contrasts with Pietist devotion. The Anabaptist privileges the church, the Pietist privileges the believer. The

[15] From the 1979 Annual Conference Paper, "Biblical Inspiration and Authority," reprinted in Joan Deeter, *Biblical Interpretation and Authority: A Study Guide to the 1979 Annual Conference Paper* (Elgin: Brethren Press, 1980). See Carl Bowman's very helpful discussion of the blending of influences in Anabaptism and Pietism, *Brethren Society: The Cultural Transformation of a "Peculiar People"* (Baltimore: Johns Hopkins University Press, 1995), 46-50.

[16] Dale W. Brown, *Understanding Pietism*, revised edition, (Nappanee, IN: Evangel Publishing House, 1996).

[17] Dale W. Brown, book review of Carl P. Bowman's *Brethren Society* (cited above) in *Mennonite Life*. Forthcoming.

Anabaptist strives for unity and consensus while the Pietist protects freedom of conscience. The Anabaptist wants purity and faithfulness while the Pietist desires openness and growth. The Anabaptist sets his vision on horizontal relations with the community, but the Pietist turns his gaze to the vertical relation with God.[18]

Most scholars now view these contrasting principles of Anabaptism and Pietism not as two opposing religious crosscurrents but rather as mutually reinforcing currents flowing into and from both traditions.[19] Nevertheless, I would suggest that more attention to what critics of Pietism once denounced as, "Ah, your dreadful subjectivism!" is now very timely. With many heavy hearts and burdened souls seeking salvation through communally mediated and monitored belief and behaviour, a personal saviour who redeems by grace through faith, not by ethics and discipleship, can be most welcome and wonderfully liberating.

Perhaps it is even time to invite the Radical Pietists back to the table. The influence of the great preacher, poet, and historian, Gottfried Arnold, on the development of Pietism can hardly be overemphasized. We have much to learn from him.[20] He spoke of the spiritual life not in terms of duty or even discipleship but as desire: *Die erste Liebe*, The First Love.[21] It was this "love theology" that found its way into the themes of much of early Pietist literature.

[18] See Carl Bowman, *Brethren Society*, 47.

[19] See Bowman, *Brethren Society*, 45-50. The work of Mennonite historian Theron Schlabach and Brethren historian Dale Stoffer also demonstrates that Anabaptism and Pietism were in many ways "mutually reinforcing currents." See Schlabach, *Peace, Faith, Nation: Mennonites and Amish in Nineteenth-Century America* (Scottdale: Herald Press, 1988); Stoffer, *Background and Development of Brethren Doctrines, 1650-1987* (Philadelphia: Brethren Encyclopedia, 1989).

[20] Gottfried Arnold's life, theology, and connections to medieval mysticism and spirituality are treated in Peter Erb's *Pietists, Protestants and Mysticism: The Use of Medieval Spiritual Texts in the Work of Gottfried Arnold (1666-1714)* (Metuchen, NJ: The Scarecrow Press, 1989). Also see Peter Erb, ed., *Pietists: Selected Writings (Classics of Western Spirituality)* (New York: Paulist Press, 1983).

[21] Arnold published *Die Erste Liebe* as a book in Frankfurt in 1696. He speaks of the Christian life in the language of "a first love" (Rev. 2:4). His links to the great love mystics are evident in this work, and this "love Pietism" was warmly received by the early Brethren.

Arnold's mystical piety was refreshingly suspicious of both religious community and theological creeds. As a poet and preacher he recognized that the order of community and the language of creeds threatened to collapse *theos* into *logos*. This is always the great temptation of church and creed, to bring Infinity into submission to a historical totality.[22] Arnold also understood very clearly how the formal language of church and creed had been used in the history of the church to punish dissidents and nonconformists who were often true believers. He therefore preached a stubborn but enlightened noncreedalism. His historical work pointed to the absence of disciplinary creeds in the apostolic church and to the terrible violence and persecution that creedal Christianity produced.

This concern is at the centre of Arnold's massive work of historical theology, *A Nonpartisan History of Church and Heresy*.[23] Applying the principles of love theology to the entire history of the church, his thesis was that the heretical movements had actually perpetuated the true church, while the orthodox church that disciplined and punished them was in reality the anti-church. He charged that orthodoxy had more to do with the politics of power and position than with the true spiritual church.[24]

Following Arnold's thesis about the manifestation of God in the world, it might be said that the orthodox who control the order of salvation have great political interests in managing a system of church doctrine and discipline wherein all yield submissively to an established theological cycle of sin, repentance, and redemption. Arnold's creative theological criticism demonstrates that in the history of spirituality, *theos*, in moments of kairos, refuses the *logos* of orthodoxy and enters history and the human soul not through the established formula of sin, repentance, and

---

[22] Postmodern theology and philosophy share some of the concerns of the premodern mystics and Pietists about the problems of "naming God" in language and "thinking God" through creed and church. Note also David Tracy's concerns about the captivity of *theos* in *logos*, which is the grand temptation of the discipline of theology. "The Hidden God," *Cross Currents* 46 (Spring 1996): 5-16. And "The Return of God," in *Naming the Present* (Maryknoll, NY: Orbis Books, 1994), 36-46.

[23] Gottfried Arnold, *Unparteyische Kirchen und Ketzer Historie*. 3 vols. (Frankfurt am Main: Thomas Fritsch, 1699-1700).

[24] Donald P. Durnbaugh's new narrative history of the Brethren, *Fruit of the Vine* (Philadelphia: Brethren Encyclopedia, 1996) captures how redemptively oppositional and subversive Arnold was in his historiography, which championed many heretics as true believers and condemned many orthodox as the anti-church.

redemption, but through a heretical revolution of transgression, excess, and gift. Heretics, ecstatics, saints, mystics, pietists, and poets remind us that often God comes first as transgression, then excess, and finally, gift![25]

The poet's gift

We in the Anabaptist historical and theological guild often forget that preachers like Denck the mystic and Arnold the Pietist were also poets. Clarence Bauman's *The Spiritual Legacy of Hans Denck* includes some of Denck's "humanistic" Latin poems. Gottfried Arnold titled his book of poetry *Divine Sparks of Love*. The great poets Goethe and Novalis received Pietistic educations, and it was Novalis who reminded us that in the quest for soul, we must never separate heart from head, body from spirit, or communal participation from self-creation, for he explained: "The seat of the soul is where the inner world and the outer world meet. Where they overlap, it is in every point of the overlap."[26]

It is not at all surprising, therefore, that one of the first persons to define Pietism favourably against its critics was University of Leipzig poetry professor Joachim Feller. He begins his definition in his poem of 1689:

> The name of the Pietist is now well known all over town.
> Who is a Pietist? He who studies the Word of God
> And accordingly lives a holy life.
> This is well done, good for every Christian.
> For this amounts to nothing if after the manner of the rhetoricians
> And disputants one puts on airs in the pulpit
> And does not live holy as one ought according to the teaching.
> Piety above all must rest in the heart.[27]

---

[25] A creative study showing connections between postmodern categories such as deconstruction, transgression, excess, gift and the experiences, expressions and discourses of saints and heretics is Edith Wyschogrod's *Saints and Postmodernism* (Chicago: University of Chicago Press, 1990).

[26] Cited in Phil Cousineau, *Soul: An Archaeology (Readings from Socrates to Ray Charles)* (San Francisco: Harper San Francisco, 1994), 31.

[27] Cited in Brown, *Understanding Pietism*, 13. The German poem is in Erich Beyreuther, *August Hermann Francke* (Marburg: Francke-Buchhandlung GmbH., 1956) 67.

It is not surprising that Pietism was first defined in the language of poetry rather than in the propositions of theology or philosophy, because the language of the soul emerges first as poetry, praise, lamentation, narrative, and testimony. The discursive language of theology and the careful language of the creeds are at best third-order language, preceded by the theopoetics of testimony and story.

Long before the postmodern death of metaphysics, the seer, sage, and preacher Ralph Waldo Emerson declared that a philosopher or moral theorist must work by art, not metaphysics. Unhappy with both moral philosophers and philosophical theologians, Emerson wrote, "I think that philosophy . . . will one day be taught by poets."[28] Postmodern philosopher Richard Rorty continues the Emersonian call for the strong poet in society. Like Emerson, Rorty is not simply referring to one who writes verse, but to those individuals engaged in the creative reconfiguration of the past and the imaginative construction of more decent and humane futures. Richard Rorty, the cool pragmatist, sounds as romantic as Emerson when he writes of:

> the poet rather than the priest, the philosopher or the scientist as the paradigmatic human being . . . the poet, in the general sense of the maker of new worlds, the shaper of new languages, as the vanguard of the species.[29]

For Emerson and Rorty, there is the conviction that the expressive individualism of the strong poet will in fact become a gift, not a liability, to the broader human community. Both thinkers suggest that it is not individualism but a conforming communitarianism that breeds intolerance and uncivil spirits in the world. A heightened individualism can in fact lead to a deeper concern for *other individuals as individuals*, rather than a concern for them as faceless, soulless members of collectives. For

[28] Emerson is quoted here by John Dewey in his University of Chicago lecture, "Emerson–The Philosopher of Democracy," May 25, 1903. See Dewey, *Characters and Events* New York: Holt, Rinehart and Winston, 1929), 70.

[29] Richard Rorty, "The Contingency of Language," *London Review of Books* (April 17, 1986), 4. Rorty argues, "We are the poetic species, the one which can change itself. . . ." Also see Rorty, *Contingency, Irony, and Solidarity* (New York: Cambridge University Press, 1989).

members of the Free Church, it can foster a deeper belief in the inherent dignity and sacredness of the human person, no matter what their sociological status or place in the community's plot.

Academic proponents of social realism like Robert Bellah, because of their profound understanding of the social construction of reality, imply that community or society is ontologically prior to any notion of individuality.[30] Perhaps. Neo-Anabaptists, because of their high hermeneutics of peoplehood, join John Howard Yoder in arguing that the church precedes the world and thus precedes the individual epistemologically and axiologically.[31] Perhaps.

But if the mystics, Pietists, and poets are right, churchly religion and communal morality alone cannot satisfy the soul nor sustain human decency and dignity. Genesis is not the beginning of religion and morality; Genesis is the beginning of Desire. The relation to the Infinite is not a knowledge or an ethic but a Desire. Because body and breath were born from the primordial art of earth and spirit, not metaphysics, may I suggest that in the ecology of true spirituality, aesthetics must precede ethics because the grand story of creation precedes the story of church and society?[32] May I suggest that eros toward the world precedes an embodied ethics? That only the id of Desire gives rise to love? That personal passion precedes public compassion? That what evokes love is a complicated beauty, not a clear morality? That aesthetic perception, not ethical vision, sustains life and love? That only a practice of virtuosity, not mere morality, will save our souls and this blessed fallen world? May I suggest that a poetics of obligation precedes any orthodoxy of word or deed and any politics of meaning? May I plead for the resurrection of the soul in the Anabaptist body?

---

[30] See Bellah, *Habits of the Heart*, 303 and 334.

[31] John Howard Yoder, *The Priestly Kingdom: Social Ethics as Gospel* (South Bend: University of Notre Dame Press, 1986), 11.

[32] I develop this theme more fully in another essay, "Theology is a Kind of Writing: The Emergence of Theopoetics," to be presented at the conference, "Gordon Kaufman's Theology as Imaginative Construction," to be held at Bethel College, North Newton, Kansas on November 3-4, 1996.

8

The Adequacy of a
Voluntaristic Theology
for a Voluntaristic Age

A. James Reimer

Introduction: Definitions and presuppositions

"Voluntarism" is a term which can readily be used to obfuscate rather than illuminate theological discussion. In the most technical sense it can refer to the theology of John Duns Scotus (c. 1265-1308) and William of Ockham (1285-1347) who, against Thomas Aquinas (c. 1225-74), argued that the divine will precedes in importance the divine intellect. This emphasis on divine willing had significant implications for ethics and was part of a larger ideological shift occurring in the late Middle Ages – the transition from a realist worldview to a nominalist one. Christian realists heavily indebted to the Greek, particularly Platonic, tradition assumed an eternal cosmic order. Moral universals such as ideal justice were part of this unchanging order (the ideal form of justice), and were considered more real than any earthly particulars, which were but imperfect imitations or analogies of eternal perfections. From the second-century Apologists to the high middle ages of Thomas Aquinas, this intellectual realism dominated western Christianity.

With Aquinas and the rediscovery of Aristotle, a theological shift began which took the empirical and observable world of the senses more seriously. It was a shift that would lead, after Thomas, to nominalism and voluntarism. Nominalists, like Scotus and William of Ockham, turned their attention from the ideal world of universal forms to particulars (particular beings rather than being in general, specific justice rather than abstract justice). Particular existents were real, universals were but "names" or "abstractions," useful in language but having no independent existence. For the nominalists, even God was understood not as universal, metaphysical essence, supreme intellect in whose mind existed all ideal

A. James Reimer is academic advisor of graduate studies at Conrad Grebel College in Waterloo, Ontario, and the Toronto Mennonite Theological Centre at the Toronto School of Theology.

forms, but as absolutely free, singular, and willing subject (or agent). Things or actions were good or evil because God willed them to be so, not because they corresponded to some eternal ideal form or essence.[1]

This shift from seeing the world as a rationally structured and ordered universe to one in which personal subjectivity and willing was at the heart of things helped to give shape to the Renaissance, the Reformation, the Enlightenment, and all of modern western thought. A voluntaristic understanding of God had deep roots in the Hebraic monotheistic tradition, which thought of God freely creating the world (visible and invisible) out of nothing through Word, creating "Adam" with free will and responsibility, and freely making a covenant with his chosen people and dynamically intervening in their history. What distinguished this long premodern Hebraic voluntaristic tradition from the voluntarism now emerging with the rise of the modern world, was that "human willing" earlier was thought to be derived from and subject to "divine willing." With nominalism began a process of seeing not only the world in terms of "volition," but human willing as independent of divine willing, a process leading ultimately to human willing without any divine horizon whatever (cf. Nietzsche and the "will to power"). Classical Christian orthodoxy creatively combined Hebraic personalism and voluntarism with Hellenistic metaphysics. This is evident in the Trinitarian and Christological formulations of Nicea and Chalcedon, and is still the case with Thomas, for whom human law is derived from natural law, in turn reflecting eternal law, superseded ultimately by divine law.

While Christian realism dominated western thought up to the modern period, nominalistic voluntarism has dominated the modern period to the present, existentialism perhaps being the most dramatic example. It remains to be seen in what direction the postmodern age will take us. If pluralism, fragmentation, and discontinuity are seen as the defining characteristic of the postmodern age (a thesis which can be debated), then nominalistic voluntarism would appear to have won the day. The above discussion of late medieval voluntarism, with its nominalistic

---

[1] For a helpful discussion of late medieval voluntarism and nominalism see William C. Placher, *A History of Christian Theology: An Introduction* (Philadelphia: The Westminster Press, 1983), 162ff.

presuppositions about God and the world, provides an essential background for the rest of this presentation.

Often, however, "voluntarism" is understood in a broader sense, as referring to those Christian traditions which have historically espoused the "freedom of the will" (radical Protestantism or the so-called "believers church") rather than the "bondage of the will" or predestination (Calvinism and, in a modified form, Lutheranism). Some version of "free will" unites the rather disparate group making up the believers church tradition, is at the heart of its distinctive theology and ecclesiology, and is considered by it to be essential for ethics and moral responsibility. Free will within radical Protestantism has generally been connected with Christian ethics and moral responsibility. The proposition *implicit* in most believers church theology goes something like this: to be virtuous is to choose the morally good over the morally evil, but in order to choose good over evil one must have the freedom to do so, otherwise one could not be considered either virtuous or culpable for one's actions. If one were not free, if one's actions were pre-determined (as in Greek notions of fate or some Christian views of predestination), one could not be held accountable for one's behaviour, neither would there be any motivation toward the good. The Fall (original sin) has distorted the human will but not to such an extent that the knowledge of good and evil, and the ability to respond positively or negatively to God (divine grace) has been altogether removed. Although qualified and interpreted in a variety of ways, this proposition or set of propositions I take to be implied in all believers church theology, ecclesiology and ethics. In sum, intrinsic to believers church theology, ecclesiology, and ethics is voluntarism of one type or another.

It is this claim – that voluntarism is indispensable for all responsible Christian ethics – that I want to examine in light of the challenge by Oxford theologian Joan Lockwood O'Donovan, who argues that a sound Christian ethic is not well-served by the voluntarism of the modern age. We in the voluntaristic tradition need to take seriously Lockwood O'Donovan's critique. I will argue, however, that classical voluntarism, as reflected in the theology of Balthasar Hubmaier (d. 1528), for instance, does not presuppose the radical nominalism present in the voluntarism of the modern period. It is grounded in a trinitarian realism that has both Hebraic and Hellenistic elements, but offers a more secure foundation for social and personal Christian ethics than do the less voluntaristic traditions.

The challenge to modern voluntarism: inadequate anthropology

Lockwood O'Donovan, a Church of England theologian, has been strongly influenced by Canadian philosopher George Grant's critique of modern liberal understandings of freedom.[2] In articles she has challenged the adequacy of an ethic premised on modern notions of voluntarism and freedom, especially with regard to the most vulnerable in the human community. Her argument deserves careful attention, for she has identified a sensitive spot in believers church theology and ethics, especially in the modern period.

Lockwood O'Donovan situates herself within the realist camp, espousing what she calls nonvoluntaristic "theological realism." By voluntarism she has in mind the modern turn to the individual person understood as "self-determining subjectivity." In one article, she examines the evolution of Catholic social theory from traditional political Thomism to modernized political Thomism. Her thesis is that the Aristotelian aspects of Thomas's political synthesis have abetted the modernization (liberal democratization) of Catholic thought at the expense of classical Christian features. In Christian thought, as systematized by Augustine, political authority was understood primarily in *juridical* terms – as restraining evil and protecting the good. Aristotle gave a more positive and creative (directive/legislative/integrative) role to political authority: "here, the essential purpose of government is less the adjudication of right and wrong on the basis of received communal understandings of divine and natural law, than the active orienting of the political whole to the order of right defined by positive law."[3] With Thomas these two traditions – the juridical (Christian) and the directive (Aristotle) – were held in tension with each other. The modernization of Catholic social theory, however, has seen the liberalization of the Aristotelian concept of law and political authority at the expense of the Augustinian-Christian understanding.

Modernization, for Lockwood O'Donovan, is the acceptance of historical progressivism, in which the inalienable natural rights of

---

[2] Her first book was *George Grant and the Twilight of Justice* (Toronto: University of Toronto Press, 1984). More recently she has authored *Theology of Law and Authority in the English Reformation* (Atlanta, GA: Scholars Press, 1991).

[3] Joan Lockwood O'Donovan, "Subsidiarity and Political Authority in Theological Perspective," *Studies in Christian Ethics* 6.1:19.

individuals take precedence over all other rights. She traces this gradual modernization process through various papal encyclicals/letters in this century, concluding with the liberal-democratic post-war Thomism of Jacques Maritain and Pope John XXIII. Both subscribed to a concept of political society in which government is authorized to make provision for the common good seen as "a body of universal natural political and social rights and obligations (principally of individuals)."[4] Modern liberal democratic society, she claims, suffers not from moral pluralism but from "moral monism, being enslaved to one universally acclaimed good, that of individual self-determination. The public hegemony of this good is both disclosed and maintained in the public hegemony of the language of individual rights."[5]

Common to biblical, patristic, medieval, and Reformation Christian thought was the "concept of natural law as the permanent moral order within which God intends human life in its individual and social aspects to be lived."[6] It distinguished between prelapsarian (the structures of created nature) and postlapsarian (fallen nature) orders. Political rule was placed within the realm of fallen nature. With Thomas and the subsequent evolution of politico-ethical thought, the distinction between created and fallen nature has gradually diminished to the point where there is a moral monism: the "hegemony of a single language . . . the language of individual rights."[7] This is the modern civil religion. "In this civil cult, the final public good, which is the measure of all others, is the self-determination of the individual subject, who stands as God, outside nature, and makes him/herself and the world around out of the resources of his/her own unlimited willing."[8]

Lockwood O'Donovan is not rejecting the value of individual subjectivity and personal right. Quite the opposite! Her concern is how these are conceptualized and safeguarded. In classical Christianity, human subjectivity and right is derived from divine subjectivity in relation to the structure of created nature and fallen nature. In modern liberal thought,

—

[4] *Ibid.*, 26-27.
[5] *Ibid.*, 29.
[6] *Ibid.*, 28.
[7] *Ibid.*, 30.
[8] *Ibid.*, 33.

natural and civil law is no longer understood in relation to the divine and eternal. Human subjectivity and right are no longer seen as derived but as inalienable – that is, as innate and intrinsic to themselves or self-determined. The ethical consequences of this are profound.

Elsewhere, Lockwood O'Donovan spells out her alternative to this modern voluntarism. She calls it "theological realism" and "Christological realism." She offers her realist alternative by revisiting the well-known 1934 exchange between Karl Barth and Emil Brunner over Christian anthropology, focusing especially on the concept of *imago dei*. In his book *Natur und Gnade,* Brunner distinguished between a formal and a material aspect of the created image of God in human beings. The formal image is that which separates human beings from other parts of creation: rationality, responsibility (subjectivity), and the capacity for language. Brunner claimed that this formal image is neutral and not destroyed by the fall and human sin – it is that which makes human beings human. The material image, in contrast, is that which makes a person truly personal, existence in love. This has been lost: "Sinful man remains a person–that is, a responsible subject–but is an anti-personal person."[9] She takes Barth's side in this debate, arguing that Brunner is not able to maintain the neutrality of this formal image, but is forced to define it qualitatively and materially–having "the capacity for recognizing God in external nature and in the events of history; the capacity for moral judgment and conduct, and for knowing one's guilt."[10] It is not the distinction between formal and material image as such that Barth rejects, but giving the formal a qualitative character.

For Barth, as for Lockwood O'Donovan, there can be no such dialectical precondition for the work of grace. Divine grace, in which the essential being of human persons is understood Christologically and relationally, has absolute, undialectical priority. This is not to deny all structure to human being, but to insist that both the form and content of human being is determined by "God's being-as-love."[11]

---

[9] Joan E. O'Donovan, "Man in the Image of God: The Disagreement between Barth and Brunner Reconsidered," *Scottish Journal of Theology* 39 (1986): 437. Cf. "Nature and Grace" in E. Brunner and K. Barth, *Natural Theology*, trans. P. Frankl (London: Centenary Press, 1946).

[10] *Ibid.,* 439.

[11] *Ibid.,* 457, 459.

Why is it imperative that we in the believers church address this issue? It concerns how we understand the uniqueness of being human in an age where the assault on human dignity by scientific and technological advances is pervasive. More specifically, it has to do with how universally inclusive our understanding of the *humanum* (the nature of the human) is. Brunner's "transcendental structural concept" of person forces him to make freedom, responsibility, and capacity for decision-making the criteria for defining human persons. But this excludes some children of Adam. Only a transcendent-relational or Christological-Trinitarian conceptualization is adequate to safeguard the unique humanity of human beings, says Lockwood O'Donovan.[12] This is what she calls theological or Christological realism. It focuses on God's transcendent act rather than on human decision-making responsibility:

> Barth's Christological realism is a significant theological gain in the ethical realm, particularly in the realm of judgments concerning those individual beings at the borders of human life: the unborn child, the severely defective infant, the very old and senile, the comatose patient. For it forces upon us the consideration that these individuals are human beings created in the image of God, that they have a share in human uniqueness because elected in Jesus Christ, the objects of God's judgment and mercy. It forces this consideration upon us by disallowing all immanent conceptions of human being, either structural or qualitative, which would place such creatures beyond the pale of humanness. It stands as a refutation of the favourite argument of the technicians and humanists of our age: that only those beings are persons, are uniquely human, that manifest the qualities of subjectivity, of personality. Against this argument it pits an uncompromising theological understanding of the particularity and uniqueness of human being in terms of its transcendent determination by God's covenant of grace in Jesus Christ. It sets forth human uniqueness as the incomprehensible particularity of God's

[12] *Ibid.*, 435.

elective Will, the transcendent mystery of the person as the mystery of God's gracious action.[13]

This is the challenge that Barth, as interpreted by Lockwood O'Donovan, places before us in the voluntarist tradition. At issue is this question: Is there a way of safeguarding the humanness of all "children of Adam" within the voluntaristic heritage, one which places such a high price on personal decision-making, illustrated most dramatically in the insistence of adult baptism at the age of accountability upon personal confession of faith?

The Christian anthropology of classical voluntarism

Here I want to explore the Christian understanding of human being within the classical voluntarist heritage, by which I mean that understanding which precedes the post-Enlightenment, predominantly nominalistic, worldview. I take the believers church tradition, at least in its origins, to stand within this earlier stream, and I will analyze the anthropology of Anabaptist theologian Balthasar Hubmaier as representative of this classic voluntarism. In his theology of human freedom and responsibility he stands in the tradition of a long line of Christian thinkers (medieval, patristic, and biblical). Common to all of them are "realist" assumptions about the world, and at the same time a strong emphasis on human freedom, subjectivity, and responsibility to make decisions, capacities which are not immanent-structural but derived from divine subjectivity.

Hubmaier, born around 1480 in Frieberg, near Augsburg, studied at the University of Freiburg, where his teacher was the Catholic scholar Johann Eck, whom in 1512 he followed to the University of Ingolstadt, where he received his doctorate in theology. He had been ordained to the priesthood earlier, and later in Ingolstadt served both as theology professor and priest of the largest parish church in the city, in 1515/16 becoming prorector of the University. After a term as cathedral preacher at Regensburg and activities in Waldshut, he came in contact with Christian humanists and the Zwinglian Reformation, and eventually converted to Anabaptism. He was burned at the stake in Vienna on March 10, 1528.

[13] *Ibid.*, 456-57.

Hubmaier was a distinguished theologian, who of all the Anabaptists gave the most systematic attention to Christian anthropology in his "Catechism of 1526-27," and in his two treatises in 1527 on the "Freedom of the Will": the first dedicated to Count George of Brandenburg-Ansbach, a follower of Luther[14]; the second dedicated to Duke Friedrich II of Liegnitz, Brieg, and Wohlau, in Silesia, who via Caspar Schwenkfeld had been converted to the evangelical faith.[15]

What is of interest here is how Hubmaier defines the *humanum*, in a realist or nominalist fashion, in transcendent derivative terms or in an immanent-structural sense (that is, along the lines of Brunner). With two treatises on the freedom of the will, Hubmaier entered the hot debate between Erasmus and Luther on whether the will is free or bound. He clearly sided with Erasmus, using many of the same scriptures and arguments. It is also obvious that he had strong nominalist leanings: "The schools call the revealed power and will of God an ordered power and will. Not that the first will is unordered for everything that God wills and does is orderly and good. He is not subject to any rule. His will is itself a rule of all things. Therefore they call the will ordered since it occurs according to the preached Word of the Holy Scriptures in which he revealed to us his will."[16]

How did this "divine voluntarism" translate into his anthropology? Hubmaier understood the human person as the dynamic interaction of soul, body, and spirit. In conceiving the human being in this tripartite fashion, he was not original; but in the way he tried to hold together in tension both the "bondage of the will" and the "freedom of the will" he puts his own stamp on the debate. He began with the assumption that only God is good, and any good work we do is the work of God and God's grace within us.[17] How is it then that we have the responsibility to choose good over evil, as the scripture teaches? Hubmaier gave a traditional answer: humans were created free, lost their freedom after sinning, and had that freedom restored with the death and resurrection of Christ.

---

[14] Balthasar Hubmaier, "Freedom of the Will, I" in *Balthasar Hubmaier: Theologian of Anabaptism*, trans. and ed. by H. Wayne Pipkin and John H. Yoder (Scottdale, PA: Herald Press, 1989), 426-48.

[15] Hubmaier, "Freedom of the Will, II," *Hubmaier: Theologian of Anabaptism*, 449-91.

[16] *Ibid.*, 473.

[17] Hubmaier, "A Christian Catechism," *Hubmaier: Theologian of Anabaptism*, 359.

But what precisely was lost with the Fall, and what exactly is freed through Christ? And, furthermore, was what is freed in Christ seen in a realist fashion (that is, as something happening objectively to all humans as such) or in a nominalist way (contingent upon individual, subjective volition and response)? What was the *imago dei* for Hubmaier, and what was lost, retained, and restored in this image?

With these questions we come to the heart of his discussion of the tripartite nature of human being. "The human being," he stated, "is a corporal and rational creature, created by God as body, spirit, and soul, Gen. 2:7. These three elements are found essentially and in varying ways in every human being, as the Scripture thoroughly proves."[18] These three things, substances, or essences "are made and unified in every human being according to the image of the Holy Trinity."[19] Here we have a trinitarian "realism," in which humans are images of the divine in the state of innocence before the Fall. The flesh (*soma, corpus, Leib*) is the material physical body which derives from the earth. It is that which we share with the rest of creation. The soul (*psyche, anima, Seele*) is the life principle in us, that which made the dust of the ground alive when God breathed upon it. The spirit (*pneuma, spiritus, Geist*) is the image of God, the divine, in us. Hubmaier distinguished between the divine Spirit as such and the divine spirit as a component of human being. It is the human spirit which is the point of contact for the divine Spirit. The soul, the life principle finds itself hovering, as it were, between the flesh and the spirit: "the soul, which has become flesh through the disobedience of Adam, must through the Spirit of God and his living Word be reborn to a new spirit and become spirit, for what is born of the Spirit is spirit, John 3:6."[20]

In the prelaspsarian state, all three elements were good, and wholly free in the recognition, capability, and performance of good or evil. This power to will the good is not self-originating but is derived from God. It is, however, part of our created structure: "Whether now such a power for willing what is right and good is in us, it is not in us as if it were from us, for it is originally from God and his image, in which he created us

---

[18] Hubmaier, "Freedom of the Will, I," *Hubmaier: Theologian of Anabaptism*, 429.
[19] *Ibid.*, 430.
[20] *Ibid.*, 432.

originally. . . ."[21] After the Fall, because of disobedience – the wrong use of this freedom – this structure has been distorted. Free will has been lost. Each of the three elements, however, has lost it in a different sense. The flesh has been completely ruined (total depravity, one might call it). The soul has been seriously wounded, half-dead, not even knowing good or evil. Only the spirit retains its original righteousness, in which it was created. However, it is captive and can only "bear internal witness to righteousness against evil."[22] It would appear, therefore, that for Hubmaier, there was at least one element in the *humanum* which could never be destroyed, and which remains the point of contact for God's Word in Christ: the spirit.

With the restoration in Christ, appropriated by the human being through the spirit which has remained whole although captive all along, the soul regains, according to Hubmaier, its capacity to know good and evil, and the freedom to choose. The flesh remains ruined, although harmless, until the resurrection of the body. The soul remains between flesh and spirit, and can choose to follow either. If it chooses the way of the flesh, it sins willingly and is held accountable; if it did not sin willingly it would not be sin. So the human destiny now lies with the human choice: "If I now will, then I will be saved by the grace of God; if I do not will, then I will be damned, and that on the basis of my own obstinacy and willfulness."[23] Free will, in Hubmaier's view, was "nothing other than a power, force, energy, or adroitness of the soul to will or not will something, to choose or flee, to accept or to reject good or evil, according to the will of God, or according to the will of the flesh. . . ."[24] Hubmaier has nothing but scorn for those who deny such freedom, and through this denial excuse themselves and blame God for their sins, leading people to laziness and despair.

Having said this, however, Hubmaier insisted that the good that we do does is not due to our merit but is God's grace working within us. First, humankind was created free by God in body, soul, and spirit originally. Second, having lost the freedom and capacity to know good and evil, our

---

[21] *Ibid.*, 438.
[22] *Ibid.*
[23] *Ibid.*, 442.
[24] *Ibid.*, 443.

freedom was restored by "a special and new grace of God through Jesus Christ."[25] Through the sent Word of God humans are able to choose and do the good, with the exception of the flesh, which prior to the resurrection cannot do anything but sin and struggle against the spirit.[26] Like Adam, one can choose to reject the Word of the Spirit; to do so is not God's doing but one's own. The human ability to choose comes from God but not the particular choice. Hubmaier does allow a place for "God's omnipotence, omniscience, and eternal foreknowledge, predestination, providence, or reprobation,"[27] but these lie beyond human investigation and have to do with the hidden, absolute will of God, who owes no one anything.[28]

Hubmaier was without a doubt a voluntarist with nominalist leanings; but he was a voluntarist in the premodern sense – that is, there is a strong component of what might be called trinitarian, theological, or Christological realism. The ontological structure of being human (body, soul, spirit) remained the same for all humans. This structure is not self-determined or innate in the modern sense, but derived from God originally and restored by a new act of God's grace in Christ. Furthermore, the good which human beings do after the restoration of their freedom is not of their own merit but is a response to the sent Word of God within them. The "spirit" (the divine image in human beings) remains unspoiled by sin throughout and is the point of contact for God's Word.

Conclusion: What about the idiot?

The most difficult question remains unanswered: Where do those on the boundary of humanity, those exemplars of humanness who are without free will in the ordinary sense of the term (the unborn fetus, the infant, the mentally handicapped, the insane, the comatose), belong when the very essence of the human – the image of God – is defined as the capacity to make responsible decisions? Anabaptists such as Pilgram Marpeck had a simple answer: Such people are covered by the objective work of God's grace in Christ. In the words of Marpeck:

[25] Hubmaier, "Freedom of the Will, II," *Hubmaier: Theologian of Anabaptism*, 454.
[26] *Ibid.*, 456.
[27] *Ibid.*, 467.
[28] *Ibid.*, 472.

[T]he law is given for those who can know and not for those who cannot (such as children or idiots, for whom there is no law either with man or God). . . . All who know and recognize their sin can only then receive comfort and security. To this part of human recognition and faith belongs the baptism of the apostolic church, and not to young children or the ignorant, who have no law or knowledge of sin even though they are under law and sin. That is why young children had to be circumcised under the Law, for whoever received circumcision is responsible for the whole law, but only after he knows it. Where in the old Law was any child punished for his own transgression? Much less so in the new, where the children never bear the penalty of the parents nor the parents of the children.[29]

According to Marpeck, children and the ignorant (it is not clear what he did with those who had never heard the proclamation) "are without justification pronounced blessed by Christ, and regarded as belonging to the sanctified of the Kingdom of God."[30] At the point where persons reach the age of accountability – are able to know good and evil, and choose the good over the evil – human beings become responsible for their actions; prior to that or outside of that they are "simply received by Christ." Although Paul asserted that without faith no man can please God, "Children and the ignorant are not required to believe or disbelieve these words, but those who are born from the knowledge of good and evil into the innocence and simplicity of faith are required to believe."[31] Only when children receive the knowledge of good and evil, only at that point do "sin, death, and damnation begin."[32] Only where there is knowledge is there sin.

---

[29] "Pilgram Marpeck's Confession of 1523" in *The Writings of Pilgram Marpeck*, trans. and ed. by William Klassen and Walter Klaassen (Scottdale, PA: Herald Press, 1978), 127. Whether this view of the innocence of children does justice to the interrelatedness of all of creation in its fallenness both past, present, and future must remain a topic for another occasion.

[30] *Ibid.*, 128.

[31] *Ibid.*, 129.

[32] *Ibid.*, 131.

Although Marpeck was theologically not as sophisticated as Hubmaier, especially in spelling out the nuances of God's prevenient grace operative in choosing good over evil, the general sentiment and logic was the same. Believers church ecclesiology is premised on the assumption that at some point in the development of personhood, one gains the knowledge of good and evil, and the capacity and responsibility to respond to God's grace voluntarily. Prior to this a kind of Christological realism is assumed (the ignorant are saved by God's objective act of grace); after this there is a shift to a kind of nominalistic voluntarism, in which a particular person truly becomes a subject (a free moral agent) in the fullest sense. Is this not an incoherent conceptualization of the *humanum*?

The believers church tradition, as exemplified historically in its origins by Anabaptists like Hubmaier and Marpeck, is caught in a dilemma bordering on an internal contradiction. In its very concern for strengthening ethics at one end of the human spectrum (emphasizing the free will and moral responsibility of adults), it weakens the ethical foundation at the other end (its definition of full personhood in terms of free will in effect places fetuses, infants, and others with less than full rational and volitional powers outside the fully human and thereby threatens their very existence). It is a dilemma which in the classical voluntarist tradition was mitigated by certain realist assumptions. In the premodern voluntarist tradition, free will was ultimately derivative and subordinate to the mystery of divine will, election, and providence (as we have seen in Hubmaier). This derivation, however, never annulled human accountability, even for those in the nonvoluntarist traditions.

With the radical nominalism of the modern period and the loss of all sense of transcendent realism, voluntarism as understood by the believers church is in danger of undermining the very ethic it once sought to undergird. It is in danger of moral situationalism, not to speak of arbitrariness, when it comes to defining and preserving the human. Only by heeding the warnings of nonvoluntaristic theologians, particularly when it comes to defining what it means to be human, and by preserving strong theological realist assumptions as a foundation for Christian ethics within our voluntarist tradition, are we in a position to face the moral challenges facing the church. The only way a voluntaristic theology can be adequate to these contemporary challenges is if it retrieves and preserves its classical understanding of human agency as derivative from, dependent upon, and accountable to divine agency.

9

A Postmodern Critique of Educative Church Experience as Voluntary

Joyce E. Bellous[1]

Introduction

Voluntarism has had a pervasive influence in Western society, including education in the church. In order to understand the effects of voluntarism on Christian education, I want to inquire into the relationship between voluntarism (willing) and reason (thinking)[1] in what I call "educative church experience." The term voluntarism is ambiguous; it refers to the human activity of willing or taking purposive action, and to the concept of voluntarism as it has developed over time. In the believers church tradition, voluntarism is typically understood to imply that people are free to choose to become members of the church through adult baptism; adult or believers' baptism is an act based on a free confession of faith. Becoming a member of a faith community continues to be seen as an act of volition freely chosen without coercion, and in particular without the constraints of having the decision made for us by the church or our parents, or due to pressure from the community. That is, the concept of voluntarism is grounded on a strong view of personal freedom, based on the radical individualism implied in the idea that, for example, we can freely choose our associations without influence from other people.

This form of individualism flourished during modernity. Specifically, theories surrounding the idea of voluntarism were based on the

---

Joyce E. Bellous is assistant professor of Lay Empowerment and Discipleship and director of the MRE Programme at McMaster Divinity College, Hamilton, Ontario.

[1] I agree with Hannah Arendt that "[t]hinking, willing, and judging are the three basic mental activities [and that] they cannot be derived from each other and though they have certain common characteristics they cannot be reduced to a common denominator." See *The Life of the Mind* (New York: Harcourt Brace Jovanovich, 1978), 69. For the present purposes I do not discuss the mental activity of judging. I will use "reason" as a synonym for thinking and to apply to thinking (reasoning) on one's own. Also, I use "reasonable" to include a social capacity for thinking with other people and responding to them, in a way which influences both thinking and willing.

presumption of the freedom to separate from the former, pre-modern socio-religious order if people chose to, as well as on the latitude that allowed the mind to follow out its own thinking without fear that free-ranging, public inquiry would be corralled by church doctrine and practice, as it had been during the pre-modern era.[2]

As part of the modern criticism of pre-modern religious hegemony and it effects on the individual, Immanuel Kant (1724-1804) wrote an essay entitled "An Answer to the Question: 'What is Enlightenment?'" in order to warn his generation of a tendency towards immaturity. He defined immaturity as "the inability to use one's own understanding without the guidance of another."[3] He chided those who were caught up in the enthusiasm of the Enlightenment but who failed to see that, even though emancipation from the old order was possible, they retained their reluctance to rely on their own understanding as a guide to daily life. To him, the motto of the Enlightenment was "Have courage to use your *own* understanding."[4]

My perspective is postmodern, and I will clarify what that means. At the heart of postmodern critiques is a criticism of two elements of modernity that many postmoderns see as some of the failures of that era from approximately the French Revolution (1789) to the mid-twentieth century (1968-1972, in some views). The first criticism is of language that pretends to be the product of a "sovereign rational subject" who is "atomistic and autonomous, disengaged and disembodied,"[5] and this commentary grounds the critique of modern individualism. The second criticism identifies the main project of modernity as one of liberation and posits that it has failed. Modernity is seen as an attempt to liberate humankind most specifically from the economic, religious, sexual,

---

[2] See J.E. Bellous, "'On Thinking Other Wise.' A response to Elmer Thiessen's 'Academic Freedom and Religious Colleges and Universities: Confronting the Postmodern Challenge,'" in *Paideusis* 10.1 (Fall 1996).

[3] Hans Reiss (ed.), *Kant: Political Writings* (Cambridge: Cambridge University Press, 1991), 54.

[4] *Ibid.*

[5] Kenneth Baynes, James Bohman, and Thomas McCarthy, *After Philosophy: End or Transformation?* (Cambridge, Massachusetts and London, England: The MIT Press, 1989), 4.

political, and social structures of the pre-modern world.[6] One way of interrogating the modern project of liberation is to ask whether people can achieve maturity, *on their own*, as Kant proposed. The question of maturity underlies the motivation of this essay. As a consequence of the criticism about language, I will use first person pronouns throughout to acknowledge the embodied and engaged status of the author of this particular text. That is, it would be inharmonious with that perspective to make a postmodern critique of educative church experience as voluntary, using third person pronouns. As to the criticism about liberation, I will explore the role that power relations play in exercising the will and the inevitable influence that others have on us in the constitution of personal and social identity. I suggest that maturity is more of a community project than Kant allowed.

The central issue in Christian education continues to be the issue of maturity that Kant identified; the human activity of willing plays a crucial role in the realization of Christian maturity. At its best, Christian teaching aims at human maturity grounded on the fullness of Christ. But the very existence of the specifically Christian discovery of the will, which Kant defined as a "power of *spontaneously* beginning a series of things or states,"[7] is contested by many thinkers who appear reluctant to support a uniquely Christian perspective.[8] While it is beyond the scope of this essay to probe philosophical criticisms of the faculty of the will at length, I will refer to these arguments in proposing that educative church experience unites thinking and willing in a plausible way so as to allow for intellectual growth toward maturity in Christ, and at the same time takes account of social influence in the project of becoming mature. While we

---

[6] See for example, J.E. Bellous, "Jean Baudrillard: Reclaiming Evil Talk," in *Lire Baudrillard aujourd'hui/Reading Baudrillard Now: recherches semiotiques/semiotique inquiry* Journal of the Canadian Semiotic Association Vol. 16, Nos. 1-2 (1996): 27-47; Jean Baudrillard, *The Transparency of Evil* James Benedict trans. (London: Verso, 1993), 3-13; Michel Foucault, "The ethic of care for the self as a practice of freedom," in *The Final Foucault*, James Bernauer and David Rasmussen, eds. (Cambridge, Mass.: The MIT Press, 1988), 1-20; Jean-Jacques Lyotard, "Answer to the Question: What is the Postmodern?", in *The Postmodern Explained*, Don Barry et al. trans. (Minneapolis: University of Minneapolis Press, 1988), 1-16.

[7] *The Life of the Mind*, Willing, 6.

[8] *Ibid.*, 11-39.

cannot be cavalier and ignore criticisms levelled against the concept of willing, neither can we simply give in to them. Rather we need to prize the Christian discovery of the will and explicate ways that willing and thinking work together to respect what is necessary in becoming mature Christians, i.e., learning how to be authentic in our choices and to recognize the role that circumstance and other people play in our decisions.

What sort of church experience will educate people to think and act for themselves, and grow toward Christian maturity, given that their thinking (e.g., the taken-for-granted, enculturated, and conventional ideas of faith and practice) and their willing (e.g., the choices they make) need to be redeemed through the work of God, in Jesus Christ, through the power of the Holy Spirit? In short, what kind of church experience enables Christians to attach themselves to the community and then grow in faith and practice toward spiritual maturity that they willingly choose for themselves, yet also share with the community they join? In light of this dual educational task to constitute members that own their faith but also share it with others, the relationships between willing, thinking reasonably, and experience form an important concern. Regarding church experience that is educative, I suggest that the concept of voluntarism poses problems but at the same time provides a pathway ahead. I want to examine the concept to show how it both helps and hinders our attempt to become people of mature faith and practice. To anticipate the argument, on one hand, the individualism associated with voluntarism misdirects us with respect to becoming mature Christians for two primary and related reasons: it fails to take seriously the role that power plays in human relationships, and it does not take a full enough account of the social nature of becoming a mature person in the context of a faith community. On the other hand, willing remains central in the project of becoming a mature Christian, since faith and practice must be authentic for it to be effective in securing for each person the rich resources of God's grace, and for commitment to the faith community to be grounded on the freely chosen, active, and sustainable ministry of each member.

The significance of voluntarism

The existence of the will has been contested by eminent philosophers, notably in this century by Gilbert Ryle (1900-1976) in *The Concept of*

Mind, in which he asserted that the will is an "artificial concept."[9] In outlining the history of the concept of the will, Hannah Arendt (1906-1975) points out that resistance to the concept may have been primarily due to its absence from ancient Greek thought, although she suggested that Aristotle's idea of *proairesis* was a kind of forerunner of the will.[10] Since the will had no firm base in ancient Greek thought, many philosophers were unpersuaded by what was a uniquely Christian discovery. As Arendt pointed out, however, one aspect of their critique relied on an analysis of human consciousness, which did not exist in ancient Greek thought either.

A second aspect of this criticism of the will deplored the degree of freedom that the concept implied. As Arendt noted: "Willing, it appears, is characterized by an infinitely greater freedom than thinking, and . . . this undeniable fact has never been felt to be an unmixed blessing."[11] She accepted the reliability of the concept of will, and what stands out in her analysis of the history of the concept of willing, as distinct from thinking, is that willing is future-oriented and action-focused. She noted that "the normal mood of the willing ego is impatience, disquiet, and worry (*Sorge*)" because the will assumes that what it aims to achieve is possible but not guaranteed; thinking, on the other hand, tends to quarrel with it when will tries to do what it wants; to her "the will always wills to *do* something" and holds in sheer contempt the faculty of thinking which depends on past remembering, and essentially, on doing nothing.[12] It is this aspect of will as future-oriented and action-focused that I attend to when I describe the union of thinking and willing through educative church experience.

In everyday language, when we say that an act or decision is voluntary, we usually mean that the agent involved acted of his own accord, without compulsion, constraint, or under the undue influence of others. That is, willing aims at future action, and voluntarism assumes that the agent of the action exercises a high degree of independence.

I use the male, singular pronoun throughout this discussion because the language generally associated with voluntarism fits male experience

[9] Gilbert Ryle, *The Concept of Mind* (Harmondsworth: Penguin Books, 1949), 61.

[10] *The Life of the Mind,* Section Two: Willing, 6.

[11] *Ibid.,* Willing, 26.

[12] *Ibid.,* Willing, 37.

more than female experience. Married women in the Western world tend to be economically dependent on men and solely responsible for the care of small, dependent children, although this is changing. In light of this interlacing of dependence, women find it difficult to speak about, or think of themselves as able to act on their own accord without compulsion or constraint, and it raises the further (very troubling) question of what constitutes undue influence from other people's lives, as in the abortion dilemma. When women make the choice to abort a fetus, they may be acting as though they are nothing more than individuals, in the same radical sense that surrounds voluntarism. Christians are well advised to consider with utmost care what it means to act on one's own for those who bear and birth other people. Yet if voluntarism, as understood historically, is positioned as a part of the disposition of mature human beings, and if we insist that women do not act entirely on their own in the same way that men are thought to do, women as a group are left out of the picture of what it means to be mature human beings. The exclusion of female experience from the concept of voluntarism is important historically and philosophically; to include unreflectively the feminine pronoun in this discussion is to make the error of false gender neutrality.[13] We mislead ourselves if we refer to women as if their gendered experience fits the development of the concept. I am aware that women were, and are, involved as volunteers in numerous movements and have benefitted greatly from this participation. In making the point about false gender neutrality, I in no way wish to eclipse the significance of female voluntarism. Rather I want to make a philosophical point about the appropriate use of language. Actually including women's experience in how we think about human willing would help us arrive at a more useful concept for voluntarism.

To continue describing the concept as understood to this point, voluntary acts are taken by someone who determines his own destiny. In this way, belief in an independent free will is at the core of our general conception of voluntarism. Voluntarism implies the absence of compulsion in any form. For an act to be voluntary, its agent is not even prompted by outside influences. Voluntarism presupposes that an individual is capable

---

[13] Susan Moller Okin, *Justice, Gender and the Family* (New York: Basic Books, 1989), 10-13.

of separating himself from the influence of others in order to use reason to make decisions of his own. These decisions, and the actions that follow, may emerge spontaneously from his character or from the situation in which he finds himself. Acts understood to be voluntary are motivated from within, are free, unprompted from without and unconstrained; they are deliberate or intentional. In addition, mature human agents are thought to have a developed capacity for acting on their own volition. This assumption is so pervasive in Western society that whenever other people act, we perceive them to be doing so voluntarily, i.e., we believe that they are freely choosing to do what we see them doing. But we also assume that a person can have too much will. If we say that, as an example, a young boy named Jack is wilful, we mean that he chooses to act without proper regard for other people. We judge that Jack's will is wild and immature. Parents and teachers must tame it. This is the role that education is typically given. Education domesticates Jack by instilling obedience in the place of wilfulness: he must learn to engage in purposive action by becoming obedient to others.

Yet educational practices aimed only at teaching people to be obedient are potent with mis-educative possibilities. The relationship between obeying and willing is not a simple one. The tension between autonomy, or thinking for one's self, and obedience to others is at the heart of Kant's concern about immaturity. In part, this essay attempts to work out his view of the boundaries around when and where mature people should be obedient versus when and where they should use their own reason as a guide for daily life. If our boy Jack is to learn to use his intellect as a member of a Christian community, merely learning to be obedient to others will not suffice. Jack's will must be preserved in ways that enable him to participate meaningfully in the project of becoming like Christ, on his own and when he is by himself, as well as when he is in the presence of other Christians. Christian education is concerned with his character: Jack must come to see that his actions shape his future possibilities and that they affect other people.

In considering what we believe about voluntarism, recall the two dimensions of the term – the activity of willing and the concept, or the cloak of theories, that has built up around the term over time. The activity of willing, taking purposive, future-oriented action, is informed by the concept and is understood in its light. My primary discomfort with voluntarism is with the cloak of theories and doctrines that surround the idea of willing. Even initially, Christians should have at least two problems with the concept of voluntarism and its role in educative experience. The concept of willing originates in Paul's insight (Romans 7:15-25) that he found himself not doing what he wanted to do and doing what he did not want to do. This self-awareness was in conflict with his own Greek education. In Plato's view, to know the Good was to do the Good. Plato's confidence in the relationship between knowing and doing was challenged by Aristotle, who thought that doing the Good followed from practice, or habit, rather than from knowing alone. But Aristotle's criticism of Plato's view is different from the Apostle Paul's. Unlike Plato, Aristotle admitted certain limitations to doing what we know is Good, i.e., we cannot do everything we know because we do not have the power to do so.[14]

What is odd about Paul is that he countered the sufficiency of knowing as a basis for acting rightly, and posited that even actions within his power to do he sometimes did not do. Christians should be cautioned by Paul's insight in making judgements about their own and other people's actions. When we see someone act, can we assume they are acting voluntarily? Of course, certain body functions are involuntary or voluntary, but this point does not apply to taking purposive action in the sense I am using it.

The second concern with glibly accepting theories that surround voluntarism can be posed in terms of obedience. What is the relationship between obeying other fallen human agents and obeying God? Is this relationship clear to us?[15] I do not pursue these important questions here except to intimate conceptual boundaries around willing, wilfulness, and obedience, and to suggest that training people to be unreflectively obedient discourages them from moving beyond a merely conventional understanding of what it means to be Christian. Neither does it provide them with sufficient defence against social pressure.[16] If the concept of voluntarism has had a strong influence in Christian education, we would expect to find an emphasis on obedience, self-control, and individual

---

[14] Aristotle, *The Nicomachean Ethics* (Oxford: Oxford University Press, 1991), especially 28-58.

[15] Dorothee Solle, *Creative Disobedience* (Cleveland: The Pilgrim Press, 1995).

[16] I pursue encouraging educative resistance in "Should We Teach Students to Resist?" in William Hare and John P. Portelli, *Philosophy of Education* 2nd. ed. (Calgary, Alberta, Canada: Detselig Enterprises Ltd., 1996), 369-81.

responsibility.[17] I think this emphasis is what we uncover. To test this hypothesis, there is no quicker way to increase the intensity of a discussion than to dispute the role obedience should play in the Christian life. We have emphasized the concept but not the character development that educating the will would involve.

To return to our historical analysis: in addition to signifying a solitary, unconstrained decision-maker, an act is voluntary if there is no state control over the agent's behaviour, no conscription, force, interference, or even the suggestion of influence by someone outside the agent. As an example, the relationship between church and state is voluntaristic if there is an economic separation between the two institutions: the church hopes that the state will not interfere politically if it does not support the institution financially. This hope assumes that power is grounded in economics, something both Marxists and functionalists have tended to assume.[18] In addition to the political and economic, voluntarism has theological and philosophical roots. The theological aspect asserts that God's sovereign will rules the world and the nature of will is freedom.[19] We have then two dimensions for the concept of will, God's and man's. In the historical development of the dynamism between divine and human will, Duns Scotus (c.1266-1308), asserted that "God is will; man is will; the former 'dominant', the latter 'subject'"; and further, "[t]he absolute free-will of God appoints, works, and organizes the whole; and all things are means for the attainment of the final end, the blessedness of predestination."[20] If we focus on the idea of voluntarism implied in Scotus's statement, man is represented as absolutely free with respect to "the immediate connection, of which man is in the act of becoming

---

[17] It is not clear to me that these attributes are like the more recent emphasis on spiritual formation, which echoes pre-modern modes of spirituality. In self-control or obedience the emphasis is on not doing (i.e., on not being disobedient) and the emphasis for spiritual discipline is on doing, fasting, meditating, and the like.

[18] Michel Foucault, *Power/Knowledge* (New York: Pantheon Books, 1980), 88-89.

[19] "Scholasticism," in *The New Schaff-Herzog Encyclopedia of Religious Knowledge*, Samuel Macauley Jackson, ed. Vol. X, 1950: 259-69, 260.

[20] "Scholasticism," 264. I do not intend to suggest that Duns Scotus made the whole moral law depend on the arbitrary choice of divine will, since his contribution to thought was taken up and elaborated by others, notably by William of Ockham (c.1290-1349); see Frederick Copleston, *A History of Philosophy* (Garden City, New York: Image Books, 1962), 199-274; and Arendt, *Life of the Mind*, Part III, Intellect and Willing, 125-46.

conscious; absolutely, man is wholly subject to the unity of the great objective plan."[21] That is, man is free in regard to the unfolding of his consciousness but his freedom is exercised within the freedom God has to design the larger context in which human activity has meaning. Educative church experience, as I describe it later on, is based on G.W.F. Hegel's (1770-1831) idea of *conscientia* (or knowing with), an attempt to reconcile divine and human freedom. From the human perspective alone, *conscientia* connects willing and thinking. Hegel's idea of experience, as well as the role thinking plays in taking purposive action, were shaped by his view of the possibility for reconciliation between divine and human willing.[22]

A postmodern critique

In terms of postmodern critiques generally, it is as if at certain points – for example, in the fifteenth and sixteenth centuries[23]– there is a flood of new thought, made possible by intellectual, socio-political, economic, and technological change. The dam controlling the flow of human thought breaks from the pressure. This breakdown is felt in the perception that current knowledge is incapable of effectively speaking to the human condition in order to make sense of these moments. The river of knowledge rushing through the dam widens to include new thought, as well as former thinking missed in the previous mainstream. The flood period is one of destruction, renewal, revision, and invention. Martin Heidegger (1889-1976)[24] contended that the future direction for the mainstream is best speculated upon by examining the flow of the past. Diverse postmodern thinkers propose vastly different moves for us to make. One group urges us to simply pack up camp and go to a new location. They assume the history of human thought needs an entirely new beginning, for example, with a new language to describe human experience. Another group wants

---

[21] "Scholasticism," 264-265.

[22] Charles Taylor, *Hegel and Modern Society* (New York: Cambridge University Press, 1979), 1-68.

[23] This flood of change can also be conceived as a "struggle for a new subjectivity." See Michel Foucault, "The Subject and Power," in Hubert L. Dreyfus and Paul Rabinow, *Michel Foucault: Beyond Structuralism and Hermeneutics* (2nd. ed.), Chicago: University of Chicago Press, 1983), 213.

[24] Martin Heidegger, *Identity and Difference* (London: Harper & Row, 1969).

us to tinker with what we already know and try using new language tools to make the project work. A third option accepts that revision of the mainstream must be deep but will come from within the borders of the flood tide of thought. This group is busy sorting through the flotsam and jetsam of earlier periods, as well as the present one, in order to spot past misdirections and to make sense of new opportunities. I follow the last option and below I will draw the concept of voluntarism[25] into the postmodern flow of revision and invention in order to note some of its contributions to, as well as its misdirections for, the mainstream of thought.

The uniquely Christian discovery of the will[26] provided the ethical and philosophical roots for voluntarism. This discovery is based on Paul's declaration about himself in Romans mentioned earlier. In outline, ethical voluntarism posits that what we desire is what is good and what we feel an aversion to is what is bad, and *vice versa*. On this view, prudence, or the selection of appropriate means for the attainment of whatever goals we happen to have (for example, self-preservation), is the proper director for moral agency.[27] A postmodern critique of voluntarism cannot accept this ethical stance because it under-analyzes the role that power plays in social relations. In addition, philosophical voluntarism focuses attention on will as the centre-piece of human experience, and the specifically metaphysical roots of voluntarism assert that will is the ultimate and underlying reality behind the whole phenomenal world.[28] In philosophical voluntarism, human will is primary over reason, a view which is a shift away from Plato's and Descartes's view that reason directs what we are calling the will but what Plato would have described as the passions. Because he thought reason directed the passions, Plato believed that those who knew the Good would do it. When voluntarism claims that will has primacy over reason, as exemplified in David Hume (1711-1776) and Arthur Schopenhauer (1788-1860), reason is understood in a narrow way, i.e., as

---

[25] William Brackney, *Voluntarism – The Dynamic Principle of the Free Church* (The Hayward Lectures, Acadia Divinity College, 1992). I thank William Brackney for his careful reading of this text and his helpful comments and clarifications.

[26] See Arendt, *The Life of the Mind*, 1-146, especially 6.

[27] *Encyclopedia of Philosophy*, Paul Edwards, ed. Vol. 8 (New York: Macmillan Publishing Co., and The Free Press, 1967), 270-72.

[28] *Ibid.*, 271.

a mere technique.[29] To Schopenhauer, reason had a primarily biological function. It acquired a surplus of energy which permitted it to deal with complexity in the phenomenal world as a "disinterested spectator."[30] To Hume, reason was not the director of the passions; it was merely an inductive and deductive technique that cannot provide ends or goals.[31] Describing reason as mere technique limits its use in experience in a way similar to the limits that the scientific method has come to play in modern life. Science, as we think of it, entered the West in the seventeenth century as a way of knowing that promised men mastery across the range of human experience, but it has not provided a way of increasing our insight into ourselves or our insight into God. How could it? Science is "restricted *in principle* to telling us about a part of reality only, that part . . . that is beneath us in freedom and awareness."[32] A postmodern critique of voluntarism is uncomfortable with reason as technique, and prefers to have reason and will collaborate rather than exist in a hierarchical relationship in which one directs the other.

The problem is not how to use reason or will as an ethical technique or to see how one controls the other. Rather, it is to see how reason operates along with the will as we reflect on experience, so that we can make gains in becoming better people through following Christ's example. In making a postmodern critique of voluntarism, I am removing the will from its important role in human experience and replacing it with reason, especially if reason is conceived as mere technique. Following Hegel, I object to making one aspect of being human central in human experience, by itself. In addition, and in contrast to the image of the solitary individual who wills in an unconstrained and uninfluenced manner, Hegel addressed the inescapably social and embodied character of human experience and

[29] In terms of a more expansive view of reason's role in learning, John Dewey, who was significantly influenced by Hegel's concept of experience, characterized propositions as "*means* to furthering and completing some given inquiry [as an essential part] of a general theory of how information accrues and is used in problem-solving contexts." Tom Burke, *Dewey's New Logic: A response to Russell* (Chicago and London: University of Chicago Press, 1994), 2.

[30] Frederick Copleston, *A History of Philosophy,* Volume 7 (New York: Image Books, 1965), 35.

[31] *Encyclopedia of Philosophy*, 270-71.

[32] Huston Smith, from the Preface, in Edmund Colledge and Bernard McGinn (trans.), *Meister Eckhart: The Essential Sermons, Commentaries, Treatises, and Defense.* (New York: Paulist Press, 1981), xi-xii.

configured the concept of reason toward what I call an education for growth.

In contrast to what is voluntary, recent criticism maps the way power operates in modern society and refuses credibility to those who claim that they act from the inside, on their own, unhindered and unconstructed by the social world. Voluntarism may have served well as a reaction to the excesses of *sovereign*, or pre-modern power, but it fails to fully address power's exercise in the modern period. The power games of modernity, described by Michel Foucault (1979)[33] are *pastoral and disciplinary power*. To Foucault (1926-1984), the exercise of *pastoral* and *disciplinary* power invests the individual (like a parasite invests the body) with the result that we learn to mistrust ourselves and fail to come to know ourselves from the inside. This analysis posits that every social relation has compulsion at its core – whether existential (e.g., in terms of alienation), epistemological (e.g., through lies and deception), psychological (e.g., through emotional harm), or physical (e.g., through bodily harm). On this view, those who imagine it is possible for them to act alone, unconstrained from the outside, fail to notice how power operates within them and as a result never know themselves. Not to know what is within is to abandon ourselves to the mercy of forces from without: Man alone is man unknown to himself. Modern power operates so as to tempt us into believing in our own absolute sovereignty. Voluntarism plays into a strategy of self-ignorance by scorning the givenness of human experience, the cultural and social embeddedness of persons, and the inevitable play of compulsion in every social relation.

As well, the concept of voluntarism keeps us from recognizing the ubiquity and innovation of power's games. Misrecognizing power games traps us in a no-win situation. On one side, voluntarism intimates that something has gone wrong if an act is prompted, constrained, or even suggested by another person. It assumes that it is possible to act in an uninfluenced state. By implication, when power is exercised, it threatens the intention to act on one's own. In this view, power is harmful to individuals and is sometimes described as a social pathology.[34] That is, if

---

[33] J.E. Bellous, *Power, Empowerment and Education* (PhD Dissertation, University of Alberta, 1993), 16-39.

[34] J.E. Bellous, "Encompassing Power," in *Philosophy of Education, Proceedings*, Audrey Thompson (ed.) (Urbana, Illinois: Philosophy of Education Society, 1993), 114-22.

voluntary acts alone are good because they come from within and are motivated by the will, all events that are not voluntary are coerced, and therefore harm someone's interests. Power exercised on us from outside harms our interests because others can have only their own interests at stake. The assumptions here are that scarcity and competitiveness define the public sphere of human action. Thus it follows that being good requires that we give away our power (because power is harmful). We are trapped: we can never relax when we exercise power. We exercise it to defend ourselves from its use by other people, but people who exercise power cause harm, so we are bad when we use it.

But the situation is even worse. In terms of experience, usually we have to work hard to win a powerful position; after all that work, power adheres to us and to our position. If we try not to be powerful, and give power away, neglect shapes our social interactions. Neglect is felt in others as abandonment, which produces unwelcome effects in all our social relations. As a result, people in positions of power fluctuate between coercion, which has force at its core, and a *laissez-faire* use of power, which has neglect and abnegation at its core. Leaders are in a constant state of anxiety with respect to the exercise of power. As a consequence, they hang on to power so no one else can wield it over them, to harm and devalue their interests, yet they must appear to give it away so they can be seen, and can see themselves, as good people. The prevalence of power games characterizes leadership patterns in many Christians.

From an educational perspective, power inevitably plays into the teaching/learning relation. The tendency to fluctuate between coercion and neglect can shape interactions between teachers, pastors, and those who are potential members of the community through believers' baptism. But there is a third option. Empowerment is grounded in attempts to remove obstacles people face in trying to secure their own interests, in concert with their willingness to support other people's interests. Empowerment is exercised through attentiveness in which teaching is directed by a clear sense of what is involved in Christian maturity; it is guided by observing what the learner is interested in, already knows, and still needs to learn. How do we educate the young without coercion or neglect, and so that they willingly choose to belong to a community, while at the same time develop the competencies inherent in an authentic Christian character? This third way in power relations engages learners in the activity of teaching along with us as soon as they are capable of participating meaningfully, which begins for many when they are in grade four.

Many postmodern critiques assert that power is not merely evil but its exercise is inevitable.[35] Power plays everywhere, through everyone. Thus, there are two ways to conceive power: (1) as the willingness and ability to pursue and attain communal human goals through the mastery of our environment,[36] and (2) as the willingness and ability to get my own way despite resistance from others. In the first view, power is social and cooperative. In the second, it is personal, assumes adversarial relationships, and is characterized by zero-sum games of winning and losing: the powerful win, the powerless lose. In the first view, through the cooperative organization of communal goals we can secure common interests so that power is created by the compelling effort of a community and is enhanced in everyone who participates. The second view coheres with the concept of voluntarism as the willingness to do what I want in isolation from others and without so-called undue influence from them. This aspect of the concept, linked with the reckless exercise of self-absorbed and adversarial power, is myopic and unreasonable. It is an exercise of power that mis-educates us, preventing us from attaining educative experience because it frustrates communion among us. Getting what I want despite resistance from others in the context of conceiving my self as a solitary and uninfluenced decision-maker does not help formulate educational approaches blending transmissionist and transformational aims of teaching people to mature together in Christ Jesus.

Educating for growth

The point about spiritual growth is caught in the expression "the fullness of Christ." While this terminology is not found in the New Testament text as such,[37] the expression captures two aspects of Christian commitment, namely that we must become members of the body of believers through the

---

[35] Michel Foucault, "The ethic of care for the self as a practice of freedom," in *The Final Foucault*, James Bernauer and David Rasmussen, eds. (Cambridge, Mass.: The MIT Press, 1988), 18.

[36] Michael Mann, *Sources of Social Power* Vol. 1 (New York: Cambridge University Press, 1989), 6.

[37] I recognize the expression "the fullness of Christ" does not appear in the New Testament (NRSV) in this form. By this expression I include several biblical ideas: maturity, image, mind and fullness: a) Maturity: Eph 4:13, Phil 3:15, Col 1:28, Col 4:12, Heb 5:14, James 1:4; b) Image: Rom 8:29, 1Cor 15:49, 2Cor 3:18, 2Cor 4:4, Col 1:15, Col 3:10; c) Mind: 1Cor 1:10, 1Cor 2:16, Phil 2:5; d) Fullness: Eph 3:19.

volitional act of baptism and that we must learn how to live out our membership in the Body of Christ. That is, salvation and education are two sides of one task which originates in the experience of being in Christ and moves forward as we are becoming a new creation in Christ Jesus – a goal most clearly picked out in the Incarnation of Christ. We become believers (at a given point in time) and we are becoming believers (over time) as we grow into the fullness of Christ. For this reason, Christian education involves the aim of transmitting inherited knowledge and traditional spiritual practices in which we conserve what is essential to an identity in Christ. In addition, Christian education deploys the transformative aim of enabling believers to change in the direction of becoming like Christ through reflecting upon their personal ownership of that inherited knowledge and their spiritual growth through the Christian practices that are part of their heritage.

To address the dual aims of transmission and transformation, I agree with Richard Foster[38] that the task of being Christian needs a theology of growth, but I would add that a theology of growth requires support from the *praxis*[39] of an education for growth. Spiritual growth does not result from theological ideas about it, by themselves. It also resides in action that nourishes it. While I initially focus on transformative learning in educative church experience, I do not wish to denigrate transmissionist aims; as I will show, there is a relationship between them that is central to educative church experience.

Why do we need an education for growth to anchor Christian maturity? At the core of the growth model is an observation of an odd element in Christian culture that I also see in myself: I am shocked by mistakes, sin, and conflict in the community and in me. If these failures catch us unawares, it may partly be due to practices that reduce being Christian to the initial act of salvation or baptism and treat this act as a *fait accompli*, with the outcome that new or baptized Christians are thought of as finished products. The concept of voluntarism plays into this tendency, first because it pays so much attention to choosing to become a member at a given point in one's history, lending itself to the idea of a *fait*

---

[38] Richard Foster, "Becoming Like Christ," in *Christianity Today*, Vol. 40, No. 2 (February 5, 1996):26-31. Richard Foster is currently at Azusa Pacific University in Azusa, California.

[39] For a comprehensive discussion of the term *praxis*, see Tom Bottomore (ed.), *A Dictionary of Marxist Thought* (Cambridge: Harvard University Press, 1983), 384-89.

accompli, and secondly because the believers church tradition provides little or no idea of the spiritual status of children prior to the moment of their acceptance of Christ. While the need for salvation for children from unchurched homes may be obvious, it is not at all clear what the children of Christian parents are converted from, and it is less clear how the process should be structured intellectually in order for new believers to eventually sense the possibility, importance, and attractiveness of maturity in Christ. As adult baptizing believers, we must acknowledge that the spiritual status of children is explicit in infant baptizing traditions and that education plays the more obvious role of realizing fully what has already taken place in the child's spiritual state. I do not want to suggest that, as a result, education in the other traditions is better. Rather, Christian education needs revision if we want people to become mature believers in, and practitioners of, faith, and we cannot use either force or neglect to secure educational aims if we want children eventually to be mature believers.

In assessing an education for growth, our disappointment when we sense our ineffectiveness in addressing sin and conflict may also be an *accoutrement* of spiritual pride. Yet in either case, why does failure surprise us? We must learn about sin and learn not to sin; facing sin is not something we know how to do instantly or in advance. An education for growth relieves us of *naivete*, pride, and despair about ourselves and our communities because educational growth *occurs only* in the context of conflict. We discover the need to grow through seeing that something we are doing continually misses the mark; conflict inspires growth through our longing for an integration of faith and practice as surely as it threatens disaster through the disintegration of word and deed in the form of spiritual hypocrisy. An education for growth enables us to see and secure the willingness, ability, and courage to turn our conflict, sin, and mistakes into the new creatures that we are called to become – a growth which takes place through the work of the Holy Spirit and through the encouragement of God's acceptance of us, despite the (accurate) belief that we are unacceptable on our own.

Becoming like Christ, which is focused on the fullness of Christ, is a process requiring an engagement in educative church experience in order to sense the lively truths of Christianity through seeing the truth about ourselves. Growth in Christ relies on self-knowledge. The fullness of Christ is both the destination for our pilgrimage and the path along which we move, since we need Christ's presence within to begin the trip at all.

There are educational elements that ground spiritual growth. One is the unfolding of intelligence, which has two aspects in a Christian context, namely thinking or reason, which is essentially the ability to give reasons for what we are doing, saying, and believing on the basis of past experience and cognitive knowledge. Another, according to Christian tradition, is an aspect of intellect called spiritual perception. Spiritual perception knows things by directly sensing them and can understand divine truths by means of immediate experience, through what might be called self-observation. In the first sense, the use of the intellect generally entails deploying cognitive knowledge and practices for addressing situations that help people identify and resolve problems in ways which lay the foundation for the acquisition of new cognitive knowledge.[40]

The second sense of intellectual activity has been particularly hard to define in modern Western societies that have underestimated its value: the intellect engages in a type of reflection that pays attention to the depths of the soul or the innermost aspect of the heart.[41] This second sense may also be identified as "personal intelligence," a term provided by Howard Gardner[42] (1983). Gardner identifies two types of personal intelligence: intrapersonal intelligence, in which we become able to discriminate between our own feelings and therefore make sense of ourselves, and interpersonal intelligence, in which we discern aspects of other people and effectively make sense of them. For him, personal intelligences tend to develop naturally from infancy to adulthood without explicit teaching. As he notes, "one simply allows them to emerge."[43] Yet Gardner thinks that societies should encourage this development through "literature, rituals, and other symbolic forms," through which "the culture helps the growing individual to make discriminations about [his or her] own feelings or about

---

[40] For the relationship between intelligence and problem-addressing, see Howard Gardner, *Frames of Mind: The theory of multiple intelligences* (New York: Basic Books, 1983).

[41] For more definitions of heart and intellect, see G.E.G. Palmer, Philip Sherrard, and Kallistos Ware (trans. and eds.) *The Philokalia*, Volume 1 (London and Boston: Faber and Faber, 1979), 361.

[42] Howard Gardner is currently co-director of Project Zero at the Harvard Graduate School of Education, and adjunct professor of neurology at the Boston University School of Medicine.

[43] Gardner, *Frames of Mind*, 253.

the other persons in [his or her] milieu."[44] The aim is to develop a sense of self through the self-knowledge that enables the development of reason in the sense I will describe later on. This second aspect of intelligence is the site for understanding the development and exercise of the will.[45]

In Christian traditions, the second aspect of the intellect develops through attentiveness to the heart as the centre of being human; the heart encompasses body, soul, and spirit and thus has an all-embracing significance for spiritual formation. It is a form of attentiveness that results in the self-knowledge central to spiritual growth, when aided by the Holy Spirit. The point of self-observation is to allow insight to shape character so that we can both will and do that which is pleasing to God. One of my assumptions is that pleasing God also produces an authentic life and thus leads those who observe themselves to move beyond enculturated and conventional knowledge of what it means to be Christian. In order to achieve some freedom from culture,[46] the methods of the intellect in this second sense are nourished by the spiritual disciplines of worship, prayer, fasting, meditation, community life and service, to name some of them. In these practices, we pay attention to what goes on around us and in us and use this information to allow concepts about the Christian life to move past taken-for-granted knowledge. As an example, prayer of the heart means prayer not just of the emotions and affections but of the whole person, including the body. In analyzing the relationship between willing and thinking, in the context of educative church experience, I will spell out the most helpful way of seeing how the intellect can operate in an

---

[44] *Ibid.*, 253.

[45] A further explication of intelligence of this second type is found in Daniel Goleman's *Emotional Intelligence* (New York: Bantam Books, 1995). Goleman uses the term "character" as a synonym for emotional intelligence and makes the case that Gardner's idea of the intelligences really rests on a notion of cognitive rather than affective intelligence. His book explores the affective side of intellectual life. Recent brain research intimates that thinking and feeling are not separable functions and that each influences the other, sometimes in dramatic ways.

[46] I am thinking here of Peter Brown's view that sexual renunciation in early Christianity was more of an attempt to resist the cultural pressure to perform in the marriage bed in order to do one's cultural duty to perpetuate the social group, than it was a rejection of sexual intercourse as such. What should we resist in our day in order to find some freedom from culture at the end of the twentieth century? See Brown, *The Body and Society: Men, women, and sexual renunciation in early Christianity* (New York: Columbia University Press, 1988).

education for growth by using a model provided by Hegel. He proposed a way of experiencing these two aspects of intellect in terms of one process which is now the crux of attempts to design transformative learning.[47] But we cannot put transformative learning at the centre of educative church experience without first unravelling the relationship between thinking and willing, since the latter concept is embedded in our assumptions about what it means to commence and continue in the Christian life.

In proposing an education for growth towards fullness in Christ, or Christian maturity, one of the competencies to develop, which I call "experiencing," emerges from our capacity for educative experience that is grounded on *conscientia*, the central aspect of Hegel's concept of experience. *Conscientia* unites willing and thinking.[48] If we map out the relationship between thinking and willing, we may find new directions for the educational growth of reasonable members of church communities. By "church experience," I mean the holistic educational program of a local community of believers. Finding an educational vision for this community is my purpose. A working hypothesis for the relationship between thinking and willing, based on a postmodern critique of church experience, would dispute what voluntarism has assumed about power relations and would not accept that "[n]othing other than the Will is the total cause of volition."[49] We are dramatically affected, in what we decide to do or not do, if other people coerce or neglect us.

Educative church experience

What is educative church experience? Interactions are educative if there is some movement towards reasonableness in the learner. Educative experience engages learners with the form and content of what is to be

---

[47] For an explanation of transformative learning's relationship to Hegel, see *Dewey's New Logic*, especially 18-21.

[48] I am interested in analyzing only a small piece of Hegel's thought, specifically his concept of experience as picked out by Martin Heidegger in *Hegel's Concept of Experience* (New York: Harper & Row, 1970). I acknowledge the limitations in taking a small slice of such a large work and the inevitable over-simplification that often results.

[49] Duns Scotus, quoted in Arendt, *The Life of the Mind*, "Mental Activities in a World of Appearances," 69.

learned in such a way that new thought is possible. Form and content are typically presented to the learner by other people. Experiencing new thought, in the context of what the learner already knows, making new connections, seeing something new for oneself, is what it means to learn something. In short, learning is done by the learner in community with others.

In educating Christians, we transmit content (knowledge and practices) in a particular form to them and also teach them to be reasonable with respect to that transmission. As a measure of being reasonable members of a faith community, Christians must be willing and able to identify themselves as among the faithful, reflect on that faith commitment, and willingly participate in a faith community. Willing and thinking work cooperatively in the reasonable Christian. Therefore, in teaching people to be reasonable, the development of cognitive knowledge alone is not sufficient; educators must also pay attention to the will which, from the perspective of a postmodern critique, requires both that people learn to exercise their will in the context of acting *with* others rather than by themselves and that educators pay attention to power games in the teaching/learning relation. Teachers work *with* learners without being either coercive or neglectful. Further, the willingness to participate reasonably does not develop by training people merely to be obedient. But how can thinking learn to collaborate with willing in the process of educative church experience? In pursuing this question, which is essential to the growth of mature Christians, I will spell out how thinking (reason) that is collaborative with willing, and sensitive to power's exercise, would operate.

In describing how reflecting on our consciousness works to unite thinking and willing, according to Hegel,[50] I am concerned with only a small portion of his thought, namely his view of experience, because of its role in an education for growth. In asking what it means to be reasonable, a distinction must be made between two words, *dianoia* and *nous,* which are both terms for reason. In the tradition that influenced Hegel, *dianoia,*

---

[50] As Arendt asserts: "No philosopher has described the willing ego in its clash with the thinking ego with greater sympathy, insight, and consequence for the history of thought than Hegel." *Life of the Mind,* "Willing," 39. I follow Arendt's argument only in terms of how Hegel unites willing and thinking in so far as I focus on the role that the future plays in his thought. As Arendt noted, Hegel does not mention the will in his description of consciousness's awareness of its own consciousness, but it is Arendt who suggests that willing is what Hegel is really talking about (41), and I follow her move on this point.

discursive reason, deals with mathematics and lies between perception and the more intuitive *nous*, which is deployed in philosophy. The German words for understanding (*Verstand*) and reason (*Vernunft*) retain a distinction between higher and lower faculties as do *dianoia* and *nous*. In Plato's successors, in the language and mysticism of Meister Eckhart (c.1260-1327) that influenced Hegel,[51] the higher faculty brings us into contact with the intelligible order; it is ascribed to God and is the divine spark in human beings. The lower faculty is characteristic of human beings and is sometimes thought to be shared with other animals. In using the higher faculty it is possible to think about thinking; *nous* enables reflection upon itself.

Hegel distinguished reason from reasoning or argumentation, and from the verb "to reason" or "argue." He also distinguished his view of reason from Enlightenment rationality and from common sense. He disdained all other uses of the term reason. He thought of reason as connected with faith, and as able to give consciousness an immediate and complete view of the whole truth. It is the role that reason plays in seeing things whole that is significant for educative church experience. Reason builds whole concepts, or works in that direction, by reconciling the oppositions within and between concepts with each shape of the concept that is brought to the movement of thought. As an example, reason operates by reconciling the shape I have for the concept of trust as I converse with the friend who did not meet me for lunch when she said she would.

Reason that is capable of working *with* the will cannot be taken in the narrow sense of reason as technique, which amounts to learning a system of prescribed linear thinking.[52] Learning to be reasonable has as much to do with the heart as with the head. For Hegel, reason was rooted in self-knowledge – the knowledge of one's consciousness of one's self.[53] To him, "philosophy contemplates what is present, in its presence."[54] To clarify a

---

[51] *A Hegel Dictionary* (Oxford, UK; Cambridge, MA: Blackwell, 1992), 8-11.

[52] Nel Noddings, *Educating for Intelligent Belief or Unbelief* (New York and London: Teachers College Press, 1993), xiv.

[53] According to Taylor, it was a basic principle of Hegel's thought that the subject and all the subject's functions are necessarily embodied as a rational animal who thinks, and as an expressive being whose thinking always and necessarily expresses itself in a medium. Charles Taylor, *Hegel and Modern Society* (Cambridge: Cambridge University Press, 1979), 18.

[54] *Concept of Experience*, 27.

description of experience that educates, and is grounded on contemplating what is present, consider the difference between two types of conversation. In the first, we are speaking with those who do not look at us, do not seem to hear anything we say, categorize us in ways we find objectionable, and generally misinterpret who we are, even though we are standing before them, trying to let them see us as we are. In this type we are misrecognized. Others neither see us nor hear what we are saying, so that they cannot sense what we are in our uniqueness. In the second type of conversation, we are engrossed with those who really look at us without making us uncomfortable, who hear what we are saying and sense what we are doing even when we cannot be articulate about the complex feelings and thoughts that we have. As we converse, one or the other of us is able to put into words what we recognize as that which we really are. Through conversation we see ourselves in a new way, and the other person is central to this self-recognition. Hegel's philosophy of consciousness is similar to this second type. Experiencing[55] is a dialogue within ourselves and with others in which the liveliness of the other's presence, in union with attentiveness to our own thoughts and feelings, enables learning to take place between us. The other person does not coerce or neglect, but pays attention to us; both participants pay attention to themselves and to each other in a way that is empowering to new thought. To refuse to receive the other's presence, to refuse to pay attention to ourselves, is to open up the possibility of coercion or neglect.

Since Christian educators want to teach learners to take reasonable purposive action, and since being reasonable is social, the teacher's presence needs to be valuable to learners, and learners need to prize each other. In having significance to learners, teachers become aware that learning takes place in the growth of the learner's consciousness. The growth of consciousness towards reasonableness is realized through a dialogue within self-consciousness between what Hegel calls "natural" and "real" knowledge. Teachers need to discover the content of the learner's current natural knowledge (what the learner feels, thinks, and takes for granted) in order to interact educatively with it. This insight can only come when learners are doing some task or involved in conversation. If learners merely sit still and say nothing, teachers cannot discover the content of the concepts learners currently hold. In educating willing and thinking, the teacher's role is to discover ways to let real knowledge show up to learners

---

[55] *Ibid.*, 23.

and to attend patiently to the struggle that the dialogue between natural and real knowledge initiates.

At the outset of reflecting on our concepts, natural knowledge provides us with ideas that show up without effort on our part. This knowledge is actually a configuration of the historic evolution of particular concepts, experiences, and cultural orientations passed on to us from other cultural members, and constitutes what we take for granted as the truth. Natural knowledge is our taken-for-granted view of the way things are; it is effortless and no work is involved because we assume we already know the object of our glance in advance of really looking. Real knowledge, by contrast, is what we receive from paying attention to the other. It lives behind the back of the taken-for-grantedness of our ordinary experience of phenomena and refers to the way phenomena essentially and really are apart from our incomplete or unfinished opinion of them. It is the difference between looking at the moon while lying on our backs in the grass on a summer evening, and walking on its surface.

In the dialogue between natural and real knowledge, natural knowledge shows up as incomplete or unfinished. This consequence for natural knowledge is made possible through *skepsis*, which is the seeing, watching, and scrutinizing to see what and how beings are as beings.[56] There is a constant tension between natural and real knowledge, and this tension is natural knowledge's resistance to real knowledge and to *skepsis*. But *skepsis* is not mere scepticism. This point is important to the discussion of voluntarism. The dialogue between real and natural knowledge is thorough-going but is distinguished from the scepticism which an individual may wield against any and all forms of authoritative voice. Such scepticism is a refusal to pay attention to the other. This latter type is unreflective; it is a silly habit. Unreflective sceptics refuse to receive knowledge from the other; they dismiss others' views since relying on these views implies a capitulation to undue influence from other people. Hegel observed that in habituated scepticism one tries "to examine everything for one's self and follow only one's own conviction, or better yet, to produce everything by oneself and hold one's own act alone as true."[57] To hold and act on a conviction merely because it is mine alone, and to carry forward concepts unreflectively, is no better than blindly

[56] *Ibid.,* 65.
[57] *Ibid.,* 14.

following the authority of other voices. The only benefit of being enslaved to one's own opinion is the conceit it affords.[58] This sort of scepticism fails to recognize its dependence on the historical weight of its concepts. Thus Hegel criticizes Kant's position that we can become mature *on our own*, by implication, as radical individuals.

I agree with Hegel that all our knowledge is passed on by a social world that nurtures us. What is transmitted is crystallized in our concepts. It is precisely this historic crystallization that educative experience must contemplate. We may think about the concepts we are given, but we remain dependent on a social world for them. To think beyond what we have been given requires an exercise of the will. To exercise will, we continue to need others to converse with about what we are thinking and wanting to do; and we must come to recognize the responsibility for actions that we take because they affect other people's lives.

The concept of voluntarism is vulnerable to habituated scepticism in its desperation to be unconstrained by influences from outside the individual. At the extreme end, fundamentalist thinkers may be driven either by blind obedience and unswerving other-directedness or by unreflective self-domination. Hegel's comment that "one barren assurance . . . is of just as much value as another"[59] can apply here. In essence, fundamentalism is an unrelenting refusal of educative experience. It is mis-educative; it is a dysfunction of the intellect. Fundamentalism is the refusal to let the object of our gaze guide us in our thinking and acting: receiving (real) knowledge from the other is rejected in favor of thinking that we already know everything we need to know about the object. By contrast, the educative aspect of reflecting on consciousness is not a method or approach but simply lets us follow the movement of the object that we are studying[60] without trying to control it according to our predispositions about it. Yet real knowledge makes natural knowledge uncomfortable even in people not given to fundamentalism. Hegel observed that there is even a kind of violence between the two ways of viewing phenomena in which natural knowledge tries to refuse real knowledge and the movement of conceptual shapes characterizing the

[58] *Ibid.*, 14.

[59] G.W.F. Hegel, *Phenomenology of Mind*, trans. J.B. Baillie (New York: Harper Colophon Books, 1967), 135.

[60] *Hegel and Modern Society*, 54.

growth of consciousness. In educative experience, the refusal is overcome whereas in fundamentalism it is sustained.

When we allow experience to move us forward in our thinking and acting, we catch sight of something, a person or a thing; for example, the way someone's mouth is turned up at the corners, and in observing that object, our sighting of it brings the phenomenon into view. In being conscious of, and fully attentive to, the turning up of this person's mouth – in the shape of a smile, for example – we do not just see the person but we sense what the person really is, or at least we observe more of what that person is; we perceive in a new way. Now it is the other's presence that directs our gaze, not our own thoughts or notions about the phenomenon. Our contribution to the process of self-consciousness's examination of the phenomenon is precisely *not* to overlay our observations with our notions and thoughts about the phenomenon but to let the other person's mouth speak for itself.

Both real and natural knowledge play an important and enduring role in dialogue, but natural knowledge must let go of its certainty – which is what seems impossible to the fundamentalist thinker. In willing, which is future-oriented and action-focused, we let go of our certainty about the current shape for a concept. We need to put trust in something other than the comfort of our current ideas in order to make this move. In willing, learners move toward the future, motivated by real knowledge of the concepts of faith and by letting go of what appears to be certain but what is actually incomplete. Our incomplete concept of what God is doing during periods of painful struggle is one example. As we observe our own consciousness, we put trust not in the knowledge we possess but in the activity of being present to God and in God's willingness and generosity in being present to us.

In the activity of willing, we also put our faith in hope for the future. We learn to try; trying is learning. The way we experience the activity of willing is to pay attention to what we want and to try to achieve it. Teachers are crucial in the activity of willing when they let learners sense what they want to do. Teachers encourage trying: the teacher's role is to show them that it is attractive to be saved by Christ and to show them what it is possible to try once Christ dwells within. To engage the will is to make claims on our future possibilities. In this way, educating the will is related to the possibility of hope. In allowing willing (the future) to give shape to thinking (the past), we realize the aim of experience.

In educating the will, moralizing tones of voice, facial expressions, gestures, and texts are disastrous. The teacher learns through trying how to attract learners to Christ, particularly by paying attention to the learners themselves, and certainly not through moralizing discourse. The teacher draws the learner into the presence of Christ who is the lover of our souls. In drawing the learner forward hopefully, doubt, fear, and failure are accepted as inevitable aspects both of trying new projects and of letting go of old ideas in order to gain new ones. For these reasons trust in the teaching/learning relation is an essential component of educating Christians.

Through experience, willing and trying take us forward to new realizations. On Hegel's view, experience differs from doubt as understood by Descartes. In doubt we have thought X (my friend is worthy of my trust) and in our activity of doubting we fully consider not X (my friend is not worthy of my trust) to be the case. After we reflect on not X, we doubt our doubt (we mistrust our mistrust of our friend) and return to X (my friend is worthy of my trust). When doubt ends, things are much the same as they were before. In experience, on the other hand, as we pay attention to X, our consciousness of X shifts and changes shape. The direction of the change arises from the nature of X, as it really is, rather than from our need to return to what is comfortable. The new shape of X annihilates the old shape of X so that the old shape for X dies in us and a new shape takes its place. We now have a new shape for consciousness to consider.

It may be that our first awareness of the movement of shapes comes through seeing an old concept die.[61] This realization can cause us pain. That is, I may think my friend is trustworthy because she always meets me at the precise time we agree upon. I trust her because she never fails to show up. Trust rests on never having been let down. If she does not come one day, I become attentive to her not coming and to the relationship between the conceptual shape I have for trust and to her not being where I expected to find her. In dialogue I may come to see that she has a complex life, so do I, and that trusting her does not mean never being let down. It means something more: it signifies confidence that has more hope than certainty in it. Disappointment makes trust wise. But I risk pain and

---

[61] I am thinking here of Nietzsche's well-known announcement that God is dead or Michel Foucault's announcement that man is dead, which he makes in the last line of *The Order of Things* (New York: Vintage Books, 1973).

loss in the process, and I cannot look forward to a comfortable place to which I may return. I cannot go home to my old concept of trust, but neither is the new one entirely strange and without any relationship to the old one.

Through experience, neither trust nor mistrust are lost entirely. What is lost is my inadequate view of trust. Yet a new shape for it emerges through the reconciliation. Experience is not destructive in the end, but it is imperative that I sense what I currently feel and think about trust in order to liberate my inadequate conception of it. It is in the presence of mistrust that I can do this, just as it is in the presence of a Catholic friend that my Protestantism shows up more clearly for what it is. Experience requires the Other. If experience is to be educative, I must be able to dialogue with those who differ from me, in order to see myself as I am.[62] In this way, experience does not annihilate personal identity or the identity of my faith tradition, but neither do these identities merely continue the same in my understanding of them. The direction of change is shaped by remaining focused on the aim of Christian education, which is to become like Christ. The trajectory of change is shaped by that end. It is because of the relationship between personal identity and the movement of thought through experience that transmissionist aims for Christian education retain their significant place in transformative education. We pass on a tradition to be processed by the movement of thought in young Christians by telling them the whole story of Christian faith and practice, so that they can reflect on what we transmit in light of their experience and be transformed into the likeness of Christ.

Conclusion

Educative church experience is a process of reaching forward, reaching and arriving somewhere new; it is not so much the accumulation of knowledge but a mode of being fully present to the inevitable failures that make up the stuff of ordinary Christian lives.[63] Educative church experience is not achieved by getting the right curriculum. It requires us

---

[62] The problem educationally is not whether to encounter those who are different, or Other, from me, but when to do so. If I am too young and unstable in my identity, will I merely be confused by our differences? On the other hand, do we give children enough credit for being able to be empathetic and complex in their thinking?

[63] *Concept of Experience*, 119.

to use the Biblical text in light of our need to address the surprises that come through our life together. Being a reasonable and willing member of Christian community implies a developing willingness and ability for the social[64] and personal growth of consciousness as opposed to individualistic and dogmatic attachment to settled shapes for concepts.

The concept of voluntarism should no longer couple with power as the willingness and ability to get our own way in spite of resistance from others. If Christians are to be reasonable and willing members of the church, they need to develop a capacity for experiencing the phenomena of church life so as to move past empty and unjust practices and press forward toward the fullness of Christ. In order to be educated for the next century, we need to recognize what is personal and what is social in spiritual growth.

---

[64] Growth of self-consciousness is social, as far as Hegel is concerned, because consciousness has three notable features: it proceeds through increasingly adequate stages (i.e., it 'grows') and it is dependent on the social world for the maturation of this growth potential; it is essentially interpersonal and requires the reciprocal recognition of self-conscious beings (an I that is a we; a we that is an I); it is practical and cognitive: self-consciousness exists in a world of alien others and finds itself in those others. The other is essential to consciousness. To Hegel, this implies the establishment and operation of social institutions as well as scientific and philosophical inquiry. *Hegel Dictionary*, 62-63.

10

The Voluntary Church
in the Twenty-first Century

James W. McClendon, Jr.

I

I grew into Christian faith in what many would call a "voluntary" church. This was the old original Baptist church in Shreveport, Louisiana, a city that displayed many of the woes and joys of the American South. There I was baptized in the years between two World Wars. Certainly we young Christians in that church were taught to value liberty: we were told that Baptists had played a major part in gaining religious liberty in the American nation and elsewhere; we saw for ourselves that our own church membership was freely chosen, not something pre-arranged for us by our parents or by any others; we were taught, also, that we had an obligation to defend others' liberty of worship or of abstinence from it. We were free to be Baptists; they were free not to be, free even to be Methodists or whatever else they would. Later I would learn that our liberty and that of our neighbours was not quite so absolute as it had seemed; yet in those early years it was like the truth of the Bible itself, unquestionable – indeed, it was the truth of the Bible itself: did not John 8:32, King James Version, say "And ye shall know the truth, and the truth shall make you *free*"?

Even there, though, the voluntariness of a voluntary church had limits. No one in Shreveport supposed that a group of us, or even a church full of us, could do as we liked in all cases. "Voluntary" didn't mean that someone who wasn't a member in good standing could barge in and vote in church business meeting. "Liberty" didn't mean that whoever was preparing the Lord's supper could fill those little glasses we drank from with wine from the liquor store instead of using the customary grape juice from the grocery store. In fact, someone made that experiment once at our church, and the consequences were not at all happy! We were committed to voluntarism, but that was only one among several commitments as strong or stronger.

James Wm. McClendon, Jr. is Distinguished Scholar in Residence at Fuller Theological Seminary in Pasadena, California.

Still that boyhood church seems remarkable to me. I have described only a fragment of its common life, which was far richer than I have said. Partly this was because of the worship: our pastor, M.E. Dodd, had a truly catholic gift for worship. He brought to our services a sense of the holy; he brought a way with words that drew on the riches of King James English and expanded it with his plain Tennessee eloquence; he knew how to draw our large congregation into one body of wonder, prayer, and praise. All this took place in a lovely domed worship space that modestly echoed Saint Sophia of antiquity.

Partly, too, our church life was richer because everybody then learned the Bible: we Baptists (and Methodists and Presbyterians, too) could quote it even if many lacked the skill to locate the chapter and verse of their quotations. Our church was richer, too, because we shared a pervasive sacramental life, though we did not call it that: the rites of baptism and Lord's supper were observed in such a way that at least one Louisiana youth would never be able to forget whose child he was. Moreover, our religion was richer because it was strongly related to Shreveport politics and government and culture: when there was a question of government that would be fair to all people, or a question of saloons that threatened the health and livelihood of the city's weaker members, or a question of a college that would provide education for young women, we knew in each case the side our church would be on. In summary, our church in its time and place was broad gauge. It was strongly evangelistic; it was persistently educational; it was richly sacramental; it composed a seamless whole. When I learned there to defend the voluntary church, I was learning the rationale for churches that were in a certain sense "catholic."

But were our churches voluntary? Certainly so, if that meant we consented to be the Christians that we were. In that sense, though, the membership of every church in our town, every church in North America, was and remains voluntary. No tax supports a state church; no law constitutes us Lutherans or Buddhists or Catholics or Baptists. In North America those old battles had long ago been fought and won. If that is all "voluntary" means, it has no present use and we can turn to other matters. Contrariwise, if by "voluntary" any mean to deny the influence of others' lives upon their own, that is simply mistaken: I owe what I now am, including my so-called "free" choices, to a variety of influences and conditionings that make me so; beneath all these influences, as I believe, are the everlasting arms of divine election and divine providence. Our spiritual ancestors were not stupid folk; they did not use such high and holy words as "voluntary church" lightly and unadvisedly; we must take care to see what they meant if we are to mean anything useful by such words now.

Earlier in our century, theologian Harris Franklin Rall, in search of a way to characterize Methodists, contrasted "gathered church" and "given church." In eighteenth-century England the given church was the existing, institutional Church of England spread in its parishes across the land; the gathered church was the class meetings and open air exercises of the Wesleys and their followers. Harvard historian George Williams, in a 1991 essay, agreed with Rall that the gathered-given distinction might be used to analyze not only eighteenth-century England but other ecclesial situations. For the Radical Reformers the given church either was Roman Catholic or was the new state churches of the Magisterial Reformers; in each case the radicals found the given church deficient and their response was gathered churches called Anabaptist, communities that were in the words of Walter Klaassen "neither Catholic nor Protestant." Williams found still other uses of "given" and "gathered." Over against the Old Roman church of late medieval times stood the magisterial churches themselves; Lutherans and Reformed were "gathered" from the "given" Roman church. The church of Pentecost, on this way of reckoning, was both given and gathered: as constituting a new divine beginning, it was God's gift, the given church; yet it was a community gathered from Israel and from the existing nations with their many tongues and many myths.

One of the advantages of this given-gathered classification is its flexibility. While Ernst Troeltsch's well-known typology seems to make the church type forever church, leaving the Anabaptists forever a sect, the given-gathered scheme allows what had been the gathered church in one era to become the given church of another. The radical people called Methodists, forming a gathered church in eighteenth-century England, found themselves in mid-twentieth century America worshipping in stately urban edifices, though often, by this century's end, those same buildings were barely a tenth filled on Sunday morning, replicating the deserted architectural monuments of the English church: gathered church had become given church once more. The same was true of the radical Baptists of New England and the South: these dissenters who had forsaken the stately meeting halls of colonial America to gather elsewhere for hot revival preaching and soul-shaking song now often find themselves lonely in their neo-classical piles. For these folk "gathered" has become "given," while the new Christian phenomena may be charismatic churches or house-churches or still other movements.

So the gathered-given terminology, by its flexibility, has an advantage, but such changing labels are a disadvantage as well: if the teams will not keep their own names, how can their fans remain loyal? If we are committed to a gathered church, does it cease to deserve our loyalty because its mansions are now more stately? Am I not a baptist because I do not worship in a brush arbour? I do believe the term "gathered church" bears an ongoing witness: its passive verb form declares that it is not we who gather but God who gathers us: the church is called out before it can call others; it is gathered before it witnesses to God on earth.

Such considerations apply to the concept of the voluntary church as well. Like the term "gathered," "voluntary" was a word employed by those for whom the existing or given structures had failed. Such dissenters turned deliberately (that is, voluntarily) to more faithful ways, building communities that could fulfil the Great Commission, fellowships to stand clear of the state and its authority, assemblies that read the Bible with opened eyes, obeyed biblical commands, and practised gospel solidarity with other believers. Their freedom was not a good or goal in itself or in isolation from the gospel; freedom was exactly a part of that good news. Such revolutionary changes have recurred repeatedly in Christian history, and what is meant by "voluntary" must be determined case by case:

> *Swiss Brethren* forsook control of Christianity by their state government: they volunteered to convene churches not authorized by the city council and voluntarily became missionaries to their district and their world.

> *Hutterites or Hutterian Brethren* turned away from the capitalism and attendant militarism they saw overtaking Europe: they volunteered to experiment with collective ownership unprotected by any sword.

> At *Schleitheim* radical believers abandoned previous attempts to go it alone and voluntarily formed a unity sealed in the atoning blood of Christ (their motif was *Vereinigung*, at-one-ment): they pledged a distinct way of living that

included daily home Scripture reading and a weekly Lord's supper.

Waldshut, a town in South Germany, led by its parish priest Balthasar Hubmaier, gave up a corrupt clerical religion: following their pastor they volunteered a new pattern of life and thought summarized in his "Eighteen Theses."

Terrible experience of government by militant saints (at *Münster*) led many North German and Dutch baptists to renounce the use of force: led by a genius elder named Menno these Dutch radicals voluntarily formed communities of such peaceable stability that they have survived to this hour.

Meantime, radical Christians in England and newfound America shared similar renunciations and volunteered similar experimental communities of life and faith, giving rise to people subsequently called Baptists.

More broadly all the above were called "anabaptists" or "baptists," for in the course of nearly three centuries, the fifteenth through the seventeenth, most of them had turned back to believers' baptism. They had recovered the primitive incorporative act, deliberate on the part of candidate and community alike. As a practice, it fit them well, because like the risky life of faith that followed, baptism required the wholehearted (and once immersion was re-instituted, the whole-bodied) participation of each.

Then came the early seventeenth century, and here a great rift, unnoticed by some surveys, makes our baptist story less smooth, less uniform. (I use the word "baptist," small b, of all those lately called "believers church.") Until the early 1600s, the term "voluntary," like "gathered," flags several episodes in the radical history, though it has different work to do in different cases. Now we need to pay attention to a change in the intellectual and social weather in which all Western Christians made their way. This rift appeared in the Enlightenment and it is with us to this day. It brought with it (1) a new sense of the human self, called *individualism*, (2) a new, science-oriented way of construing human speech that *segregated religious utterance* from representative language, and (3) a new way of struggling with doubt about much that we know, called *foundationalism*. Here some care with words is required. If with historians we call this cluster of mental habits "modernity," we must not confuse it with the religious term "modernism," which was only one form that modernity took. In course of time, as we will see, modernity also took shape as fundamentalism.

The impact of the new way of thinking is illustrated by the struggle over the human will that occurred in the churches that formed the (big-B) Baptist denominations. What chiefly distinguished the two main sorts of English Baptists (each with strong Dutch connections) had to do with the freedom of the unregenerate human will. The Baptist Confession of 1611, drafted in twenty articles by John Smyth, denied any "sin of origin or descent" because all sin is "actual or voluntary," and it affirmed that "men of the grace of God are able . . . to repent," while alternatively they are able to resist the Holy Spirit. A generation later (1644) the London Confession of the Particular Baptists affirmed contrariwise that "all since the Fall are conceived in sinne, and brought forth in iniquitie" (Art. IV) and that "Faith is the gift of God wrought in the hearts of the elect by the Spirit of God" (Art. XXII), yet omitted even the least mention of human ability (Lumpkin, 1969:157-63). This difference was explicit. Similar struggles were occurring in other Christian camps: The Synod of Dort (1619) had already rejected the attempt of the Arminian Dutch Reformed to take the path the General Baptists were to follow. These struggles are still with us: what needs to be seen is that they arose in new cultural weather, in a modernity that gave such conflicts a definitive role they had not had in earlier baptist centuries.

Much that is thought and said about the "voluntary" church in the centuries following (say from 1650 onwards) is thought out and argued in this new climate. These new thoughts are worked out by new men (for they conceived their human nature differently), they are declared in a new language (for the very grammar of religious utterance had changed), and they are argued or proposed with a new dread, the terror of uncertainty (for the era of *philosophical* foundations had arrived). The old labels, Baptist, Mennonite, Brethren, and the like, continued in use, but now they were applied to a people divided on two sides of a crevice that was shaken open by these wider climatic changes. It was as though modernity was an earthquake rumbling across the world and opening vast fissures in earth's soil, so that some baptists found themselves on one side of that fissure, some on the other, though both sides endured the same modernity.

The chief areas in which the differences appeared were the freedom of the will (already mentioned) and the nature of Scripture. The former difference issued in the continuing struggle over Calvinism within the evangelical spectrum; the battle over the Bible would issue in the fundamentalist-modernist controversy. Neither side of either battle, I have claimed in *Ethics* and again in *Doctrine*, could do full justice to baptist convictions; neither side could express the original vision that had made the old brethren (to use their own word) brethren, neither side in these battles was in good position to make the believers church the believers church. Baptists (large or small "b") might by the grace of God survive the modern era that has run from 1650 to our own time, but only with great difficulty could they be baptists in it.

II

This long unsuitability of the present age to baptist (or biblical) existence is central to what I have to say, but here I give only three concrete examples of the difficulties our predecessors faced, leaving a full exposition to another time and place. My first example comes from John Leland (1754-1841), a Virginia Baptist preacher. For Leland, liberty, the realm of the voluntary, could be argued in Jeffersonian fashion by appealing to self-evident principles. Just as Jefferson had written in the draft constitution of 1776 that "We hold these truths to be self evident . . . that all men . . . are endowed by their creator with inherent and inalienable rights" (in Wills, 1978:374), Jefferson's political ally John Leland proclaimed church freedom in a 1791 title, *The Rights of Conscience Inalienable.* Leland put this philosophically fragile claim of inalienable rights forth in the first instance not as essential biblical teaching (which of course it was not) but as an apologetic argument for freedom for non-established churches in the new United States. Yet what began as external apology inevitably became, in the minds of many Christians, doctrine proper and timeless; they could no longer distinguish apology from Christian teaching. Thus E.Y. Mullins's 1908 book, *The Axioms of*

Religion (1908), took up the Leland line again, arguing that Baptist principles were simply self-evident and American.[1]

Someone may say that it hardly matters whether baptist truth is discovered in the pages of Scripture or looked up in a philosopher's table of self-evident axioms, but it matters a good deal both to Christian doctrine and to those who must construe the law of the land. For example, an appeal to the rights of the individual conscience (Leland's appeal) provides no adequate defense of the liberty of pacifist Mennonites or Hutterites who mean to live on the land in a community free from military conscription; by individualizing the claim of the kingdom of Christ, these axiomizers unwittingly diminished it.

This points the way to my second example, drawn from the modernist-fundamentalist struggle in Canadian life earlier in the twentieth century. Rather than embarrass any living survivors of this battle, I call to mind two names from the past: T. T. Shields and D. C. Macintosh. Thomas Todhunter Shields (1873-1955) was for many years the highly gifted pastor of Jarvis Street Baptist Church in Toronto. Self-taught, exact, and eloquent, Shields is well remembered for his vigorous (and divisive) attacks on McMaster University, the predecessor of the present College, which he believed had not stayed true to the faith of its founders. His leadership in the Baptist denomination opened rifts that in some cases remain unhealed to the present day. Representing his fundamentalist position as the faith once delivered to the saints, Shields placed ultimate reliance on the infallibility of Scripture (later partisans would call it biblical inerrancy), and he related the remainder of his theological convictions to this one. Thus he defended the truth of the Bible (and his own doctrinal preaching) on ground that was itself neither biblical nor self-evident, namely the theory of infallibility. By it he found he could validate his teaching in a satisfactorily modern fashion.

Mark Parent has shown that the English-born Shields came quite late in his ministry to this distinctive (and divisive) view of the nature of

---

[1] When I was a young seminary professor, I thought Mullins's axioms were self-evident to any reasonable mind. Then one fine Berkeley day I mentioned Mullins's title, *Axioms of Religion,* to a lawyer acquaintance, an intelligent non-Christian man of Hispanic descent. He asked to see the Mullins book; I lent him my copy but was surprised to have him return it shortly. What seemed to me, birthed by the church and nurtured on the Bible, to be self-evident seemed to this intelligent atheist mere unproven claims.

Scripture. It was the person and work of Jesus Christ that had founded Shields's early theology, and not until after the First World War did he begin to change. Earlier he had declared that the Bible is not to be regarded as a textbook of science, but is "solely a textbook treating of sin and salvation." Typology, not biblical literalism, had dominated Shields's early reading of the Old Testament. By 1922, however, he had begun the course that shaped the rest of his career. Now for him the first principle was the inspiration and authority of the Scriptures, and it was only in the second instance that there came an insistence upon the essential deity of Jesus. One cannot help but wonder if the militancy Shields had brought to making war on the Germans in 1914 had later turned into defeating German literary and biblical scholarship. In any case, as Shields preached in 1930, the Bible "could not be more utterly unlike every other book had it literally dropped from the skies." In the end, Shields's broad evangelicalism narrowed itself to his preferred foundation, inerrancy, so that the talents of this eloquent preacher and Baptist leader were used only to support an ever-shrinking constituency of withdrawn fundamentalists.

Contrast with this the thought of Douglas Clyde Macintosh (1877-1948). Born in Ontario, Macintosh was savingly converted as an adolescent (as he would later say, he made the "right religious adjustment" to God). After graduating and teaching for a time at McMaster University in Toronto, he went to Chicago in its liberal heyday to earn a Ph.D. In 1909 he was called to Yale Divinity School, where he served out his long career as professor of systematic theology. Macintosh as a Baptist was strongly attached to the Bible, but his ultimate line of theological defense was not scriptural infallibility, which he rejected, but the religious experience of each individual faithful believer who made what Macintosh called a "right religious adjustment" to the experiences of sin and grace. Thus he invoked what he considered a scientific criterion, an indefinitely repeatable empirical experiment, to validate the truth of Christianity in a modern or foundational fashion. In his case, philosophical training and interest led him early to grasp the foundation (which for him was experience), and then gradually to widen it, recovering more of the evangelical faith of his childhood. Toward the end of his life Macintosh set out to write a three-volume theological work that would deal in successive volumes with social religion (1939), personal religion (1942), and finally a summary theology that would encompass both. Regrettably, the third volume never appeared.

In each case the foundation satisfactory to one side was refused by the other, even though both sides shared many believers church practices. Their strategies were each based on the intellectual culture of their day, which demanded a supposedly self-evident epistemic foundation; in this regard they were indistinguishable.[2]

This reflection on Canadian theological conflict and its causes may introduce my third example, the more recent and equally bitter conflict in the Southern Baptist Convention in the last half-century. Prior to the battle, as sociologist Nancy Ammerman has shown, most Southern Baptists did not explicitly belong to either of the camps later labelled moderate-liberal and fundamentalist-conservative. Then in the early 1980s a fundamentalist minority set out to capture the machinery of the denomination's convention, using both persuasion and other tactics. The ensuing battle forced the majority in the middle ground to take sides, and in the end the fundamentalists had gained political control of the Southern Baptist Convention with its vast bureaucracy of publications, mission funds, service organizations, and social action agencies. Noteworthy in this complex and dark struggle is the appeal the winners made to biblical inerrancy. The beauty of inerrancy was not that it offered hermeneutical guidelines but that it made Scripture a *foundation* for knowledge–the very sort of foundation that the modern period demanded of its reasoning as earlier times had not. Ammerman, after describing the fundamentalist victory, writes that "While 'modernity' might be the long term victor in the [American] culture, this institutional segment of the culture [the Southern Baptist Convention] had been reclaimed by a fundamentalist movement." Her judgment, though, needs correction at this point. The fundamentalist movement *is* a modern movement; it is a *part of modernity*, so that its victory reflects modernity's triumph even more than a moderate outcome could have done.

The Southern Baptist Alliance, an organization formed to resist the fundamentalist capture of the Southern Baptist Convention, in 1987 issued a declaration of principles or "Covenant" (for it was a time, they declared, "when historic Baptist principles, freedoms, and traditions need a clear voice"). The first two elements of this new Covenant were commitment to the freedom of the individual and the freedom of the local church. Once

[2] See Nancey Murphy, *Beyond Liberalism and Fundamentalism* (1996).

again in this third example, foundational principles, in this case freedom and the voluntary church, were being invoked in protest by believers church people who faced a new given "church," the newly captured Southern Baptist Convention.

III

Yet some felt that this invocation of traditional principles by the Southern Baptist Alliance and others failed to confront the deeper difficulties. Thus, some young Baptist scholars in the southern United States drafted a declaration, "Re-Envisioning Baptist Identity: A Manifesto for Baptist Communities in North America." It warned against "two mistaken paths" that imperiled Baptist life. Plainly the paths were those of the now hardened opponents in the late Southern Baptist controversy: those who would "shackle God's freedom to a narrow biblical interpretation," opposed by those who would "sever freedom from . . . the community's legitimate authority." In effect, the document said the politics of separation had failed to settle the deeper issues, said that the two sides were alike mistaken, and called on both to recognize and renounce the underlying "idolatry" that had made their war possible.

I want to consider that document briefly, for it moves away from the kind of modernity that has kept all kinds of baptists from their true business. The theological battles over (1) human nature and its freedom and (2) over the Bible and its divine and human status were predestined by the Zeitgeist. This battleground was staked out by modernity itself, and if modernity is ending we may soon be able to hear one another speaking in authentic baptist voices again.[3]

Two pervasive features distinguish this "baptifesto": Its New Testament saturation, together with (less frequent) allusions to the oldest baptists and to the Old Testament, give "Re-Envisioning" some shelter from the heavy weather of modernity (it escapes the triple alternatives of foundationalism or scepticism, of biblical literalism or private

---

[3] I acknowledge that I am listed as one of the dispatchers of this declaration. Yet I am not its author; my main role has been to write books that the authors say gave them some guidance. Consequently what I say here is my independent criticism, some positive, some negative, of this arresting statement.

interpretation, of social individualism or social collectivism). It claims each of these alternatives is idolatrous; hence like stone idols each is a dead alternative. Its theme is free-church liberty. This freedom requires an exodus; once again the voluntary church must say no to the assumptions of the day. The way into the future requires burying the idols and leaving the grave site.

"Re-Envisioning" offers four affirmations, each introduced by an italicized slogan explained in the paragraphs that follow. These slogans have evoked more reader resistance than any other part of the document. They mean to challenge the reader's complacency, mean to startle minds, not settle them. In one draft version the four affirm:

1. *Bible study* in *reading communities* rather than private interpretation or supposed "scientific" objectivity.

2. *Gospel witness* as the call to *shared discipleship* rather than invoking a theory of competent souls.

3. *A free common life in Christ* in *gathered, reforming communities* rather than withdrawn, self-chosen, or authoritarian ones.

4. *Liberty without coercion as a distinct people under God* rather than relying on political theories, principalities, or powers.

Each motto names a standard baptist practice. Each motto then takes a cue from the New Testament and earliest baptist life to re-envision that practice. Modern approaches both left and right wing that deny these are set aside.

These four practices have persisted for baptists through good days and bad, through pre-modernity and modernity alike. The four are shared Bible study (we are a people of one book), an evangelism that summons into a new shared life, an understanding of church as divine fellowship, and a counter-cultural, counter-political church. (Between the time of the address here recorded and the publication of "Re-Envisioning" in *Baptists Today* [June 1997], a fifth, the practice of baptism, preaching, and the Lord's table was inserted.) These practices have been supported by all baptist sides throughout the modern period, yet no side could adequately protect this heritage. One wing could not practice Bible reading freely because it had adopted a modern theory of inerrancy; another wing could not practice it freely because it had adopted a modern device called private interpretation. One sort of baptist could not practice evangelism freely because they believed outsiders had no free will; the other sort could not practice evangelism effectively because they reckoned outsiders had inviolate rights of privacy. One wing failed to realize Christian community because it was individualist; the other failed to do so because it was collectivist. One wing could not practice the politics of Jesus because it had succumbed to deism; the other could not practice the politics of Jesus without offending individualism. I do not suppose that the authors of "Re-Envisioning Baptist Identity" have overcome all these difficulties at a stroke, but I believe they point a hopeful way for the voluntary church. It is a way, as their title suggests, that will require some re-thinking, some re-envisioning.

In particular, biblical *Bible study* is related to what some have called the Rule of Paul: the claim of 1 Corinthians 14 that when believers meet, each brings a contribution (cf. Yoder, 1984:22; 1987). These contributions will not be identical, will not be in the same tone of voice, will not come from the same authoritative commentaries. Harmony comes not from ministerial authority but comes when at the Spirit's behest contributors aim to build up the church (1 Cor. 14:26-29). As the "baptifesto" puts it, "When all exercise their gifts and callings, when every voice is heard and weighed, when no one is silenced or privileged, the Spirit leads communities to read wisely and to practice faithfully the direction of the gospel."

Next, the biblical *priesthood of all believers* grows from practising the way of Jesus: it is not that each of us makes his or her way to God independent of all the rest of us; rather such priesthood means we are members one of another in Christ. "Re-Envisioning" puts it positively (we are priests one to another, confessing faith and fault to each other in the church) and then adds a negative: "We reject all accounts of freedom that construe faith as a private matter between God and the individual or as an activity of competent souls who inherently enjoy unmediated, unassailable, and disembodied experience with God." It rejects "identifications of the priesthood of believers with autonomous individualism."

The biblical *practice of church* as lives bound together is undergirded in this document by the practices (not the mere doctrines) of believer's baptism and called-out church membership. Granted, the baptifesto challenges those who seem to lack these practices (will they consider acquiring them?), but before that it challenges any who too confidently think they already have these practices. Thus baptists must "close off nominal Christianity in their own ranks. [The baptifesto] is only second a gesture toward other traditions and communities to the end that they might make disciples of those whom they baptize."

This declaration has most trouble, I think, in saying what it intends about church and state in Western society. It yearns to show that there is a *kind of liberty* that, just because it follows Jesus, cannot be content with modern church states and state churches. Nor can followers of the crucified be content with current Western institutions such as the culture-church as a social bulwark or civil religion as the state's underlying myth. It wants to say all this clearly, forcefully, and biblically, wants at the same time to affirm the obligation to support others' freedoms as well as our own, yet it has not easily reduced these to the brief space of two columns. I am glad for what it says: "The disestablishment of the church is constitutive of its identity as God's called-out community which foreshadows the coming reign of God as does no other community." Yet I wish (for example) it might have been more explicit about the peacemaking task of Christ's church.

IV

If "come out from among them" is thus always the path of the voluntary church, if we always say no to some given ecclesial home in order to say yes to a gathered church, will the voluntary church not repeatedly fall into heresy and schism? What is to keep such a fluid and evolving movement oriented to the wholeness of Christian faith? Protestants have their *sola gratia* and Catholics their *magisterium*; what have we radicals to keep us integral and true? Is the call to radical protest a call to isolation and to *Schwärmerei*, fanaticism? For answer, consider Ephesians 4:1-16, that I believe points to our Christian future. This paragraph speaks of the unity of the church, and indeed of the great confessional unities that Ephesians says should bind all together: one body, one Spirit, one hope, one Lord, one faith, one baptism. It concludes with appeal for growth "completely into Christ, who is the head" (4:15 New Jerusalem Bible). Yet I will approach this paragraph neither from its beginning or its end. Rather I begin with a famous but hard-to-translate verse in the centre: 4:13. In the New Jerusalem Bible this reads:

> until we all reach unity in faith and knowledge of the Son of God and form the perfect Man, fully mature with the fullness of Christ himself.

Here "perfect Man" – I might have wished to translate it "perfectly human One" – is the striking word. It is even an offensive term to the New Revised Standard Version translators, who when they reach the Greek word *andra* do not translate it at all (they simply skip it, for they recognize that *aner* is not *anthropos*, not man in the generic sense, human being: what stands in Ephesians is the distinctively male Greek word)! Embarrassed by this, the NRSV folk passed over it in silence. Yet I think the New Jerusalem Bible misleads us as well, for it lets us believe this "perfect Man" is only God's holy people. Then why the singular? What a translator's puzzle!

Markus Barth, in the Anchor Bible commentary on Ephesians, argues for a reading quite different from all these (1974:II, 484-96). The main verb in the verse, he points out, is "come" or "reach"– the Greek is a form of *katantao*, meaning to arrive at a given point, or sometimes "to meet a person." In every use of this verb, Barth writes, "movement is presupposed" (485). But who or what makes a journey to encounter a *perfect male human being*? In answer, he suggests two images from the ancient world. The first envisions "a festival procession that is under way in solemn fashion for a solemn purpose. Those partaking in the cortege go out to meet a very important [traveller, who will bring] them bliss, joy, security, and peace." Such a procession might, for example, go out to receive a king who was approaching a city. Psalm 68, just quoted in Ephesians, describes such a royal procession. There is also another possibility: it might be a bridal party that goes outside the walls to meet the approaching bridegroom. Both sorts of solemn march were social customs in Paul's day, and both would be familiar to the first readers of Ephesians. Barth tells us we need not choose between them, since in Psalm 45, and again in the Song of Songs, and also in the rites of many ancient cultures as well, the two sorts of procession, marital and political, were combined into one. He adds that the movement of the procession toward the Expected One was matched by the Expected One's own approach to the procession and the city. Then he reminds readers that

> the "coming of the Lord" is fundamental to the life, faith, confession, worship of the [early] church. The saints pray, *"maranatha,* [our] Lord, come!" (1 Cor 16:22; Rev 22:20). The hoped-for coming of Jesus Christ is usually called his "parousia" (1 Thess 4:15-17; Matt 24:27, etc.). (486f.)

Here, in brief, is the direction of the believers church in the "coming" century—indeed, its true or proper direction in any century from first Advent to last Advent. We are to move together toward the full knowledge of the *huios tou theou,* the Son of God—so says Ephesians 4:13. When that last, full meeting comes, and only then, will our goal be reached. But all is not then ended, for as Markus Barth points out,

> [J]ust as a king or bridegroom, by his advent and through his meeting with those expecting him, fulfils the hope and changes the status of many, so according to Ephesians 4:13 does the Son of God, the Perfect Man, the Messiah. He makes his people participants in his perfection and riches. All that is his becomes theirs. The transformation of the many, effected by the meeting with [this unique] Man, is in this case distinct from a gradual improvement. It resembles a sudden change comparable to the effect of forgiveness and sanctification (487).

Paul in Romans calls this still-awaited "sudden effect" glorification. When that comes, the assets of the Coming One will be bestowed upon the citizens or upon the bride, so that (in the language of Ephesians) the Messiah himself is perfected by incorporating his people into himself, one Christ. Thus the New Jerusalem Bible and the New Revised Standard Version are not all wrong, though their translations are deficient, for finally what each translation proclaims will also come true—they have simply jumped ahead of the writer to Ephesians!

In just what, one might wish to ask, is that great and sudden change in the people of God to consist? Ephesians has already answered. For 4:13

serves as the centre, the fulcrum, by which we may understand the entire passage, 4:1-16. What the apostle urges in the verses before and after it discloses the changes already under way in the lives of those who join the cortege and move outside the city walls to meet their coming Prince. None of these ongoing changes is independent of the Coming One's presence and his help: he whom we are to meet is quietly, as if incognito, already present in our midst. Let me briefly list these expected changes as Markus Barth (with Ephesians) presents them.

First, there is *the binding character of Christian ethics*. Israel was set free from bondage in order to observe God's law; not set free to ignore the Ten Words. God's messianic people must now (4:3 Revised English Bible) "make fast with bonds of peace the unity which the Spirit gives." So the theme of unity, which runs through Ephesians, is linked here with other still-to-be-realized Christian themes. It is linked to peace, so little acknowledged till now save by a few radical Christian communities; it is linked to the acknowledgement of the Spirit which is being recovered by Pentecostals for us all; it is linked to bondage or servanthood, namely to the old anabaptist way of the cross. So–if your congregation plans to march to meet the coming One in the solemn procession of verse 13–you must look well *now* to Christian unity, to peacemaking, to Spirit-giftedness, to suffering servanthood.

Next follow the *seven unity themes of Christian doctrine*: one body, Spirit, hope; one Lord, faith, baptism; one Father God "over all and through all and in all" (4:6 REB) Later Christians have seen these seven centred around the holy trinity: God the Spirit, God the Lord or Word, and God the Father. What these verses bring out is that the radical church that marches to meet its Saviour must be a church holding fast the treasure of biblical doctrine: the Bible is a treasure of faith as well as a treasure of practice; the story the Bible tells is God's own story, told as God pleases to tell it.

There follows this seven-fold theme a *doctrine of ministry* suitable for an assembly marching to meet its bridegroom-king. Our Catholic and Protestant forebears quarrelled over orders of ministry–twofold ministry, threefold ministry, and the like. Ephesians knows nothing of this, but it does distinguish two sorts of ministry: an equipping or training ministry functionally divided into *apostles* (who plant churches), *prophets* (who declare God's truth), *evangelists* (who make certain we do not remain an ethnic enclave but share our good news), and *pastor-teachers* (who instruct and guide each flock). Ephesians then places alongside all these a still greater emphasis upon the full ministry of the saints, "God's holy people" equipped by the just-named preparers and trainers (4:12 NJB). For a different audience than this, I would emphasize this apostolic abolition of the "laity," this rejection of supposed Christians who receive without needing to give. I emphasize instead how urgent it is to acknowledge ourselves members of "a church without laymen and priests": no special privilege accrues to us helpers. We are only *servi servorum dei*, servants of the servants of God.

Now to the final three verses of our paragraph, where we meet the *organic doctrine of church* that coheres with this futuristic vision. I will leave these last three verses (4:14-16) unexposed, except to quote the English translation made by Markus Barth:

> 14 No longer are we to be babes, tossed by waves and whirled about by every doctrinal gust, [and caught] in the trickery of men who are experts in deceitful scheming.
> 15 Rather by speaking the truth in love we shall grow in every way toward him who is the head, the Messiah.
> 16 He is at work fitting and joining the whole body together. He provides sustenance to it through every contact according to the needs of each single part. He enables the body to make its own growth so that it builds itself up in love.

Is that the shape of the voluntary church in the century just ahead? After all that has happened in our era – our experiment with modernity, our dominant science, our terrible wars, our broken human compacts, our empty human hearts – are we to turn back in the end to such well-worn words as these that speak of the great coming parousia, back to a passage that points toward an ethics, a doctrine, a practice of ministry, a community preparing for a coming day – the day when, though we know not when, he *comes*? Are we voluntary church folk destined to become part of the cortege or (as we say in our day) to be part of the committee designated to go and meet this Coming One, meet him lest he reach our national walls, reach our ghetto walls of pride and privilege, reach our very soul's walls and find us unready for the Great Day?

References

Ammerman, Nancy Tatom (1990) *Baptist Battles: Social Change and Religious Conflict in the Southern Baptist Convention*. New Brunswick, N.J., and London: Rutgers University Press.

Barth, Markus (1974) *Ephesians*. Volume I, Introduction, Translation, and Commentary on Chapters 1-3; Volume II, Translation and Commentary on Chapters 4-6. The Anchor Bible, vols. 34 and 34A. Garden City, N.Y.: Doubleday.

Ferm, Vergilius, ed. (1932) *Contemporary American Theology: Theological Autobiographies*. Vol. 1. New York: Round Table Press.

James, Robison B., ed. (1987) *The Unfettered Word: Southern Baptists Confront the Authority-Inerrancy Question*. Waco, Tex.: Word Books.

Klaassen, Walter (1981) *Anabaptism: Neither Catholic Nor Protestant*. Revised Edition. Waterloo, Ontario: Conrad Press.

Lumpkin, William L., compiler (1969) *Baptist Confessions of Faith*. 2nd. rev. ed. Philadelphia: Judson Press.

McBeth, H. Leon, ed. (1990) *A Sourcebook for Baptist Heritage*. Nashville: Broadman Press.

McClendon, James Wm., Jr. (1986) *Ethics: Systematic Theology Volume I*. Nashville: Abingdon Press.

_____ (1994) *Doctrine: Systematic Theology Volume II*. Nashville: Abingdon Press.

McClendon, James Wm., Jr. and John Howard Yoder (1990) "Christian Identity in Ecumenical Perspective." *Journal of Ecumenical Studies* 27:3 (Summer).

Macintosh, Douglas Clyde (1919) *Theology as an Empirical Science*. New York: Macmillan. Arno Press ed., 1980.

_____ (1939) *Social Religion*. New York: Charles Scribner's Sons.

_____ (1942) *Personal Religion*. New York: Charles Scribner's Sons.

Mullins, Edgar Young (1908) *The Axioms of Religion*. Philadelphia: American Baptist Publication Society.

Murphy, Nancey and McClendon, James Wm. Jr. (1989) "Distinguishing Modern and Postmodern Theologies." *Modern Theology* 5 (April).

Murphy, Nancey (1996) *Beyond Liberalism and Fundamentalism: How Modern and Postmodern Philosophy Set the Theological Agenda*. Valley Forge, PA: Trinity Press International.

Parent, Mark (1994) "The Irony of Fundamentalism: T.T. Shields and the Person of Christ." *Fides et Historia* 26 (Fall):42-57.

"Re-Envisioning Baptist Identity: A Manifesto for Baptist Communities in North America." Numerous signers. *Baptists Today*, June 1997.

Shurden, Walter B. (1993) *The Baptist Identity: Four Fragile Freedoms*. Macon, Ga.: Smyth & Helwys.

Williams, George Huntston (1991) "The Believers' Church and the Given Church." in *The People of God: Essays on the Believers' Church*., Eds. Paul Basden and David S. Dockery. Nashville: Broadman Press, 325-32.

Wills, Garry (1978) *Inventing America: Jefferson's Declaration of Independence*. New York: Random House.

Yoder, John Howard (1984) *The Priestly Kingdom*. Notre Dame, IN, University of Notre Dame Press.

_____ (1987) *The Fullness of Christ: Paul's Vision of Universal Ministry*. Elgin, IL: Brethren Press.

11

Believers Church Ecclesiology as Ecumenical Challenge

George Vandervelde

1. Believers church tradition as ecclesiological bridge

One of the intriguing features of the believers church tradition lies in the peculiar combination of the two terms in this designation. The first term, "believer," indicates the strong emphasis on the voluntary nature of membership. Nevertheless, in this tradition one of the scenarios of Pharaoh's dreams is not repeated. The lean "believers" do not devour the "church." For, in the voluntary tradition, "church" is not conceived of simply as a secondary result – almost a by-product – of individual decisions for Jesus. This more substantial sense of church is especially important in North America, where in many strands of evangelicalism the church is little more than a "fellowship" in the thin sense. The church becomes a term for the collectivity that results when like-minded Christians gather.

To the extent that the church constitutes a magnitude beyond this local gathering, evangelicals all too frequently reach for the notion of the invisible Church and its unity. At a gathering of the World Evangelical Fellowship in Manila some years ago, a committee of which I am a member submitted a recommendation along these lines: "Evangelicals need to labour more concertedly to manifest the visible unity of the Church." This motion was strongly opposed. "Visible unity," it was claimed, means supporting the quest for unity espoused by the World Council of Churches. Two counter arguments were presented. First, evangelicals would not want to suggest that the World Council of Churches has the monopoly on visible unity.[1] Second, the unity for which Christ prayed

George Vandervelde is professor of systematic theology at the Institute for Christian Studies in Toronto, Ontario.

[1] In fact, the Lausanne Covenant contains this statement, "We affirm that the Church's visible unity (Eph. 4:3,4) in truth is God's purpose (Jn. 17: 21, 23)," which is accompanied by the commitment, "We pledge ourselves to seek a deeper unity in truth, worship, holiness and mission"; see James A. Scherer and Stephen B. Bevans, *New Directions in Mission and Evangelization 1: Basic Statements 1974-1991* (Maryknoll, New York: Orbis, 1992), 256.

could be nothing other than visible unity: " . . . that the world may believe that you have sent me." But such arguments were to no avail. The motion to work for greater visible unity went down to defeat.

Given this North American evangelical tendency towards ecclesiological minimalism, the believers church tradition is ideally positioned to provide a healthful antidote. While sharing the evangelical concern about fully committed believers, the voluntarism in this tradition in no way diminishes the concern for the church as a visible reality, a reality deeper and broader than an aggregate of individuals, an ecclesial whole greater than the sum of its members. One could argue that the accent on "believers" is itself an *ecclesial* concern. The insistence on "believers" is rooted in the concern for the "church," for its unique character as a visibly distinct community. Accordingly, the Dordrecht Confession of 1632 affirms: "We believe in and confess a visible Church of God, consisting of those who . . . have truly repented, and rightly believed; who are rightly baptized, united with God in heaven, and incorporated into the communion of the saints on earth. I Cor. 12:13."[2] More succinctly, Article 8 of the Confession adopted by the Mennonite General Conference in 1963 affirms that the church "is the visible body of those who are Christian disciples."[3]

Voluntarism distinguished the believers church first of all from the state, from its coercive aspects expressed not simply in overt acts of power but in the very basis of the state, namely involuntary inclusion: membership is given by the fact of being born within a specific territory. But the distinctness of the believing community extends beyond its contrast to the state. As the frequent designation "radical reformation" suggests, the believers church distinguishes itself explicitly from the magisterial reformation, especially from the "involuntarism" of pedobaptism. It is in this specific context that I want to discuss voluntarism. I wish to explore the interrelationship of the two primary biblical emphases within the believers church tradition in order to present this tradition as a bridge that could span the chasm that yawns between a minimalist evangelical ecclesiology and a maximalist ecclesiology. By maximalist ecclesiology I mean the sacramental ecclesiology represented

---

[2] John H. Leith, *The Creeds of the Churches* (Garden City, N.Y.: Doubleday, 1963), 299.

[3] *Mennonite Confession of Faith* (Kitchener, Ontario: Herald Press, 1963), 14.

by traditions that play a major role in the ecumenical movement, such as the Orthodox, the Anglican, and the Roman Catholic communions.

Before I elaborate why insights from the believers church tradition are crucial in ecumenical discussion, I need to own up to another tradition that will play a role in this examination – my own. I belong to the Christian Reformed Church, a denomination which has its origins in the Dutch Calvinist tradition. In North America, this denomination situates itself within the conservative evangelical context. In this paper, the Calvinist tradition inevitably affects my analysis. But I proceed from this legacy not as a normative point of departure, but as a tradition that at various points needs the correctives and challenges that the believers church tradition can provide.[4] I will attempt to let the "magisterial" tradition in which I have grown up function as a kind of a heuristic instrument, rather than as a dogmatic given that obtrudes in such a way as to do injustice to the believers church tradition.

I am not certain whether within the believers church tradition I need to adduce arguments to establish the urgency of working for the unity of the church, not only *within* a tradition that is often as sadly divided as my own but simultaneously *beyond* that tradition. In some way, the very origin of the believers church fosters a wariness of the ecumenical quest. The believers church in large measure represents a protest against established and sacramentalist church assumptions. And it is precisely these churches that have played a significant role in the ecumenical movement. At the same time, the restorationist elements of the believers church tradition provide an ecumenical impulse, a vision of the unity of the church in its origins. Of course, this vision's effectiveness is blunted by the assumed prerequisite for unity, namely to be "like us." In this it duplicates the pre-Vatican II call that issued from the Roman Pontiff, namely "Return to Rome." Similarly, the denomination to which I belong at one time operated "ecumenically" from the same assumption: We seek the unity of the church – and it will come about when all churches become like us: Reformed.[5] Yet, in recent believers church literature, voices call

---

[4] Throughout this essay, I have tried to take to heart Richard Mouw's warning against a paternalistic approach that fails to take up the fundamental challenge which the believers church tradition presents; see his introduction to John Howard Yoder, *The Royal Priesthood* (Grand Rapids: Eerdmans, 1994), viii.

[5] See *Acts of Synod, 1944*, Christian Reformed Church, 330-67. A strikingly different approach is evidenced in the later "Ecumenical Charter," *Agenda for Synod 1987*, 170-75 and *Acts of Synod 1987*, 588-90.

for a greater and more generous involvement in the quest for the unity of the Church.[6] The real question is not whether, but how, the believers church tradition can most constructively engage in this quest without betraying its own heritage.

Let me begin by indicating the need for believers church engagement in the ecumenical discussion by briefly reviewing a sample of evangelical engagement. The World Evangelical Fellowship, by means of its Task Force on Ecumenical Issues, provided an official response to the WCC's *Baptism, Eucharist, and Ministry* document.[7] The WEF response takes strong exception to sacramentalism. It circumscribes sacramentalism as the view "that sacraments are efficacious signs, conveying the grace that they contain, and that grace is communicated by virtue of the rite."[8] The critique of sacramentalism is particularly strong with respect to the crucial sacrament of initiation, namely baptism. The WEF document objects to formulations that feature baptism as subject and an active verb as predicate: baptism "unites," "initiates," "gives participation in." While appreciating *BEM*'s attempt to do justice to the call for conversion and faith, the WEF response judges that this call is undermined by "the sacramentalist thrust of the entire document."[9]

It is interesting to compare the WEF response to a more typical believers church response. The General Mennonite Society of the Netherlands also takes exception to *BEM*'s approach to baptism, yet its criticism is positively formulated. The Dutch Mennonite response sets forth its understanding in ecclesial terms; baptism "expresses and records that from then on the person baptized belongs to the congregation and is accounted a 'new creation.'" The Mennonite response clearly distinguishes this human confessional act from the Holy Spirit's recreative act which effects the actual transition to "new creation." Having stated this understanding, the Mennonite response proceeds by claiming the freedom to interpret within its own believers church framework the strong *BEM* statements regarding what baptism is and does.[10]

---

[6] See for example, Max Thurian, ed., *Churches Respond to BEM*, 6 vols. (Geneva: WCC, 1986-1988), III, 289-90.

[7] *Evangelical Review of Theology*, 13 (1989): 291-313.

[8] *Ibid.*, 312.

[9] *Ibid.*, 295-97.

[10] *Churches Respond*, III, 290.

The ecclesiological issues at stake in this discussion come to the fore in some interesting U.S. Roman Catholic-Baptist dialogues.[11] After setting forth some areas of common understanding, the U.S. Roman Catholic-Baptist dialogue pinpoints "Areas That Require Further Study." This heading may be understood as an ecumenical euphemism for "Areas of Disagreement." In any case, the disagreement singled out in the very first sentence comes as no surprise: "There is a marked difference between us on the meaning of the sacraments."[12] The key difference lies "in the very understanding of what the sacraments are, and of their role in the economy of salvation." The dialogue describes this difference as follows:

> In the Catholic tradition, the sacraments are mysteriously effective of the grace which they ritually signify, and in which the faithful have a personal encounter with Christ who confers on them his saving grace. In the Baptist view, the ordinance of baptism is a dramatic emblem to the one baptized of his fellowship in Christ's death and resurrection, and the Lord's Supper is a holy symbol in which bread and wine are used to commemorate together Christ's dying love for mankind. The ordinances do not, however, actually effect or confer the grace which they symbolize."[13]

Later the dialogue understandably connects this difference on sacraments directly with a difference in ecclesiology:

> Catholics view membership [in the church] more as the result of baptism, which explains their practice of baptizing infants. Baptists regard a person's profession of trustful faith and repentance as fundamental to Church affiliation. . . . for them the Church is a gathered community of those who believe in Jesus Christ."[14]

---

[11] For the Baptist-Roman Catholic and the Southern Baptist-RCC dialogues, see Joseph A. Burgess and Jeffrey Gros, FSC, eds., *Building Unity: Ecumenical Dialogues with Roman Catholic Participation in the United States* (New York: Paulist, 1989), 39-44 and 45-51, respectively; hereafter referred to as *BU*.

[12] *Ibid.*, 43.

[13] *Ibid.*

[14] *Ibid.*, 43-44.

Compared to the WEF response, these Mennonite and Baptist ecumenical statements reflect greater ecclesiological self-awareness. Such ecclesiological concern equips the believers church tradition to play a unique role: it may be able to advance the ecumenical discussion by providing a third way between ecumenical sacramental ecclesiologies and the minimalist ecclesiology that curtails the ecumenical effectiveness of the much-needed evangelical contribution.

The co-inherence of church and voluntary faith

For the believers church tradition to fulfill its ecumenical role, however, requires further examination of the relationship of ecclesiology and voluntarism, the relationship of church and the voluntary act of faith. I argue that it is possible, on believers church terms, to affirm the primacy of the church with regard to the voluntary act of faith. Such primacy appears to be entirely contrary to fact, of course. Voluntary acts of faith seem primordial, while the church is secondary, the product of such decisions. Ecclesiology appears to be derivative. Yet, is this really so? Above we noted a sense of church in which it is, if not primary, certainly more than the sum of individual decisions. Is it possible to take the next step to argue that in a significant sense church is the primary given? John Howard Yoder opened his plenary address at the 1978 "Believers Church Conference in Canada" by stating, rather unabashedly, "The Church of tomorrow [note the singular form and the capital "C"] cannot but be a Believers' Church."[15] Supported by an appeal to theologian Karl Rahner, Yoder's claim called for a further probing of the believers church tradition for its ecclesiological substance. Uncovering the ecclesial matrix of voluntary faith is crucial, lest ecclesiology fall prey to individualist disintegration. Furthermore, Yoder's claim was not a triumphalist take-over prediction by a tradition that has itself been oppressed and marginalized in the past by the imperialism of others. Since the "be like us" mode of ecumenism is excluded, the believers church tradition too needs to be open to the ecclesiological issues raised in ecumenical discussion.

[15] Jarold K. Zeman and Walter Klaassen, eds., *The Believers church in Canada* (Brantford, ON: Baptist Federation of Canada, 1979), 3. Cf. *Royal Priesthood*, 67.

Here I want to consider some statements by representative believers church spokespersons that may indicate not only that voluntary faith decisions are constitutive of church, but that church is constitutive of such voluntary decisions. One theme worth pursuing is that of "covenant." Often this term is used to refer to the voluntary human act. Covenant then becomes the equivalent of voluntary "agreement," a contractual arrangement. As such it does not transcend an individualistic approach to community. When "covenant" is synonymous with a human contract, community can indeed be seen as a by-product of individual decisions: community is created by a "social contract." Accordingly, "covenant" is used as an equivalent of personal commitment. It is in this sense that Yoder, for example, spoke of "covenanted fellowship."[16] But there are indications in this same essay that he had in mind a deeper sense of Christian community. He speaks of community not simply as a product of individual decisions but in effect as a product of God: "The work of God is the calling of a people, whether in the Old Covenant or the New." By this he does not mean simply that since those individual decisions are a work of the Spirit, the resultant community is a work of God merely in a derivative sense, in the same way as a meeting or a conference is the product of an invitation. Yoder highlighted the uniqueness of the church by contrasting it to other gatherings. The church, he insisted, is not "simply the *result* of a message, as "an alumni association is the product of a school or the crowd in the theater is the product of the reputation of the film."[17]

The import of this emphasis on the corporate nature of church can be illustrated by examining a startling argument Yoder employed when he articulated the relation between the existence of the new community and "the nature of the gospel itself":

> If it is not the case that there is in a given place men of various characters and origins who have been brought together in Jesus Christ, then there is not in that place the new humanity and in that place the gospel is not true. If, on the other hand,

---

[16] John Howard Yoder, "A People in the World: Theological Interpretation," in James Leo Garrett, Jr., ed., *The Concept of the Believers' Church* (Scottdale, PA: Herald, 1969), 257.

[17] *Ibid.*, 258.

this miracle of the new creation has occurred, then all the verbalization and interpretations whereby this brotherhood communicates to the world around it are simply explications of the fact of its presence.[18]

This statement articulates the inextricable relation between gospel and community. More importantly, it underscores the relationship between the voluntary principle and ecclesiology. Voluntarism is not adequately expressed in the sequence: believers → church. Rather, the sequence is also: church → believers. In other words, believers are not the foundation of the church except insofar as the church is the foundation of believers. As Harold Littell contends, the church is not a "bag of individual grains of sand, but a corporate entity of such intensely binding quality that the metaphor of a living body springs to mind."[19] According to Yoder, people are called by God to a "new social wholeness," and it is from this call to peoplehood that "personal conversion" is derived.[20] This could still be understood as affirming the primacy of individual conversions, except that conversions take place in relation to the missionary *community* called "church." The two terms of the self-designation, "believers church" go both ways: it is a *believers* church, i.e., believers obviously make up the church. But they never constitute a church *de novo*; their voluntary acts of faith do not create the church. For that reason, the authentic Christ-community is a believers *church*, i.e., a faith community constitutes the matrix of believing. Believers do not take up membership in a Christian club; rather, they are *incorporated into* the church.

Let me try a different tack on the foundational role of the church. One of the strong points of the believers tradition is its concentration on the story of Jesus in the Gospels and the story of the Church in Acts as a paradigm for the Christ-community today, and as a guiding norm and source for theological reflection. It is instructive, then, to note the specific role of voluntary choice in the Gospels.

---

[18] *Ibid.*, 259-60. Cf. *Royal Priesthood*, 75.

[19] Franklin H. Littell, *The Free Church* (Boston: Starr King Press, 1957), 11.

[20] *The Concept of the Believers' Church*, 258.

Christ's ministry is indeed a continual summons to commitment. His person, his actions, and his words challenged all whom he encountered to a choice. That is clear from all the descriptions of encounters with him. But it is supremely captured in the announcement and call that sum up his ministry: "The Kingdom is at hand – repent and believe the gospel." This challenge to commitment is especially clear in Christ's relation to the disciples. And since the twelve clearly represent the new people of God in embryo, the centrality of the summons to commitment is paradigmatic for the centrality of the voluntary principle as emphasized in the believers church tradition.

Yet, there is surely more. The summons to commitment is quite different from any modern sense of "choice." The supreme moment of voluntary action is not that of the followers but that of Jesus, *his* choosing. Almost imperiously, he chooses his disciples – and they follow. So dominant and foundational is the choosing by Jesus that, by comparison, the disciples' choice can be described by negation: "You did not choose me but I chose you to be my disciples." I do not wish to get into the doctrine of election from eternity; making sense of these "timely" stories is quite enough of a challenge. At this historical level, the priority and primacy of God's electing action in Christ's choosing is manifest.

The book of Acts, while constantly recounting the conversion of "individuals," is also clear that they do not make the church but are "added to" it. Further, Luke described the great missionary breakthrough to the gentiles in this way: God *takes* "from among them *a people* for his name" (Acts 15:14). The paradigmatic nature of the choosing by and in Jesus becomes clear when Paul speaks of God's election as occurring by God's *eklogeen*, his calling-out (Rom. 9:11). God's sovereign mission movement in and through history, concentrated in the story of Christ, produces a new missionary community. As is clear in both Romans and Acts, God's electing way – through "the Way" – is not a selection process of disparate individuals who subsequently conglomerate. Rather, God's electing sweep through history is directed to nations and peoples, in order to form a *new* people in a renewed creation.

From the viewpoint of God's sovereignly saving ways, it would be a sad mistake to identify an emphasis on the voluntary principle as Arminian, if that is understood as detracting from the sovereignty of God's gracious choosing. The emphasis on the voluntariness of faith and on the distinctiveness of a committed fellowship is thoroughly biblical. Further, the voluntary principle in its origin expresses an ecclesial concern. It describes the distinctive shape of the church. Nevertheless this principle does have soteriological implications. One may even say that its foundation is soteriological. At this level it will not do to combine God's call and the believing response as a "50-50 proposition": God offers salvation and, in our voluntary response of acceptance, we meet God half way. Salvation is God's sovereign work. Faith is his gift. The Holy Spirit transforms a heart of stone into a beating heart of flesh. Christ chooses. God elects. But God's sovereignty is hardly honoured by replacing the 50-50 arrangement with a 100-0 or 60-40 proposition. Even the ever-popular 100-100 depiction, though true, is utterly unhelpful, for it fails to indicate that one of the 100s is divine, the other human: that the divine actor is the sovereign creator of the universe, while the human actor is fragile, a clay vessel. If in a perfect world the divine-human relationship would have to be described in asymmetrical terms, the post-Fall situation dramatically compounds the relationship. Now the divine actor is revealed as sovereign Saviour, Redeemer, Healer and, correspondingly, human beings are described as mortally wounded, in need of rescue – worse, as alienated, as enemies, even as dead. No equation, whether proportional or disproportional, is equal to the wonder of this divine rescue. In the words of the Mennonite Confession of 1963, "as sinner, man is self-centered and self-willed, unwilling and unable to break with sin."[21]

The non-incompatibility of infant baptism

A recognition of the primacy of community as a sovereign work of God in Christ through the Holy Spirit can go far towards making the believers church perspective fruitful in the dialogue with more sacramentally oriented ecclesiologies. Weaving the voluntary principle into the fabric of both the community principle and the sovereignty principle could open the way to a more sympathetic approach to claims regarding the "effect" of the sacraments, even the "effect" of the sacrament which the Schleitheim Confession calls "the greatest and first abomination of the Pope," namely

[21] "Brief Statement of Mennonite Doctrine," art. 4., *Mennonite Confession of Faith*, p. 11; cf. "Dordrecht Confession," art. II, in Leith, 294.

infant baptism. In fact, let us take this abomination as a test-case for ecumenical engagement on the part of the believers church. Such openness does not mean *accepting* the pedobaptist argument. Rather, as the awkward phrasing of the heading indicates, my goal is far more modest. Openness at this point means entertaining the possibility that a pedobaptist position need *not be incompatible with* a believers church ecclesiology. This approach yields benefit in the opposite direction as well: it prepares the soil for a more receptive hearing of the believers church critique of certain assumptions surrounding infant baptism.

The believers church critique of infant baptism should lead to a reappraisal of the "effect" of baptism for infants. If the biblical nature of this critique is heard, it would have to lead to divesting this sacrament of all assumptions about its "ontological" effect on the child, such as the "infusion of grace," the imprint of an indelible character, or an assumed "regeneration." This need not sheer the sacrament of all "effect." The question simply shifts to the *nature* of its effect. Some Reformation strands strongly emphasize the nature of the sacraments as a signing and sealing of God's *promises*. Within this promissory framework, the question, What does the sacrament do 'ontologically'? can be answered by a simple "Nothing." This is the right answer if the question assumes some (automatic) ontic or ethical change in the recipient.

Nevertheless, this ontological negation does not mean that nothing "happens" in the sacrament. It is conceivable that God reaches down in and through the community to embrace the one being baptized with his sovereign promise and claim. Etched on God's extended hand is the summons that it be grasped. Without re-entering the discussion as to how God is sovereignly involved even in our grasping, it must be maintained that everything in a sacramental rite, including the commitments made by congregation and parents, is aimed at the "voluntary" grasping of this hand by the one baptized. The effect of the sacrament, one might say, lives in the living community. It is the embodiment of the concretely sealed promise, a promise that inextricably entails God's claim. The voluntaristic principle needs to be invoked again and again to abolish any sense of automatism, but the principle need not impugn the effectiveness of God's promise-claim through the sacrament. God visibly testifies to his promise in such a way that the "effect" of the visible testimony and seal, the sacrament, is experienced precisely *in* the response for which it calls, namely faith.

This understanding of the dynamic effect of the sacrament requires that the sacrament not be isolated as a rite, nor instrumentalized as a ritual. Rather, the sacrament, in this case baptism, needs to be seen as an intrinsic part of a living, breathing, Christ-following community, a community where commitments and promises, the summons to nurture and the call to compassion, prayer, and care are central. Thus embedded in the community, there can be no thought of an automatic, magical effect of baptism. Moreover, this stress on the role of the living community of Christ-followers revitalizes the genius of the believers church tradition signaled at the outset, namely its passionate concern for the visible reality of the church.

The authentically biblical concern for the church as body is sorely needed to keep the voluntary principle from becoming captive to contemporary, individualistic notions of "voluntary action," of free choice. The notion of faith as personal response is readily distorted both by religious and secular impulses. As to the religious impulse, Marlin Miller pointed out that "Revivalism's preoccupation with an individual's crisis conversion has . . . diminished . . . the direct relation between baptism and church membership . . . ."[22] Likewise, secular forces have a corroding influence on our understanding of personal choice. As Jeffrey Gros warns, "The Believers' churches need to find ways of hearing the concerns about individual, consumer-voluntarism and post-enlightenment (possibly non-biblical) understandings of faith that are seen by others in the Believers' churches . . . ."[23]

No matter how one approaches the rite of baptism, the origin of new life remains a grace-filled mystery. It is after all the mystery of rebirth. Birth of whatever sort is not a voluntary act of the one being born. Baptism is a sign, not simply of the Christian's voluntary commitment, but of this new birth. For some Anabaptist leaders this sign was not merely an external audio-visual aid. As Marlin Miller indicated, for someone like Pilgram Marpeck the baptismal sign "participated in the

---

[22] Marlin E. Miller, "The Mennonites," in Merle D. Strege, ed., *Baptism and Church: A Believers' Church Vision* (Grand Rapids, MI: Sagamore Books, 1986), 23; see also Robert G. Torbet, *Ecumenism . . . Free Church Dilemma* (Valley Forge: Judson, 1968), 64.

[23] Jeffrey Gros, "Christian Baptism: The Evangelical Imperative," in *Baptism and Church,* 184.

reality of regeneration," so that "forgiveness is also given 'in' baptism." To be sure, in this view, baptism does not mediate grace. Nevertheless, according to some, Marpeck "understood baptism to transmit God's grace to the baptizand in a limited sense, namely as a divine word assuring the one of forgiveness and regeneration through faith."[24] This formulation comes very close to Calvin's understanding of baptism as a covenantal promissory act. As Timothy George puts it, "Not only are we saying and doing something to God in baptism, but God is also saying and doing something for us in baptism."[25] One can disagree as to whether baptism may be administered to infants. At the same time this disagreement ought not obscure an ecclesiological kinship that is far greater than the disagreement regarding pedobaptism would lead one to expect.[26]

By giving ecclesiologies that understand baptism (including that of infants) as a means of grace, at least the benefit of the doubt, the believers church tradition can have a renewing and unifying impact that reaches far beyond its own communities. This tradition can become a third way between the rest of evangelicalism and the ecumenical movement. But it would be a third way that does not stand between the other two as a dividing wedge but a joining bridge. Rodney Sawatsky of Messiah College concludes his essay on "Identity and Unity in Canadian Believers' Churches" by challenging these churches to fulfill a mediating role:

> [In the] post-Christian world all churches will inevitably, once again, as in the days before Constantine, become Believers' Churches. Believers' Churches in Canada need to provide a model for the semi-establishmentarian churches in this transition. Simultaneously Believers' Churches must provide evangelicals with a more biblical view of the church. In this middle ground between the ecumenical and the evangelical believers churches may well find their Canadian mission and a basis for co-operation to that end.[27]

---

[24] *Ibid.*, 19-20.

[25] Timothy George, "The Southern Baptists," in *Baptism and Church*, 50.

[26] Moreover, when some parts of the believers church tradition practise what may be called "toddler" baptism, the line between it and "infant" baptism becomes somewhat fuzzy (see *ibid.*, 47).

[27] Rodney S. Sawatsky, "Identity and Unity in Canadian Believers' Churches," in *The Believers' Church in Canada*, 241.

The role of the Baptist churches in the union of the churches of North India and Pakistan is instructive in this regard. While stating their disagreement with infant baptism and maintaining the right to practise believer's baptism, Baptists accepted pedobaptism within the unified church. One of the reasons for this acceptance is crucial. The Baptists noted in effect that infant baptism was, so to speak, geared to the subsequent faith response of the one baptized: profession of faith is required before a person is accepted to membership in full standing.[28]

Common problems: Flagging commitment

The need for openness to considering as valid what appear to be mutually exclusive understandings of church and sacrament is also fostered by the realization that the voluntary principle as such does not banish nominalism in faith commitment and church membership. In origin believers churches represent the repudiation of cheap grace, leveling a robust critique of flabby Christianity. This is indeed a problem that must be faced again and again in established churches, in sacramental churches – and in believers churches. Since the original believers churches were just that, a community of committed Christ-followers, nominalism within was no problem. But the "second-generation" church is a problem for every Christian community, be it charismatic, Pentecostal, or free church.

Kenneth Scott Latourette (1884-1968) decried the fact that for many members of believers churches their connection to the church is "through parents or friends and entails no conscious wholehearted commitment." He called this situation "a chronic problem of believers churches."[29] Recognizing the second-generation phenomenon must not lead to an adjustment of one's ecclesiology to accommodate a less than ideal situation. This would be the undoing of the believers church witness. Nevertheless, the second-generation syndrome does indicate that the problem of non-committed adherents is not unique to established or sacramentarian churches.

Another common problem concerns the assessment of the status of non-baptized children. Repudiating infant baptism does not itself banish

---

[28] Torbet, *Ecumenism*, 117.

[29] "A People in the World: Historical Background," in *The Concept of the Believers' Church*, 247.

the questions that arise on this score. Are unbaptized children within the community to be considered simply as pagans, until they make a positive voluntary commitment? That question becomes acute in the case of the death of a non-baptized infant. Is this child of believing parents to be consigned to Hell, to the "outer darkness"? If not, is the child's putative status after death totally discontinuous with its status while alive? Anything short of discontinuity, it seems, would have to lead to a reassessment of the relation of the voluntary element to the ecclesiological dimensions of God's grace. Facing squarely the status of the non-baptized children of believers calls for probing more deeply the ecclesiological matrix of the voluntary principle.

Search for appropriate ecclesial structures

The latter part of this paper is devoted to an exploration of a more practical ecumenical problem within the believers church tradition. It concerns the relationship between church and para-church and the accompanying, though not entirely parallel, relation between church unity and "cooperation."

It is difficult to give a clear definition of parachurch. As something related to, but distinct from and alongside of "church," the parachurch obtains its meaning from the definition of church from which one proceeds. The problem of definition is compounded in the believers church tradition by its historical dissociation from much of the institutional church structures. This dissociation at times has the effect of declaring institutional and structural givens as somewhat extraneous.

Within the believers church perspective, "church" in its proper sense often denotes a cohesive community of disciples, without formal structure. In the words of Robert Torbet (1912-1995), "There has remained within the Free Churches to the present time a tendency to spiritualize Christian unity and a reticence to objectify it in visible union, lest the organizational structure obscure the spiritual reality and inhibit the freedom of the people of God to be led by the Holy Spirit."[30] Torbet later pointed out that this skittishness is understandable in view of the origin of believers churches in the "protest against the authoritarianism, institutional rigidity, and identification with the state which characterized the Medieval Catholic

---

[30] *Ecumenism*, 67.

Church . . . ."[31] Coupled with the schismatic impulses that inhere in the quest for a "pure church"[32] and the localism fostered by the independence ideal, the anti-institutional bent hampers an effective ecumenical witness. This notion of the church as an organism bereft of institutional form is somewhat deceptive. If, for example, the exercise of discipline within the community is not going to be entirely arbitrary, some identifiable pattern of authority and decision-making, complete with written or unwritten policy and rules, is indispensable.

Be that as it may, something bordering on an aversion to institutions hampers the call for unity that lies at the heart of the restorationist thrust of the believers church tradition. The ambivalence regarding even small-scale ecclesial institutions translates into suspicion of the larger-scale organizations that are an inescapable part of the ecumenical quest. Consequently, instead of concerted efforts towards greater unity, the tendency is to settle for something less, what Torbet called the "halfway house of interdenominational cooperation."[33] The prominence of the term "cooperation" in believers church reflection on church unity is telling.[34] For cooperation implies a unity in deed, a joining in action, but it is the unity of distinct and possibly separated bodies.

Strikingly, the New Testament use of the "body" metaphor, highly flexible though it may be, is subject to one unbending limit: "body" cannot be used in the plural. There can be but one Body of Christ. For that reason, as important as cooperation among groups that confess the same Head is, these groups can never act as if they can simply continue to exist in separated, even isolated, "bodies." For the church, such plurality marks a deformity.

Churches of whatever tradition cannot remain satisfied with relegating the question of unity to para-church structures. If the body is one, that needs to become visible in churchly, structural ways. A body cannot exist without shape and form, without structure. Yoder was right therefore in challenging believers churches not to take "refuge in para-churchly forms"

[31] *Ibid.*, 70.

[32] Cf. *ibid.*, 72.

[33] *Ibid*, p. 104; see also his sketch of early Free Church cooperative efforts, 72-75.

[34] See, e.g., *The Believers' Church in Canada*, 48, 49, 51, 61, *passim*.

Because a believers church ecclesiology breaks through individualism, as well as through institutionalism in its various modes, it presents a gift that challenges all churches radically to rethink their own ecclesiologies. Not to face this challenge is to cut off a major tap root of ecclesial renewal.

Afterword
The Believers Church Conferences

Donald F. Durnbaugh

It was the German scholar Max Weber (1864-1920) who coined the term "Believers Church." He wanted a descriptive term to identify radical Protestants who had distanced themselves from state-sponsored church establishments or other socially dominant ecclesiastical bodies. The voluntary quality of church membership was at the heart of this grouping. Weber employed the term for those Christians who, in his words, sought "a community of personal believers of the reborn and only those."[1] Hence, in this understanding church members were those who wittingly covenanted themselves and were, moreover, those who constituted a regenerate body. Voluntary membership quite logically brought together those who opposed infant baptism (technically "antipedobaptists") or expressed more positively, those who favored "adult" or "believer's baptism." Inasmuch as such baptism was seen not as a matter of proper sacramental procedure nor of individual piety but rather as the consequence of a view of the church based upon voluntary commitment, members of the Religious Society of Friends (who do not baptize) were understood as also belonging to this family.

George H. Williams defined this strand of Christianity as "the gathered church of committed disciples living in the fellowship of mutual correction, support, and abiding hope." A more elaborate charaeterization emerged from the foundational 1967 conference on the "Concept of the Believers' Church" in a list of affirmations that included: the Lordship of Christ, the authority of the Word, church membership regenerated by the

Donald F. Durnbaugh is professor emeritus of church history, Bethany Theological Seminary.

[1] Max Weber, *The Protestant Ethic and the Spirit of Capitalism*, trans. T. Parsons (New York: Charles Scribner's Sons, 1958), 122, 144; originally published in 1930. This essay is adapted from D. F. Durnbaugh, "Origin and Development of the Believers' Church Conferences," *Servants of the Word: Ministry in the Believers Churches*, ed. David B. Eller (Elgin, Ill.; Brethren Press, 1990), xvii-xxx.

Spirit, the covenant of believers, a need for perpetual restitution of the church, the necessity of separation from the world, proclamation and service to the world, and a special, non-organizational view of church unity."[2]

Other terms have been used for this orientation: "Gathered Church," "Pilgrim Church," and especially "Free Church." The last term emerged in the second half of the 19th century from the situation in the United Kingdom among the nonconforming or dissenting bodies. The problem with the attractive usage "Free Church" was related to its most usual defining criterion – freedom from state control or establishment. In the United States, with programmatic separation of church and state by the specific rejection of establishment in the First Amendment to the U.S. Constitution, all church bodies by this prescription were technically "Free Churches." There were other problems with the term, such as its preferred use by heterodox denominations such as the Unitarians and the claims laid upon it by a wide variety of other religious groups, both liberal and conservative. For these reasons, the term "Believers Church" has gained currency in theological and historical writings as a useful and more precise designation.[3]

The Initiation of the Conference Series

The first study conference to use the term was that held by the General Conference Mennonite Church in Chicago (August 23-25, 1955). A volume containing the transactions of the conference fails to identify the precise source of the term, but several papers referred to an article by Robert Kreider published in the *Mennonite Quarterly Review* (1951); its title was "The Anabaptist Conception of the Church in the Russian Mennonite Environment, 1789-1870." In the article Kreider contrasted two different views of the church, which he called the "brotherhood type" and the "church type." He understood his typology as a conflation of the

---

[2] George H. Williams, *Wilderness and Paradise in Christian Thought* (New York: Harper Brothers, 1962), 214; James Leo Garrett, ed., *The Concept of the Believers' Church* (Scottdale, Pa.: Herald Press, 1969), 314-323.

[3] See the discussion in D. F. Durnbaugh, *The Believers' Church: The History and Character of Radical Protestantism* (New York: Macmillan, 1968), 4-8.

descriptions of previous scholars, including Ernst Troeltsch, Joachim Wach, Roland Bainton, Liston Pope, Carl Meyer, and H. Richard Niebuhr. Most of these were elaborations of the classic "church/sect/mystic" typology put forward by Troeltsch.[4]

Kreider's article had been published along with another article, this one written by Erland Waltner on "The Anabaptist Conception of the Church." Waltner identified the early Anabaptists and their descendants as a "voluntary fellowship of regenerated believers." He stated that for Anabaptists, "the church was not a 'society of the baptized,' nor was it primarily a 'church of the elect' . . . but it was to be a 'church of the believers.'"[5] A series of articles in the General Conference Mennonite Church periodical in July and early August, 1955 described the intent and design of the study conference. Elmer Ediger, one of the planners, asserted: "For generations we have been speaking of ourselves as a 'believers' church.' We have professed belief in adult baptism on confession of faith, in a brotherhood of true believers, and in a discipline which helps to build a church of true disciples. The basic question of the study conference is whether the 'believers' church' is our actual goal and intention at the present and for the future."[6]

The actual series of Believers Church conferences, however, had a different background. The impulse for the gathering came from J. A. Oosterbaan, Dutch Mennonite theologian. In 1961 he attended the Third Assembly of the World Council of Churches in New Delhi, India, best remembered for the large influx of Orthodox Churches into membership and the amalgamation of the international Missionary Council with the WCC. He was struck by the fact that descendants of the Radical Reformation had no way of uniting their concerns or entering into the ecumenical dialogue in strength, unlike those churches descended from the

---

[4] *Proceedings of the Study Conference on the Believers' Church, held at Mennonite Biblical Seminary, Chicago, August 23-25, 1955* (North Newton, Kans.: General Conference Mennonite Church, 1955); Robert Kreider, "The Anabaptist Conception of the Church in the Russian Mennonite Environment, 1789-1870," *Mennonite Quarterly Review* 25 (1951): 17-33, esp. 17-20.

[5] Erland Waltner, "The Anabaptist Conception of the Church," *Mennonite Quarterly Review* 25 (1951): 5-16, esp. 9.

[6] Elmer Ediger, "The Believers' Church Conference," *The Mennonite* (July 12, 1955): 420-421.

Magisterial Reformation ("Mainline Protestantism"). Of particular concern was his sentiment that representatives of those member churches of the World Council that held officially to believer's baptism, such as the Baptists, Disciples, and Church of the Brethren, were unwilling to consider that as "a subject formally requiring aggressive ecumenical dialogue."[7]

Subsequently, during his visit to North America in 1963 in conjunction with the Montreal meeting of the WCC Faith and Order Commission, Oosterbaan urged Mennonites, Baptists, and other "antipedobaptists" to make common cause to further the ecumenical conversation. An Amsterdam meeting of "baptizer theologians," planned at his urging for August, 1964 was called by the Baptist Theological Seminary (Utrecht) and the Mennonite Theological Seminary (Amsterdam), but was cancelled because of insufficient interest.

Through the suggestion of John Howard Yoder (1927-1997), professor Ooterbaan's idea was picked up by the faculty and administration of the Southern Baptist Theological Seminary of Louisville, Kentucky. Thus it was that the formative conference was called for June 26-30, 1967. Careful planning by two broadly representative meetings in May and October, 1966 preceded the actual conference. A prospectus developed for the 1967 meeting suggested a hypothesis to be tested:

> There exists in the heritage of those Christian groups which
> have insisted upon the baptism of believers, on confession of
> faith, into visible congregations, an apprehension of the nature
> of the gospel and of the church which is specific and coherent;
> which constitutes a theologically valid option, and a needed
> contribution in ecumenical debate.[8]

A signifcant contributory meeting had been held in June, 1964 at Earlham School of Religion for theologians and historians of the Historic

---

[7] John Howard Yoder, "Introduction," in *Baptism and Church: A Believers' Church Vision*, ed. Merle D. Strege (Grand Rapids, Mich.: Sagamore Books, 1986), 3-4; Garrett, *Concept of the Believers' Church*, 6.

[8] [John Howard Yoder], "Prospectus for a Conference on the Concept of the Believers' Church," (ca. May, 1966).

Peace Churches – Mennonites, Brethren, and Friends.[9] Some participants in the Richmond, Indiana, meeting helped to plan the Louisville conference, and many have stayed with the series of conferences over the years. Those invited to the Kentucky conference, of course, came from a broader circle of denominations, including not only Baptists of different affiliations and members of the Historic Peace Churches, but also those from the Churches of Christ, Disciples of Christ, Assemblies of God, Churches of God (Anderson), Methodists, and others. Southern Baptist sponsorship encouraged participation by members of certain denominations not active in ecumenical conversations.

The First Conference: Louisville, 1967

The Louisville Conference was carefully planned and well-organized. It attracted some 150 participants, as well as observers from the National Council of Churches of Christ in the USA, the World Council of Churches, and the Roman Catholic Bishops' Commission for Ecumenical Affairs. There were thirteen major presentations, including a keynote address by Franklin H. Littell. The conference was divided into four sections, with three papers under each section. The four were: "A Believing People," "A people in Community," "A People under the Word," and "A People in the World." A Findings Committee report attempted to list common affirmations, common points rejected, and unresolved questions. A concluding resolution asserted that conference attenders "profess to have discovered in history and in our present fellowship a common Scripturally based heritage, which is relevant for contemporary life and which is developing in churches of other traditions."[10]

The 1967 conference received wide attention in the denominational press and beyond, partly because of the presence of the invited ecumenical observers. One challenging interpretation came from the NCCC representative, Robert C. Dodds, who likened Believers Church members

---

[9] It was called a seminar on the "Church in the World." See the report by Peter J. Ediger, "Historic Peace Churches Discuss Witness in the World," *Gospel Messenger* (September 5, 1964): 24-25.

[10] Garrett, *Concept of the Believers' Church*, 324.

to "guerilla fighters" in churchly battles and thus prickly protagonists and problems for the ecclesiastical establishment. However, he found that "on balance, . . . radical protestantism proportionate to its numbers has produced more noble characters than the other streams of Christianity. The kinds of nobility – some saintly, some peaceable, some trustworthy, some generous, some yearning for righteousness of life, some striving for justice – are in short supply always."[11]

Although those present at the Louisville meeting agreed that it would be foreign to the genius of the movement to organize a formal structure to ensure an ongoing process, a voluntary "Commttee of Continuing Conversations" was named. This committee had members from several participating denominations and was asked to help plan and loosely coordinate future conferences. This could be done by assisting in the developmental stage and by mentioning possible speakers and participants. As co-convenors over the years, John Howard Yoder and D. F. Durnbaugh carried this program forward by handling communications when necessary and, on occasion, by suggesting possible themes for study conferences. Individuals and institutions used this informal means of testing suggestions for conferences and finding out what others were planning and proposing. As specific proposals came forward, these were circulated by the conveners to members of the committee for reactions.

This informal and minimal approach was understood as appropriate to an ecumenical vision that foresaw "no central administration, no defined captive constituency, and no regular calendar." The report of the Findings Committee had rejected a vision of the ecumenical task "which seeks to relate the 'faith' or the 'order' or the administrative structures of entire 'denominations' or 'communions' and which makes decisions by instructed delegates, proportional representation, and majority votes."[12] These negations were designed to buttress the essential congregational authority of church unity. This has meant that conferences have been held

---

[11] Robert C. Dodds, "Ecumenical Problems; The Radical Protestant," *The Iliff Review* 25 (Spring, 1968): 39-47. For listing of other coverage of the conference, see Garrett, *Concept of the Believers' Church*, 331-333. One of the most complete reports was Lawrence T. Slaght, "Conference on the Concept of the Believers' Church," *The Watchman-Examiner* (August 10, 1967): 483-489.

[12] Garrett, *Concept of the Believers' Church*, 319.

only as concerns have surfaced and have been tested by interested persons, or in theological terms, as the Spirit has moved.

Successive Conferences

Remarkably, given the loose and informal plan for possible continuing conferences (with virtually no structure and no budget), at intervals of two or three years conferences in the spirit and complexion of the foundational Louisville Conference have been initiated and carried on since 1967. They have ranged from Ohio to California, predominantly in the USA but also in Canada, with one related meeting in Switzerland (see the appended list). They have all been self-supporting and largely developed by academic institutions. In most cases the proceedings have been published, quite often in books or in special issues of scholarly journals. There has been a core of regular participants, many from the Historic Peace Churches, with professors predominant among them. Nevertheless, the meetings have also attracted pastors and interested church members.

Following the Louisville model, ecumenical participation has been encouraged. Jeffrey Gros, FSC, for many years director of the Faith and Order office of the NCCC, has been an active participant. The intent of faithful involvement in the broader ecumenical dialogue has been signaled by focus on key ecumenical themes. Thus the seventh conference (Anderson, Indiana, 1984) took as its basis the WCC document on *Baptism, Eucharist, and Ministry* (1982), the eighth conference (Oak Brook, Illinois, 1987) on ministry, and the eleventh (Ashland, Ohio, 1994), on the eucharist. Thus all three major foci of the *BEM* document; have been given solid consideration.

It is difficult to assess the impact of the series of conferences on the Believers Church, either upon the denominations held to belong to this family or upon the broader church. Undoubtedly, for those who have participated in at least several of the conferences, a strong feeling of fellowship and understanding has developed. There is also documentary evidence that the concept has been rather widely adopted, as some examples illustrate. A *Festschrift* dedicated to James Leo Garrett and compiled by Southern Baptist colleagues was entitled *The People of God: Essays on the Believers' Church* (1991). *Hymnal: A Worship Book* (1992) was published jointly by the Church of the Brethren, General Conference Mennonite Church, and the Mennonite Church. Its subtitle explains that it was "Prepared by Churches in the Believers Church Tradition." These same denominations, joined by some others, organized a "Believers Church Commentary Series." By the end of 1997 eight books had been issued, with more manuscripts in the pipeline.[13]

Perhaps the most persuasive evidence of the impact of the series is the simple fact of its continuation for nearly three decades. Despite the lack of organization and staffing, assisted only by sporadic and low-key efforts of the conveners and committee members, appropriate themes and necessary organization has appeared since 1967 to enable continuity. Thus the 1996 conference at Hamilton, Ontario, was able to announce that it was number twelve in the series. The many thoughtful presentations and significant publications since Louisville are in themselves a witness to the vitality of the concept.

Believers Church
Conferences and Publications

Preliminary conferences and publications

General Conference Mennonites, Chicago, IL (August 23-25, 1955): A Study Conference on the Believers' Church.

Proceedings of the Study Conference on the Believers' Church, Held at Mennonite Biblical Seminary, Chicago, Illinois, August 23-25, 1955 (North Newton, KS: General Conference Mennonite Church, 1955)

Earlham School of Religion, Richmond, IN (June 8-16, 1964): Historic Free Church Seminar: The Church in the World.

Franklin H. Littell, "The Concerns of the Believers' Church," *Chicago Theological Seminary Register* 58 (December, 1967): 12-18.

---

[13] Paul Basden and David Dockerby, eds., *The People of God: Essays on the Believers' Church* (Nashville, Tenn.: Broadman Press, 1991); *Hymnal: A Worship Book* (Elgin, Ill.: Brethren Press/Newton, Kans.: Faith and Life Press/ Scottdale. Pa.: Mennonite Publishing House: 1992); *Brethren Press Resource Catalog* (Elgin, Ill.: Brethren Press, 1997). See especially in the *People of God* volume, the article by George H. Williams, "The Believers' Church and the Given Church," 325-32.

Baptist Theological Seminary, Utrecht/Mennonite Theological Seminary, Amsterdam, The Netherlands (August, 1964): Conference of Baptizer Theologians (cancelled).

Main conferences and publications

1) Southern Baptist Theological Seminary, Louisville, KY (June 26-30, 1967): The Concept of the Believers' Church.

James Leo Garrett, Jr., ed. *The Concept of the Believers' Church: Addresses from the 1967 Louisville Conference* (Scottdale, PA: Herald Press, 1969).

2) Chicago Theological Seminary, Chicago, IL (June 29-July 2, 1970): Is There a Christian Style of Life for Our Age?"

[special issue] "The Second Believers' Church Conference, Chicago Theological Seminary, June 20-July 2, 1970," *Chicago Theological Register* 60 (September, 1970): 1-59

3) Laurelville Mennonite Church Center, Laurelville, PA (May 26-29, 1972): The Believers' Church: A Conference for Laity.

4) Pepperdine University, Malibu, CA (June 5-8, 1975): Restitution, Dissent, and Renewal: A Conference on the Concept of the Believers' Church.

[special issue] *Journal of the American Academy of Religion* 44 (March, 1976): 3-113

4a) Baptist Theological Seminary, Rüschlikon, Switzerland (July 15-17, 1975): Conference on Anabaptists 1525-1975: The Truth will Make you Free.

5) Baptist Federation of Canada/Mennonite Central Committee (Canada), Winnipeg, Manitoba (May 15-18, 1978): Study Conference on the Believers' Church in Canada.

Jarold K. Zeman and Walter Klaassen, eds., *The Believers' Church in Canada: Addresses and Papers from the Study Conference in Winnipeg, May 1978* (Waterloo, Ont.: Baptist Federation of Canada and Mennonite Central Committee [Canada], 1979).

Philip Collins, *The Church of Tomorrow: The Believers' Church* (Toronto: Baptist Federation of Canada, 1982), a study guide.

6) Bluffton College, Bluffton, OH (October 23-25, 1980): Is There a Believers' Church Christology?

J. Denny Weaver, "A Believers' Church Christology," *Mennonite Quarterly Review* 57 (April, 1983): 112-131 (with footnote references to places of publication of other conference papers).

7) Anderson School of Theology, Anderson, IN (June 5-8, 1984): Believer's Baptism and the Meaning of Church Membership: Concepts and Practices in an Ecumenical Context.

Merle D. Strege, ed., *Baptism and Church: A Believers' Church Vision* (Grand Rapids, MI: Sagamore Books, 1986).

8) Bethany Theological Seminary, Oak Brook, IL (September 2-5, 1987): The Ministry of All Believers.

David B. Eller, ed., *Servants of the Word: Ministry in the Believers Churches* (Elgin, IL: Brethren Press, 1990).

9) Southwestern Baptist Theological Seminary, Fort Worth TX (March 30-April 1, 1989): Believers' Church Conference: Balthasar Hubmaier and His Thought.

[special issue] *Mennonite Quarterly Review* 65 (January, 1991): 5-53.

10) Goshen College, Goshen, IN (May 20-23, 1992): The Rule of Christ (Matthew 18:15-20): A Conference on Church Discipline and the Authority of the Church in the Series on the Concept of the Believers Church.

[special issue] *Brethren Life and Thought* 38 (Spring, 1993): 67-107.

11) Ashland Theological Seminary, Ashland, OH (June 1-4, 1994): The Meaning and Practice of the Lord's Supper in the Believers Church Tradition.

Dale R. Stoffer, ed., *The Lord's Supper: Believers Church Perspectives* (Scottdale. PA: Herald Press, 1997).

12) McMaster Divinity College, Hamilton, 0N (October 17-18, 1996): The Voluntary Church.

William H. Brackney, ed., *The Believers Church: A Voluntary Church* (Kitchener, ON: Pandora Press, 1998).

Surveys

D. F. Durnbaugh, "Believers Church," *The Mennonite Encyclopedia* (Scottdale, PA: Herald Press, 1990), 5: 63-64

D. F. Durnbaugh, "Origin and Development of the Believers' Church Conferences," in *Servants of the Word: Ministry in the Believers' Churches*, ed. David B. Eller (Elgin, IL: Brethren Press, 1990), xii-xxx (with citations to articles on the series of Believers Church conferences).

D. F. Durnbaugh, "Believers' Church," *The Brethren Encyclopedia* (Philadelphia, PA/Oak Brook, IL: Brethren Encyclopedia Inc., 1983), 113-14.

[Merle D. Strege], "The Conferences on the Concept of the Believers' Church: Themes and Reports," in *Baptism and Church: A Believers' Church Vision*, ed. Merle D. Strege (Grand Rapids, MI: Sagamore Books, 1986), 207-208.

John H. Yoder, "The Believers' Church Conferences in Historical Perspective," *Mennonite Quarterly Review* 65 (January, 1991): 5-19.

Index

About Pandora Press

Pandora Press is a small, independently owned press dedicated to making available modestly priced books that deal with Anabaptist, Mennonite, and Believers Church topics, both historical and theological. Our books are typeset and printed using desktop technology. This allows us to produce short-run titles at a relatively low cost, while maintaining a high level of print quality. We welcome comments and suggestions from our readers.

Also Available from Pandora Press

An Annotated Hutterite Bibliography, compiled by Maria H. Krisztinkovich, ed. by Peter C. Erb (Kitchener, Ont.: Pandora Press, 1998). (Ca. 2,700 entries) 312pp., cerlox bound, electronic, or both. ISBN (paper) 0-9698762-8-9/(disk) 0-9698762-9-7
$15.00 each, U.S. and Canadian. Postage: $6.00 U.S. and Can.
[The most extensive bibliography on Hutterite literature available]

Jacobus ten Doornkaat Koolman, *Dirk Philips. Friend and Colleague of Menno Simons*, trans. by William E. Keeney, ed.by C. Arnold Snyder (Kitchener, Ont.: Pandora Press, 1998). xviii, 236pp., index Softcover. ISBN: 0-9698762-3-8
$23.50 U.S./$28.50 Canadian. Postage: $4.00 U.S./$5.00 Can.
[The definitive biography of Dirk Philips, now available in English]

Sarah Dyck, ed. and trans., *The Silence Echoes: Memoirs of Trauma and Tears* (Kitchener, Ont.: Pandora Press, 1997). xii, 236pp., 2 maps Softcover. ISBN: 0-9698762-7-0
$17.50 U.S./$19.50 Canadian. Postage: $4.00 U.S./$5.00 Can.
[First person accounts of life in the Soviet Union, translated from German]

Wes Harrison, *Andreas Ehrenpreis and Hutterite Faith and Practice* (Kitchener, Ont.: Pandora Press, 1997). xxiv, 274pp., 2 maps, index. Softcover. ISBN 0-9698762-6-2
$26.50 U.S./$32.00 Canadian. Postage: $4.00 U.S./$5.00 Can.
[First full biography of this important seventeenth century Hutterite leader]

C. Arnold Snyder, *Anabaptist History and Theology: Revised Student Edition* (Kitchener, Ont.: Pandora Press, 1997). xiv, 466pp., 7 maps, 28 illustrations, index, bibliography. Softcover. ISBN 0-9698762-5-4
$35.00 U.S./$38.00 Canadian. Postage: $5.00 U.S./$6.00 Can.
[Abridged, rewritten edition for undergraduates and the non-specialist]